HOME BY CHRISTMAS?

This book highlights the remarkable adventures experienced by some of the six hundred prisoners of war who marched out of camp PG49 at Fontanellato near Parma after the Italian Armistice on the 8th September 1943. Some went to Switzerland and internment, some joined the partisans. Others walked south to rejoin the Allied armies. A few succeeded; many more were recaptured.

It also tells of the bravery of the Italian people, many of whom were poor peasants. Without their steadfast help in providing food, shelter and clothes, often in considerable danger of savage reprisals, the ex-prisoners would have been forced to give themselves up.

The book is compiled by Ian English, who was himself a prisoner at Fontanellato, from more than sixty individual escape accounts, from whole books to short personal anecdotes. Many are published for the first time.

The Monte San Martino Trust

The Trust was founded in 1990 with the object of providing bursaries for children and grandchildren of Italians who helped British prisoners of war 'on the run' in Italy in 1943 and 1944. The bursaries enable the recipients to come to Britain for a period of study.

Since its inception some sixty bursaries have been granted. By these means it is possible for British people, especially those who were prisoners in Italy or their relatives, to repay, albeit in only a very small way, those who risked their lives by providing food and shelter to British servicemen. Any profits from the sale of this book will be given to the Trust.

Hon. Secretary, Monte San Martino Trust:
K. Keith Killby, Flat 7, 18 Lambolle Road, London NW3 4HP.

Home by Christmas?

Edited by

Ian English

HOME BY CHRISTMAS?

Privately Published 1997

British Library Cataloguing in Publication Data
A. A catalogue record for this book is available from the British Library

ISBN 0 9524073 1 0

Contents

Appendices

Plates

Maps

Illustrations

Maps 3 to 12 are reproduced from Road Map of Italy 1:200,000 edited by Touring Club Italiano. Reproduction authorised on 11 April 1997.

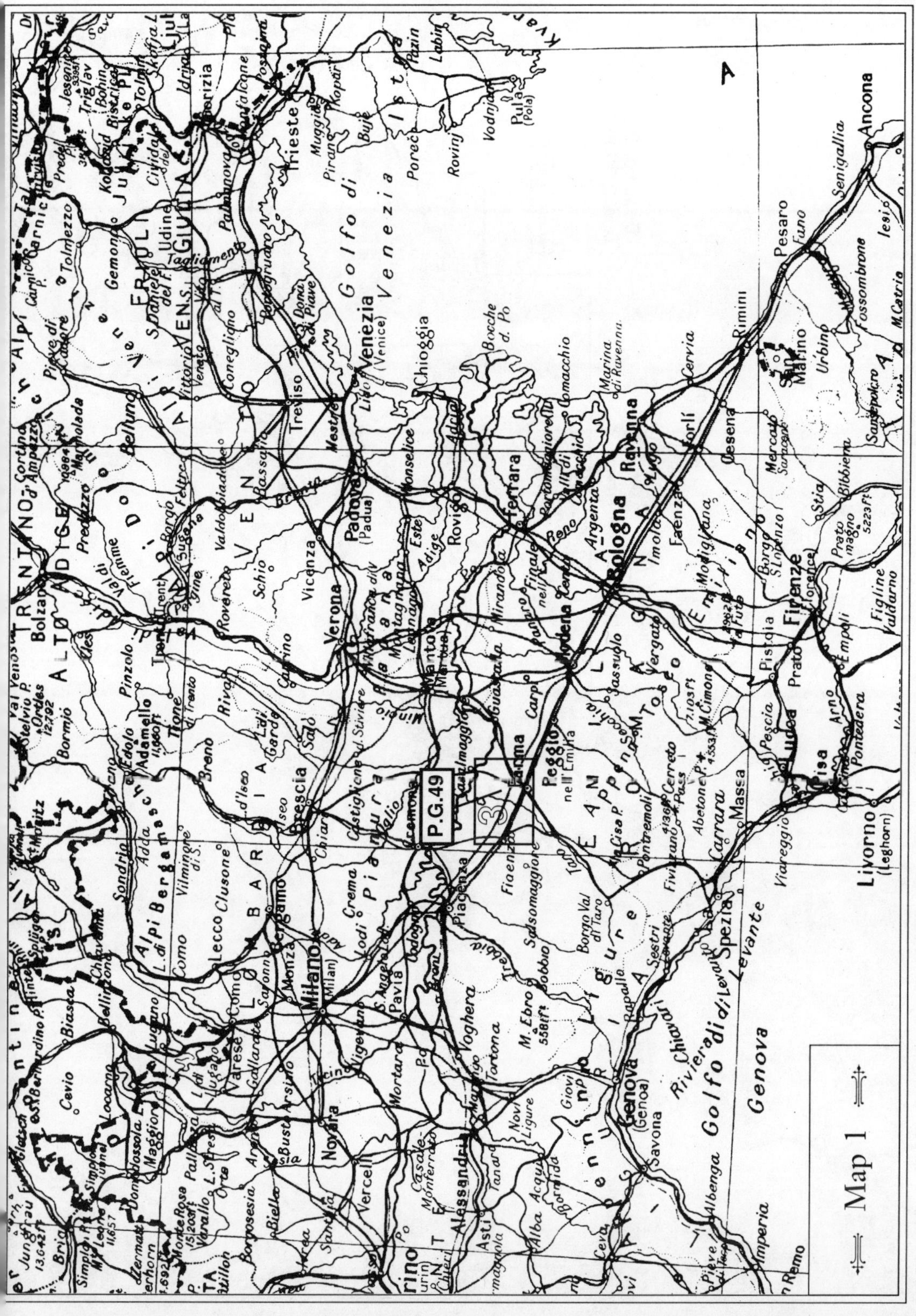
P.G.49
Milano
Venezia
Bologna
Genova
Trieste
Firenze
Verona
Padova
Golfo di Venezia
Golfo di Genova

Map 1

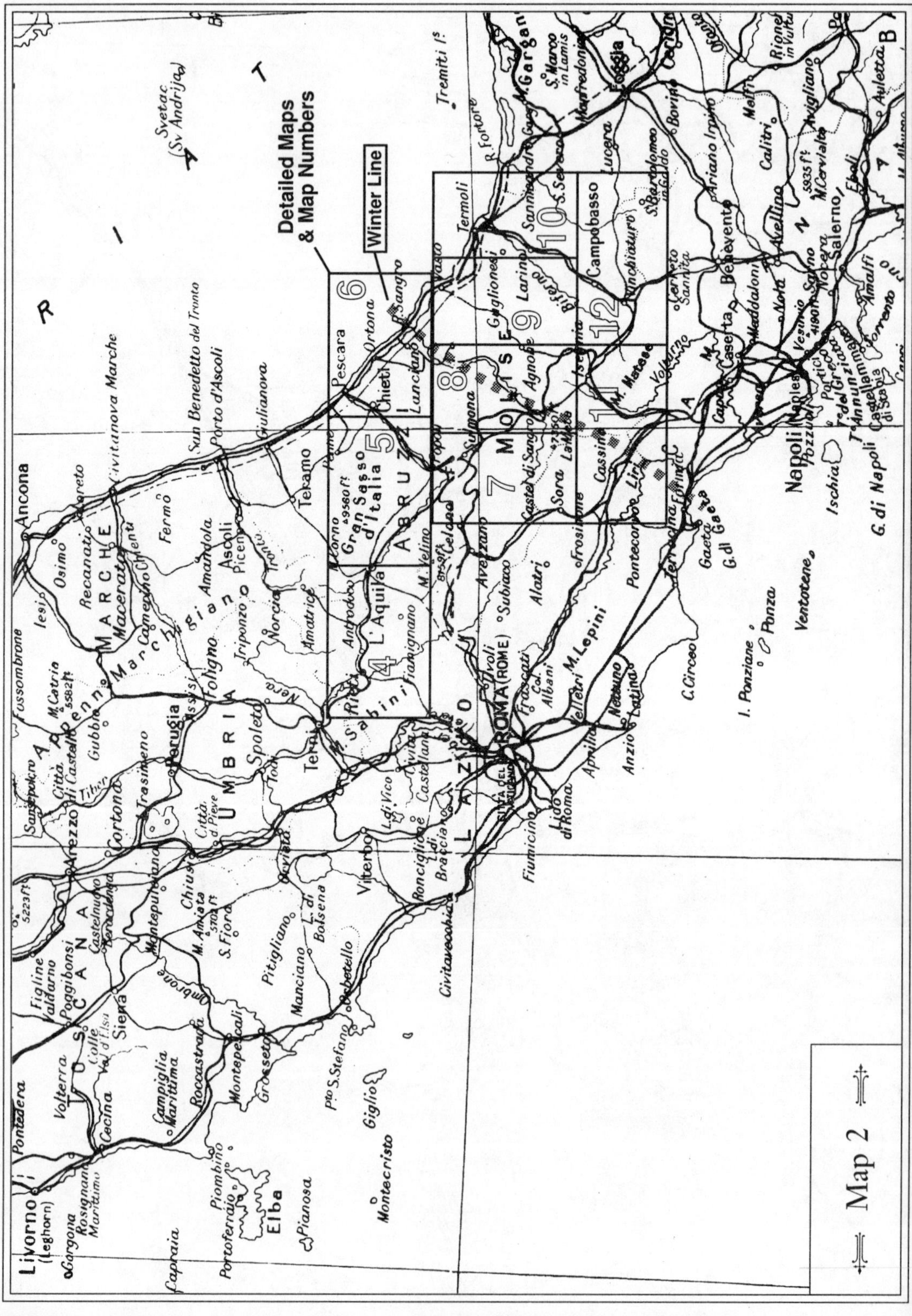
Detailed Maps
& Map Numbers
Winter Line
ROMA (ROME)
Napoli
Pescara
Ortona
Sangro
Cassino
Termoli
Campobasso
Foggia
Ancona
Livorno
Civitavecchia
Anzio
Gaeta
Salerno
Benevento
Avellino
L'Aquila
Teramo
Chieti
Lanciano
Sulmona
Avezzano
Frosinone
Terracina
Perugia
Spoleto
Terni
Rieti
Viterbo
Siena
Arezzo
Grosseto
Elba
Montecristo
Giglio
Ischia
Ventotene
Ponza
Tremiti Is
Gran Sasso d'Italia
ABRUZZI
MOLISE
LAZIO
UMBRIA
MARCHE
TOSCANA
CAMPANIA
ADRIATIC
4
5
6
7
8
9
10
11
12

Map 2

Foreword

by
Sir Denis Forman, O.B.E.

DURING the last week in October and the first in November 1943, I was in charge of patrolling on the 78 Division front on the Adriatic coast of Italy. This stretched five miles along the River Sangro as it neared the sea. In normal times the river was fordable but now, due to an autumn of incessant rain, it had become a raging torrent. Several of our men on patrol were swept away and drowned in crossing the river, and from time to time we had to suspend operations altogether. It was during one of these periods of suspended activity that I ploughed my way through the mud to patrol headquarters, a farmhouse perched like an eagle's nest on the southern escarpment of the river. I saw two Italian peasants apparently in the custody of the duty sergeant awaiting me. One was leading a donkey on a string, the other a dog, both were soaking wet and I noticed with surprise that on their feet both were wearing the vestigial remnants of a pair of British army boots. 'Two British officers, Sir, escaped P.O.W.s,' said the sergeant. We ushered them into the farmhouse O.P. and offered them tea, rum, ship's biscuits and our only delicacy—dried figs, with which the farmhouse was furnished with several dozen sacks. We listened to their tale, the first of many, and heard of the narrow squeaks, their friendship with Italian families, their fifty mile ride by bus, their march over the Gran Sasso Pass in snow, their acquisition of the donkey and the dog, whose company they believed had averted German suspicions more than once, and finally with our field glasses we tracked their route over the last five miles through the German lines, which had taken three days to cover, culminating in the whole quartet swimming across the dreaded Sangro in full flood.

Later in the year my battalion took over a huge tract of mountain territory which was more of a no-man's land than a front, and here from our base in Casoli we formed and operated a band of guerrillas. During the months January and February 1944 a constant flow of escaped British officers and men passed through our lines, in ones, in twos, in threes and occasionally a party of four or more. Two was the most common number, since it combined a degree of mutual support with the best chance of avoiding attention, and there were many evenings when I returned from a day spent ski-ing round remote units in the snow-covered Abruzzi uplands to find several pairs of escaped officers sitting in front of the blazing fire in what passed for the ante room in our battalion headquarters. Every one of the escapers had a story to tell, every one was fascinating and no two the same. There were, of course, some experiences common to all—the extraordinary kindness and support of the local population, a preoccupation with the subject of food, and frequent ups and downs in morale. Many escapers told of the black days when it seemed the only thing to do was to give themselves up—to be followed (perhaps as a result of a couple of days spent in the heart of a peasant family with plenty of food and drink) by periods of euphoria and complete confidence in a safe passage.

Travellers' tales well told are always of interest. But escaped travellers' tales have the advantage of the teller having been personally at risk. As a result of this his sensibilities were so heightened as to impress every detail and every incident on his memory. For this reason the story of an escape is vivid in the mind of the teller for all his life and he will be able to project a sense of immediacy to a listener who will come to share his hopes and fears as the tale is told. When I was first told of the nature of this book, which tells of the adventures of some of the prisoners from just one camp—PG49 at Fontanellato in northern Italy—I thought that it was one of the best publishing ideas I had heard of in recent years, and only wondered why no-one had done it before. Everything I have heard since then reinforces that view and I congratulate Ian English and his team in their enterprise and persistence in piecing together the many escape stories in this book. I also feel happy for the reader who has the good fortune of sharing in the excitement of the many escapes recounted and of marvelling at the courage and the endurance of many of the escapers.

Preface

AFTER my book *Assisted Passage* was published I received many letters and telephone calls from ex-officers who had been fellow prisoners in Campo PG49 at Fontanellato, and indeed some from other camps, telling me of their experiences and comparing them with my own. Very often their stories had great intrinsic interest, and while most had many aspects in common, several provided features which were peculiar to themselves.

I came to the conclusion that it would be a sad failure if these stories were lost for ever through the passage of time.

The actions of the prisoners of war themselves is only half the story. Equally important is the inter-relationship between the prisoners and the Italians, for the good reason that life outside the camps for the 50,000 Allied prisoners who got away after the Armistice with Italy would have been impossible without the generous Italian help which was given. Sooner rather than later the prisoners would have had to give themselves up to the Germans. Therefore I have considered it essential to include the stories of some of the very many Italians who helped the escapers from Fontanellato by providing food, shelter and clothing. In a few cases they saved the lives of the British, and in doing so, lost their own.

I fear it is inevitable that this book can never be complete, because sadly many ex-prisoners have passed on, and we have lost touch with others still alive. If one of these reads this book and does not find his name in it, I can only apologise. All I can say is that every effort has been made to make it as complete and accurate as possible. The same considerations apply to the accounts of the Italian helpers.

This book has been a cooperative venture throughout. First I must thank the thirty one ex-officers who responded to my request for information, who delved deep into their memories and then put pen to paper. They are listed in Appendix 5. Also I must gratefully acknowledge the permission given by eighteen authors who were in PG49 to use and quote from their books which have been published earlier in one form or another. All are listed in the Bibliography.

I am especially indebted to John Langrishe (otherwise known as Peter) for his enthusiasm and general support in many ways, for his chapter on 'Life in the Camp,' the story of his own adventures and for his large contribution to and management of the financial side of the project. Also to Anthony Laing for his thoughtful and helpful comments all through the production of this book, for providing the stories of the Buti family and Don Egidio, the account of his remarkable adventures, including jumping off trains (Appendix 4), as probably the farthest travelled ex-prisoner from Fontanellato. Also to Toby Graham for Chapter 2, using his previously written account of the escapes made before the Armistice.

I wish to thank Ronald Mann and Bill Cameron-Johnson for designing and painting the front cover which does so much for the impact of the book. It has received wide acclaim.

My grateful thanks go to Roger Absalom for his encouragement and advice, and particularly for his permission to use some of his ideas and thoughts which appeared in *A Strange Alliance*. His book is undoubtedly the definitive history of the whole subject of the relationship between the Allied prisoners and the Italian people in 1943–44.

Major Michael Spurrier's assiduous detective work at the Public Record Office produced the list of Honours and Awards and the Nominal Roll. I must thank him for dealing with my requests for information which he took in his stride.

The maps are taken from the *Carta Automobilistica* published by the Touring Club Italiano. My grateful thanks go to Dr. Roberto Mello, the Cartographic Director of T.C.I., for his kind permission for free use of these maps.

It has not been possible to include large scale maps covering the whole of the country from the River Po to the area of the German and Allied lines, but I hope the maps do cover the parts of Italy most relevant to the events described in the book.

I was greatly helped by my friend Hazel Ashley who patiently and expertly typed my handwritten text, correcting my several mistakes as she went along. I must also thank her for reading the proofs so carefully and promptly.

I am indebted to Sir Denis Forman who found time in his very busy life to write the Foreword. His knowledge, born of his fighting experience as an infantry officer in the Italian campaign, was invaluable.

Finally I am very grateful to Jim Balmer of Langlands Edition who from the first embraced this project with enthusiasm, who has promptly answered all my questions and given sound advice based on his long experience in book design. That *Home by Christmas?* appears as it is, is due entirely to him.

1: *Life in the Camp*

by Peter Langrishe

THE TOWN of Fontanellato lies about fifteen kilometres north-west of Parma in the lush Plain of Lombardy; between the River Po fourteen kilometres to the north and Via Emilia six kilometres to the south. Twelve kilometres south of this important road, running from Rimini up to Milan, the foothills of the northern Apennines commence.

The town has a fine moated *Rocca* or citadel at its centre, parts of which date from the fourteenth century, an arcaded square, a small model opera theatre seating two hundred and an imposing cathedral church. None of these attractions was seen by the prisoners, at least not before the Armistice, as they were not allowed into the town.

The Prisoner-of-War camp was on the eastern edge of the town and was officially designated *Campo Concentramento di Prigioneri di Guerra* 49, and was brought into use on 1st April 1943. Rumour has it that it was intended as a 'Show Camp,' for the benefit of official visitors from such bodies as the International Red Cross. At any rate it was a handsome building in its way and about as far removed from the traditional idea of a P.O.W. camp as can be imagined.

This large building had been designed as an orphanage and indeed the word *Orfanotrofio* was displayed across the front elevation. It had a frontage of about two hundred and fifty feet; built in red brick externally, with marble flooring on the stairs and corridors. There was a large central hall extending to the roof, designed as a chapel, off which were two wings, one on each side of the hall. It had a semi-basement and three upper floors. There were good washing, sanitary and cooking facilities. The inmates enjoyed the luxury of a proper bed, rather than the usual bunks, with bedside cupboards to store their meagre possessions. Most of the dormitories held about twenty four beds, but there were a few smaller rooms with six to ten beds. It was a light building as each room was well provided with windows. Leaning out of these windows was strictly forbidden. The Allied P.O.W.s were the first occupants of this splendid building.

For those who had been prisoners for two years or more in Bari, Montalbo, Sulmona and other earlier camps this was heaven.

Coupled with the war going well in North Africa at this time, this led to great improvement in prisoners' morale.

It was, of course, surrounded by the usual barbed-wire fence with guard towers at each corner occupied by the under-sized medical category C.3 soldiers allotted to guard us. Behind was a field about two acres in size which we were given permission to turn into a playing field. Here rugby, soccer and basket-ball were played with gusto. The field was also used for open-air classes. It later provided the opportunity for a small number of inmates to escape, as described by Toby Graham in the next chapter. Running across one corner of the sports ground was a small stream. The racing fraternity used to race sticks or corks down stream and had great excitement betting on the results.

The prisoners enjoyed a tolerable standard of living due mainly to the expert catering ability of Lieut. Leon Blanchaert, a Belgian serving with the British army who spoke six languages, including Italian. Our allotment of Red Cross parcels—one per man per week—was not distributed individually, but was taken into a central store under the control of C. D. 'Kit' Patterson, from where individual and personal items such as soap, chocolate and cigarettes were distributed weekly. The other contents such as cereals, butter, cheese and meat products were used to augment the somewhat meagre official Italian rations. The latter included a bread ration of one small roll a day and half a litre of wine. However, some prisoners always felt hungry. Meals were taken at mess tables in a room in the basement.

The first arrivals at this institution were some hundred and twenty officers and about thirty South African other ranks from PG41 at Montalbo, a small circular castle about forty kilometres south-west of Piacenza. They took up residence on 1st April, 1943, when PG41 was closed down. The South African orderlies were white and had been drafted in by the Italians in the hope that this would cause trouble—which it did not! These were followed at intervals by parties from other camps such as Rezzannello, Chieti, Sulmona, Capua, Padula and others. The final total was about five hundred officers and a hundred other ranks.

The daily routine varied little. There were roll-calls morning and evening, after which the day was our own to do as one wished. Voluntary classes on a wide variety of subjects were organised and well attended. Some took vigorous exercise, formal as games or informal. Seven-a-side rugger, at which the South African other ranks team was unbeaten, and six-a-side soccer was organised. Keen bridge players played endlessly with post-mortems far into the night, while others spent much of the time reading. Others merely sat about and talked in groups or just stared out of the window.

The library was a well-used facility. It was made up of books sent from the U.K. with some provided by the British Embassy in the Vatican. Most officers, having read a book sent from home, passed it on to the library. All books were examined by the Italian authorities; the hard-back covers were torn off in case a map or other aids to escape had been secreted beneath the end papers.

Morale had both its collective and individual aspects. Living conditions, which at Fontanellato were good, and the war news affected everyone. Some prisoners were now in their third year of captivity. Many had been taken in the disastrous battles of Gazala and Mersa Matruh in June, 1942, when one could be forgiven for thinking that the 8th Army was no match for the Germans. Although Allied fortunes had turned at Alamein and with the landings in North Africa, few prisoners could foresee the end of their incarceration. Boredom inevitably set in. The longer-term prisoner had read most of the books available, had tried the classes and become disenchanted with them. In a large group of men thrown together in a confined space, it was not surprising that frustrations and tensions developed. Individuals were affected differently by these conditions. Some had received no news, or only belated news from loved ones at home. Some had children born since they left the U.K. and whom they had never seen. Correspondence with home was rather a lottery. We were allowed to send a short formal letter once a month, but transport was slow and complicated, so that a reply could take two or three months and was particularly welcome when received. These and other circumstances increased anxiety and lowered morale.

It was not until later that we realised how extremely fortunate we were, compared to prisoners in many other camps in Italy and Germany; or, indeed, to the ghastly conditions endured by the Russians and Germans in each other's hands, and to the almost unbearable sufferings inflicted on Allied prisoners in Japanese hands.

One variation in the daily round was the walks. Those who wished were able to go out approximately once a week on formal walks under escort in groups of about forty or fifty, or as many as the limited number of guards could cope with. In spite of the prisoners being on parole not to try to escape on pain of the privilege being withdrawn, each walk, which began about 7.00 a.m. before the heat of the day, was headed by an Italian officer with a *carabiniere* and an escort of perhaps ten soldiers on each side and at the front and rear. Partly to take more exercise and partly to score points over our Italian guards, we walked at a smart pace along the nearby country roads, so smart in fact that we would leave our escort trailing in our wake until ordered to slow down.

There were occasional theatrical entertainments staged by the Drama Group in which were some experienced actors and producers. Remarkable ingenuity was shown in the making of costumes and stage sets. One show was a performance of Somerset Maugham's '*The Circle*.' There was an excellent band, brass and string, which gave much-enjoyed performances from time to time, sometimes coupled with a variety evening when some inmates sang songs or gave recitations. These performances were always popular because, whatever the standard, they took one out of the atmosphere of the prison camp and gave a chance to think of other things. These events were held in the large hall, which was an ideal place. A number of accomplished artists practised their skills in the camp and at least one exhibition was held.

A popular venue was a bar run by Tommy Pitman, which opened for late morning and evening sessions. One could buy vermouth which was drinkable and either the cheap vino *molto ordinario* which was quite dreadful, or more expensive wines, always provided one had the wherewithal. As P.O.W.s we were issued by the Italians with 'pay' in camp money, based on the pay received by Italian officers. We believed this was considerably less than for equivalent ranks in the British army.

An amusing and interesting feature of camp life was the activities of 'Opportunities Ltd.' or 'Opps.' This was a loose organisation run by Pilot Officer Bill Rainford or 'Rainy' as he was known—a most enterprising individual who, it was said, had been a member of the crew of a Blenheim bomber shot down over Bardia on 10th June, 1940, the day Italy entered the war. 'Opps' provided a multiplicity of services, for which he charged 10%, such as tailoring, watch repair, recovery of cigarette lighters dropped down loos, exchange of clothing, and also chocolate and cigarettes; in fact, almost anything except a means of escape from the camp.

An incident which caused some excitement occurred one hot, sunny afternoon in August, 1943, when we heard the sound of a large force of aircraft approaching from the north-east. We soon picked out a formation of thirty to forty U.S. Flying Fortress bombers heading south-west at a great height, the sun glinting on their fuselages. We could also see that one plane at the tail of the formation was on fire, and the crew began to bale out one by one, drifting down directly towards the camp!

This caused intense activity among the Italians. The camp truck set out with several soldiers aboard to round up airmen. We were disappointed that they were not brought into the camp. The sequel to this was that when the writer was in Marrakesh in mid-December waiting for transport to the U.K. he met a U.S. bomber pilot on local leave. As we talked it came out that he was on that raid. The formation had flown from a U.K. base across Germany, bombed the ball-bearing factory at Regensburg and proceeded on over Northern Italy, finally landing at Algiers. He was most interested to hear what had happened to the 'ship' that came down over Fontanellato.

We were fortunate that among the senior officers was Lt.-Col. Hugh Mainwaring who had been G.S.O.1 (Operations) at 8th Army Headquarters. Immediately after the end of the battle of El Alamein he moved forward to find a new site for Army Headquarters. Perhaps he was a little too keen and farther forward than he should have been, because he was captured by German rear guards near Mersa Matruh. He gave four lectures on the desert war from the 1940–41 campaign against the Italians up to and including the third battle of Alamein. Most prisoners had perforce a very limited view of the fighting and of the battle as a whole, and probably were captured amid considerable confusion. Mainwaring gave us a broad picture of these battles, and was able to explain the reasons for actions which up to then had been something of a mystery to many of us. Also there was a steady trickle of new arrivals, mainly wounded officers from hospitals, and those captured in the Alamein, Mareth and later Tunisian battles. From them we were usually able to catch up with news of the recent fighting.

Following the successful invasion and capture of Sicily, the war came ever closer to the Italian mainland. The Italian press began to prepare the population for the inevitable invasion. A remarkable example of this was an issue in August of the prestigious paper *Corriere della Serra* which devoted several pages to a fulsome eulogy of the British 8th Army. It was described as a superbly-trained and equipped force and reassured those Italians who might find themselves in 'occupied territory' that they would have nothing to fear from invaders. Could one imagine, say, the *Manchester Guardian* doing likewise in July, 1940, about the Wehrmacht?

An efficient news service in the camp was run by an American journalist named Larry Allen, who had been on H.M.S. *Ark Royal* when she was sunk in the Mediterranean. He posted on the notice board the official Italian communiqués and extracts from the newspapers. There was also a clandestine radio set in the camp, the whereabouts of which was a closely-guarded secret. This set had been made entirely from Red Cross parcel tins and camp wire. The only exception was the valves which by some devious means were brought in from outside.

British broadcasts were listened to on this set, and Allen skilfully worked the news received in this way with that printed in the Italian papers, so as to conceal the source of the information. He always started his accounts with the word 'Flash.' When, on 21st July, the news came through that Mussolini had been deposed, Allen posted a bulletin with the headline 'Flash, Benito *finito!*'

2: Early Escapes

by Toby Graham

AT CHIETI I had been involved in escaping activities and tunnelling with a number of others including Denis Duke and Tony Roncoroni.

The day after our arrival at Fontanellato, Duke called together the escapers from Chieti and told us there was no Escape Committee in PG49. He said he intended to talk to representatives from four camps from which the prisoners had come recently and form one. I told him I had an outline plan of escape, and he said I could go ahead with preparations once he had made certain that no one else in the camp had a prior claim. Next day Denis sidled up to me in his secretive manner and murmured that Jimmy Day and Michael Ross had registered a similar scheme the previous week with the S.B.O. He suggested that, as the playing field was not due to open for another fortnight, the two teams should work out a joint scheme on the understanding that Day and Ross would use it first.

The camp was guarded by a double barbed wire fence about nine feet high with nine feet between the two lines of wire. At each corner of the main compound, which was eighty yards long and sixty wide, was a raised sentry box with a machine gun in it. There were two entrances which are shown in the diagram.

Behind the building was a grass field which was designed to be used for exercise in day-time. It was outside the compound but the Italians told us that when it had been wired in it would be opened each morning at seven o'clock and closed soon after roll-call in the evening. Two sentry boxes would be built at the far end of the field but they would be vacated when the field had been cleared each evening. The problem for a would-be escaper was how to remain behind after the field had been cleared and the sentries at the far end removed. It would be comparatively easy to crawl across the field in darkness and wriggle under the wire at the far end, for the night sentries would be watching the compound, not the field. The solution seemed to me to be to dig a hole in the field and be hiding in it when the field was cleared and searched in the evening. The problem was how to dig the hole under the watchful eye of the day sentries in their boxes at the far end of the field and to camouflage it so that the sentries would not spot it when they cleared the field. Tony Roncoroni and Peter Joscelyne thought this idea was promising and agreed to use it.

In the week before the field was opened the five of us met to discuss plans for the escape. One problem was being able to breathe once we were in the hole and covered with soil. The other two had made gas masks in which they were planning to be buried with snouts above the ground, through which they could breathe. My scheme was to dig a long, narrow trench large enough to hold three people. The trench would be roofed in with boards and covered with earth; an entrance hole would be made at one end and closed over with earth again when we were inside, breathing in through the nose and out through the mouth in order to keep the air pure. This scheme was adopted as it seemed to be the simpler of the two.

The next thing we had to think about was how we were going to dig the hole without the guard seeing us. This was fortunately solved without much bother because the first thing that the committee was going to do when the field was opened was to construct

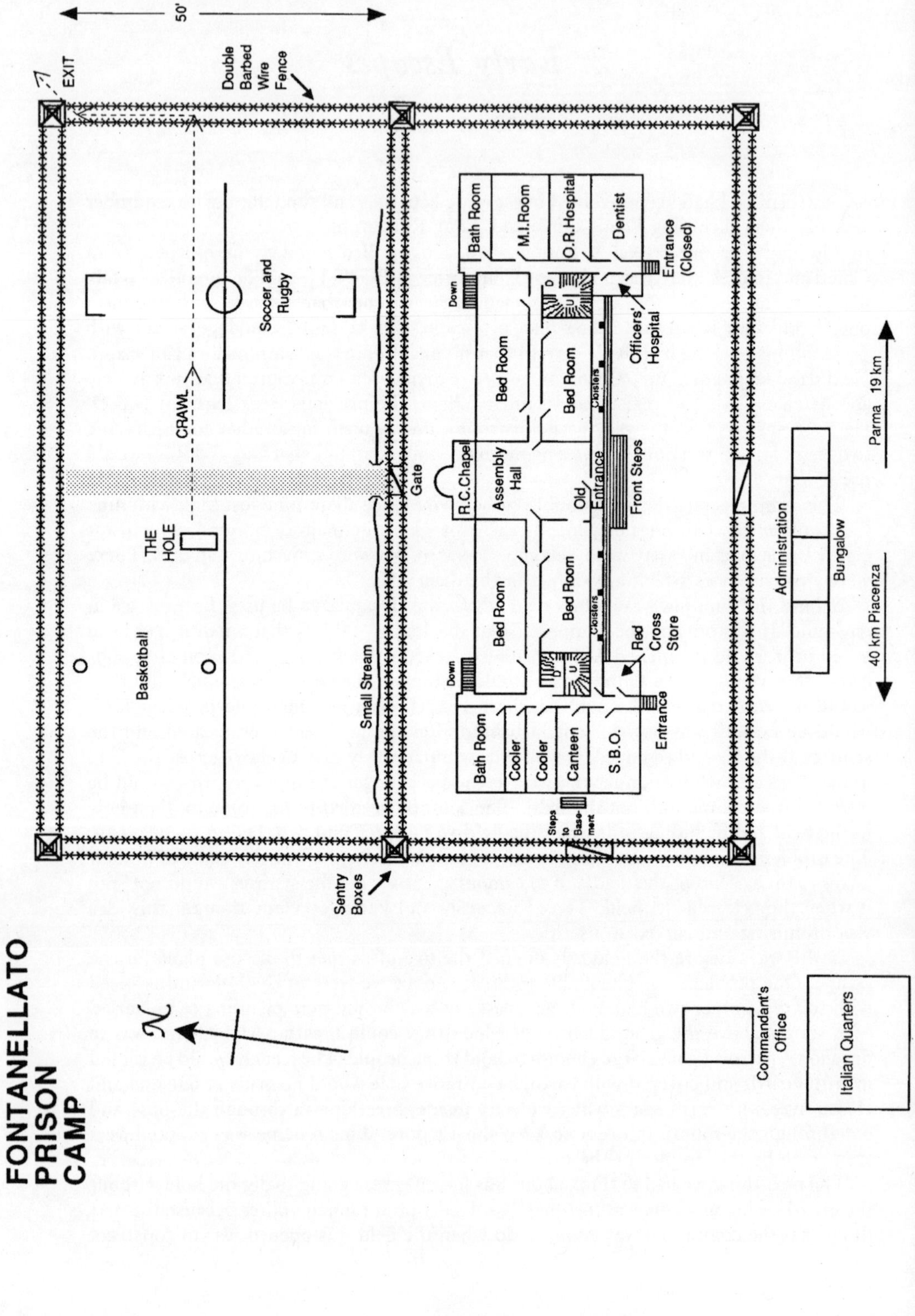
FONTANELLATO
PRISON
CAMP
N
50'
EXIT
Double
Barbed
Wire
Fence
Sentry
Boxes
Basketball
THE
HOLE
CRAWL
Soccer and
Rugby
Small Stream
Gate
Bath Room
Cooler
Cooler
Canteen
S.B.O.
Steps
to
Base-
ment
Down
Entrance
Bed Room
Bed Room
Red
Cross
Store
Cloisters
R.C.Chapel
Assembly
Hall
Old
Entrance
Front Steps
Bed Room
Bed Room
Officers'
Hospital
Bath Room
M.I.Room
O.R.Hospital
Dentist
Entrance
(Closed)
Administration
Bungalow
40 km Piacenza
Parma 19 km
Commandant's
Office
Italian Quarters

two playing fields, one for soccer and rugger and the other for basketball. A great deal of digging would be required and under cover of the activity we hoped to be able to work unnoticed.

The day of the opening of the field arrived and saw fifty officers levelling the field industriously. By the end of the day they had levelled it to a distance of twenty yards from the far end; we decided to start the next day and work exactly abreast of the levellers, so that the interest of the sentries would not be invited by the sight of two officers working by themselves.

The digging was to be done by Tony and myself while Peter, the sapper and miner, operated in the workshops producing boards nine inches by one foot six. The board-making started the day the field opened and in spite of endless friction with the theatrical-props people, who worked in the same room, Peter made enough for us to start.

The following day the levelling party was out again in strength, working this time not quite so enthusiastically for the good reason that they had to keep in line with us. The system was to dig a square hole of the right depth and breadth and place one of the planks over it. The plank was then covered over with earth and another hole of the same size begun next to it. When the second hole had been completed the thin earth partition between it and the preceding one was removed, and we then had a rectangular trench one foot six inches wide and three feet long. To save time we left spaces between the boards, relying on the heavy soil to prevent any earth falling in. Thus, although we had only laid two boards of total breadth eighteen inches, the tunnel was actually twice that length. The beauty of this method was that at no time was anything larger than one hole visible at one time, and if a sentry showed signs of interest it was the work of only a minute to cover the hole and start working innocently on the field.

The total length of the hole had to be fourteen feet; this we had measured indoors by Tony lying down with Peter on his legs, both facing one way, with me on Peter's legs facing the other.

The digging took on the nature of a routine after the first few boards had been laid. The man doing the digging, sweating with exertion and anxiety, would sit down to slide each board into place. Seated, he reached out with his left hand for the board—by this time being shuffled towards him under cover of a coat—and pushed it into position under his legs. Then he would get to his feet again and fill in the earth over the top.

Jimmy Day and Michael Ross were to enter the hole after the evening roll-call. Recently, roll-calls were being held in the playing field. This made it easier as it meant we could put the escapers in afterwards and not have to face another check until midnight. The midnight count was made by the orderly officer when he came round every room and looked at beds to see that they were occupied. Hugh Hope, who had come with us from Chieti, was very good at making papier-mâché dummies, and he made two wonderful heads with healthy mops of hair for us which we planned to put in Jimmy's and Michael's empty beds. The roll-calls on the following day were to be faked with the aid of two officers who would feign sickness in bed. As soon as the Italians had counted them on the ground floor they would race up to the top floor and jump into the other beds and be counted again.

The roll-call bugle went punctually at six o'clock and the prisoners trooped out into the field for the count. This was a good start because it was essential that the count should be completed in time for us to put the two escapers into the hole before the field was closed at supper-time. Occasionally the Italians held roll-call so late it was almost supper-time before it was over and they then closed the field immediately afterwards.

The roll-call on this occasion finished in ten minutes and the five of us walked slowly over the hole. Denis had arranged for twenty people to remain in the field playing ball games in order to attract the attention of the sentry while Jimmy and Michael were entering the hole.

The next five minutes were tense, for if anything went wrong and we made a mistake that led the sentry to suspect us, not only should we be unable to get away the following night, but the pair in the hole would stand an excellent chance of being butchered.

After a casual glance round him, Tony seated himself on top of the hole and began to uncover the entrance in a nonchalant manner. Michael, meanwhile, was lying on his stomach ready to plunge into the hole as soon as the word was given. Tony had soon cleared the earth away and with a quiet, 'Off you go Mike,' gave the signal for Michael to take an acrobatic dive forward. Jimmy soon followed him and I could hear them sorting themselves out inside. At the far end I sat ready to free the rubber breathing apparatus. Michael reported all was well but that he felt a horrid feeling of claustrophobia because the boards were only two inches from his face. There was a moment of consternation because Jimmy, on a trial run, could not move the entrance boards from the inside but Tony soon arranged things to his satisfaction so that he could get out without making too much noise and commotion when the time came.

Very soon after we had got them settled in the Italians started to clear the field. We left, each, I suspect, thinking of the hazards that lay between that moment and the following evening when we were to make our own exits.

Standing in our room we watched the field being cleared. To our dismay, as soon as all the prisoners were out of the way, a party of one N.C.O. and eight men went into the field in a most purposeful way and started fanning out across it. They walked slowly forward, diligently searching the ground. One or two of them prodded the earth with bayonets.

'Here it comes boys,' said Tony, as we watched the proceedings. 'I wonder what on earth we can have done wrong, I thought we did a good job. I could have sworn the Eyties never saw us put those two in.'

Meanwhile the N.C.O. stood on the roof of the hole while he shouted instructions to his men. Our hearts were in our mouths as we waited for the whole thing to collapse under his weight. He was a burly man, large for an Italian.

Then, miraculously, the party wheeled and started to move away from the danger area. They obviously suspected something but what that something was we never discovered. In the hole two frightened officers were waiting for the end in the form of a bayonet thrust.

That night we had a dinner to celebrate the fall of Tunis and as we ate it we thought of the two unfortunate mortals lying cramped and cold in the hole. We envied them the freedom that would be theirs in a few hours, if all went well. The moon, which was already bright enough to make the crossing of the field a hazardous undertaking, would be brighter still the following night and, unless we made our attempt then, the chance would be gone, certainly for nearly a month and possibly forever.

Once they had got out of the camp, Jimmy and Michael planned to walk all the way to the Swiss frontier, a distance of about one hundred and twenty miles. For the first twenty miles they were going to walk only at night to avoid all risk of being seen. This was to allow us to get clear of the camp if there was a disturbance over their recapture. Previous experience had shown that travelling at night across country was a slow and sometimes impossible business and so, after reaching the Po, they intended to travel by tracks and country lanes as much as possible and only trek across country as a last resort. The country in the plain of Lombardy is intersected by many dykes and rivers. The

Po, a formidable barrier, is about a quarter of a mile wide at Piacenza and this was where the pair expected trouble. However, they were both well supplied with passes and money and hoped to be able to bluff their way over a bridge or else steal a boat.

North of the Po the hills begin and the country becomes progressively more wooded and mountainous. The main industry in the mountains was charcoal-burning, and timber was cut in vast quantities and transported to the plain on wire hawsers suspended on pylons, which saved the Italians fuel expenditure. The wood, so I was told, was sometimes used instead of coal in the industries of Milan and Turin.

The frontier was to be crossed either at Como, which was the shorter and more dangerous route, or at a point north of Lake Maggiore which involved a long walk round the top of Lake Como. Their maps covered both routes and they had sufficient food to last them the fortnight it would take to cover the longer one. Their food was carried in cocoa tins—now the standard method for walkers. All things considered, therefore, they were well equipped and stood a good chance of success.

At ten o'clock that night four of us were standing at an upstairs window trying to see whether we could catch a glimpse of Jimmy and Michael on their way out of the camp. The field lay clear below in the moonlight and it seemed impossible that anyone could crawl across it without being spotted from the sentry boxes. We were straining our eyes to see whether the end of the hole had been uncovered, and trying to make up our minds whether it had or not, when a great outburst of talking and shouting arose from below. My first thought, as we raced downstairs to see what it was all about, was that in some way the Italians had discovered that two officers were missing and were beginning a roll-call to find out who they were.

At the foot of the stairs we saw a slightly drunk officer surrounded by the Italian orderly officer and his gang. In the background were the British Adjutant and his satellites looking very worried. Apparently the drunk officer was having a fight with someone when the Orderly Officer, called very aptly the 'Bed Bug,' arrived on the scene. The drunk at that moment took the opportunity of swinging wildly at his opponent, missed him entirely and sat down heavily on the floor. From the floor he surveyed the room and beheld the musical comedy legs and curiously-shaped bottom of the Bed Bug. He took hold of the legs firmly in both hands and pulled, with the inevitable result that the Italian was thrown violently on to his back. There came a roar of laughter from everyone present and the situation looked as if it might get out of hand. The Bed Bug, a rather unpleasant little man, we thought, stood on his dignity; purple in the face he put the drunk under arrest. A doctor was then procured who passed the man as drunk and he was marched off to bed. With our usual appetite for 'situations' in which the Italians were in a bad position, Tony and I followed the little party to the drunk's bedroom. To our horror we found ourselves standing a moment later outside Jimmy Day's room where of course, one of Hugh Hope's dummies was 'sleeping.' The situation, which a moment ago had abounded with amusing possibilities, was now fast turning into tragedy.

Outside, we just waited praying that a miracle would happen and that the dummies would not be discovered. Inside the room, bedlam was quiet in comparison. The Bed Bug was shouting, the orderly sergeant was shouting, the two stupid soldiers standing at the door were shouting at each other about something quite different. 'If the dummies are discovered at this stage,' I thought, 'the Bed Bug will have a fit.' At that moment he was sitting on the dummy's bed shaking with wrath like a great purple jelly. His arms, like flails, waved in all directions striking the iron bedstead a resounding crack that made him wince. The adjutant, Reggie Phillips, knew what was at stake. Like a good tug-of-war team coach he chose this moment to counter-attack with about ten minutes' concentrated talking, which sounded most plausible and ended by his leading the Bed Bug protesting from the room.

Next morning Tony went out into the field as soon as the gates were open at seven-thirty, and found to his relief a gaping hole and an empty tunnel. He quickly covered the entrance with a deck chair and then went over to the wire. There he found tell-tale marks where someone had crawled through. There was no doubt at all that Jimmy and Michael had escaped. We did not find out what had happened to them until a fortnight later. It was now up to us.

Tony, Peter and I had decided that there was actually less risk involved in travelling by train to the frontier than in walking for a fortnight with all the ensuing fatigue. Once at the frontier we were going to use the short route which had, as a matter of fact, already been used successfully by two of the four men who had got out of the country up to that time.

The plan was to walk to Parma station, ten miles away, and then make the rest of our journey disguised as Spanish workmen. Peter was to be the main prop in the scheme as he could speak Spanish fluently, German well enough to deceive an Italian and Italian well enough to deceive a German.

Mike Goldingham, another of the prisoners from Chieti, had developed in the past months a talent for forgery; equipped with a steel pen, the right type paper and some Indian ink, he proved himself able to make anything from a Gestapo pass to a bank note.

The first necessity when travelling openly in any enemy country is to have adequate papers to prove your identity and to keep you out of the clutches of the police. Prisoners were not allowed cameras and since identity documents usually have a photograph on them, this had proved to be our first difficulty. We had got over it by first searching the illustrated papers day after day until we found a German who looked like us. My photograph was of a Luftwaffe ace who appeared in the paper *Der Adler* after being awarded an Iron Cross. I cut it out and Mike doctored it up with a mixture of nail-varnish and something else which made it stiff and shiny like a real photograph. The facial similarity was really remarkable and deceived everyone to whom I showed it. Tony's was good as well and a little doctoring from Mike made the similarity almost perfect. Search as we would nothing even remotely like Peter could be found and so Mike, when he made the pass, treated the space where the photograph should have been to look as though it had been torn out. To cover this he wrote a letter purporting to come from the passport office to say that the original photograph had been lost and that the new one had not yet been developed.

The cover-plan was that we were three Spanish workmen who had been working at Innsbruck but who had been sent down to Lecce to work on the aerodrome. We had been working there for the past three months and now that the job had been completed were on our way to another aerodrome at Como. This story was to last us as far as Milan, where we became workers going on a holiday from a factory in the city. Peter was to be a South American to account for his Spanish accent. I was his nephew who had spent long enough in South America to have picked up an accent as well. We were respectively Pedro and Juan Gonzalez. Tony, who spoke no word of the language, was to be a rather dumb friend who seldom said anything.

To support our story we had a wonderful array of documents made for us. I had one from my employer at Vigo. This was an astonishingly dirty bit of paper kept in one piece by sticking plaster. It was in the sort of condition you expect after being in a mechanic's pocket for six months. The burden of the text was that I was a very diligent young man and would everyone please be kind to me. Over and above this I had another letter from my mother—written in Spanish by Peter—which was full of flowery Latin phrases. Peter who, for the purpose of this operation only, was married to a girl in South America, had a big fat envelope full of love letters written in the best Spanish style with pictures. These were mostly photographs of his *bambini*.

Our passes were made out of some paper that came off Red Cross parcels. They were beautifully done in freehand by Mike and they really did look as though they had been printed. They were embellished with swastikas which were stamped on with a rubber pad. During April, letters for prisoners had gone astray and finally arrived after travelling through Germany. At some period in their wandering they had been censored by the Germans who plastered these swastikas all over them. Mike had promptly collected all the envelopes together and made a negative of the swastikas on a rubber pad. From then onwards all documents made in the camp were German.

To strengthen our story we found someone who knew Vigo well and were able to learn the geography of the place well enough to answer questions. My employer, Señor Martin, was a real man and so, if it ever got to the stage of checking up as far back as that, we might be covered.

Our clothes were the only weakness in our scheme. The other two had made home-made coats which were tidy but not much else, but I only had a sweater of Italian make and a scarf. Our trousers were all right, but our boots—cut down British issue in my case and Italian in theirs—were not very good. The trouble was that we were not sure what foreign workmen were wearing at that time. The Italians always wore hats and ties but it was a fairly safe bet that foreigners would not be so well dressed as the natives. Clothes anyway were the hardest thing to obtain and no one in camp had a suit that they were willing to lend and risk having confiscated if we were recaptured. In fact anything which was loaned to us was lost to the owner. If we were successful and got back to England there would be no means of returning it, and if we were recaptured everything was automatically confiscated. Good clothes were as hard to obtain as a pass out of the country signed by Mussolini himself. The latter, Mike Goldingham would willingly have supplied at a moment's notice.

At six o'clock that evening we were all ready for the adventure, but when at a quarter past six, there was still no sign of roll-call we began to feel apprehensive. A delay in roll-call meant a shorter time for getting into the hole afterwards.

At six thirty we were still waiting and the Italians had not even started to parade their men outside the gates. By twenty to seven I had practically given up hope of getting out that night, and the thought of crawling across the field the following night with a still larger moon lighting up the place like day was daunting.

Then, at a quarter to seven the Italians came running into the camp at the double, little realising the anxiety that they had caused. After an amazingly fast performance the roll-call was over at five minutes to seven, leaving us exactly five minutes to get into the hole.

The same crowd of games players gathered round as on the previous evening and Denis started to uncover the entrance. I lay on my stomach ready to dive in as soon as he gave the word to go.

More than once Denis gave me the stand-by order but each time, just as I was about to get in, an Italian walked along the edge of the wire and started looking in at us, or one of the sentries in the boxes began to take an acute interest in our part of the field. The minutes ticked away until the time came for the field to close. There was no sign of the usual party of men who were responsible for clearing us out and so when the opportunity came Denis gave the 'All Clear' once more. This time I had my head already in the hole when Denis called to me in an urgent voice to come out again. I shuffled myself out and saw that both the orderly officer and the sergeant of the guard had climbed into the nearest sentry box and were staring hard in our direction. For a moment the officer turned to the guard standing beside him and said something to him in an undertone. The sentry immediately cocked his machine gun and the officer and the sergeant both loaded their revolvers. For a while all three remained motionless staring into the field, then the officer pointed straight at us and the sergeant laughed. There seemed little doubt that they had seen us. Hurriedly Denis covered up the hole and as casually as possible we left the field.

The field-clearing party came in as we walked out of the gate but they did not, as we were afraid they would, walk straight over to the hole and expose it. Instead they performed the usual quick search and then came back into the house-compound, closing the gate behind them. The sentries in the boxes at the far end were dismissed and it seemed as though the Italians had not seen anything after all. Then, on second thoughts, it seemed more likely that they had caught Jimmy and Michael, had found out how they had escaped and were now waiting for the next party in order to catch them red-handed and butcher them in the hole. However, we thought we should attempt it because it was only surmise that the Italians knew what was going on, even though they had acted in a suspicious manner.

After dinner we had a conference to discuss the matter. The Italians had not searched the field later that evening and we began to hope that perhaps after all our suspicions were unfounded. However, Major Pyman, who was now in charge of escapes, was against our making an attempt the next night because the moon would make crawling across the field too hazardous. After a long discussion we convinced him that to abandon the scheme now was more than our souls were worth and so he agreed to allow us to go.

Although we had been delayed one day and consequently the crossing of the field had become more difficult, there were two advantages that we had gained. First, Jimmy and Michael had been given another day's grace; we were reckoning to get out of the country, if we were fortunate, in twenty-four hours and so the roll-call deception was to be discontinued the morning that we escaped. The reason for this was that we wanted the Italians to discover that five people were missing without first finding out that the roll-calls had been falsified for two days. In this way we could use the same deception again. The second advantage was that on the morning following our delayed escape there was to be one of the periodic organized walks. On these occasions the roll-call for those not selected to walk out was held as usual in the camp after the walkers had departed. As very frequently more officers went on the walk than were intended by the Italians, a deficiency of one or two at the roll-call in the camp could be accounted for by the presence of gate-crashers on the walk. Therefore it could not be ascertained that a prisoner had escaped until the return of the walkers. Three hours might be gained by this.

Roll-call next day was held punctually at six o'clock, the deception party did their work again. Tony moved the earth from the entrance this time because he looked less guilty than Denis. Sitting astride the entrance he did as good a job as last time and within a minute he gave me the order to go. Inside the hole it was pitch dark and the space so confined that I found it hard to roll over onto my back. Half way along, a large sod of earth had fallen in and it took me a full minute to clear it. The other two had left behind them a bottle of water which had leaked and left a sticky patch of mud. Finally my head bumped against the end of the wall, and I heard 'Crump' Colbeck, who had been our agent with the committee for any equipment that we wanted, tell me to try the breathing apparatus. The atmosphere was close and foul and the nearness of the roof to my mouth was unpleasant. The breathing tube was full of earth at first but two good blows cleared it and the unpleasant trapped feeling left me. Meanwhile thumps and bumps proclaimed the arrival of Peter and Tony and soon we were all three wedged in like herrings in a tin. The boards were then replaced over the entrance and after one or two experimental heaves to see whether he could move them from the inside Tony reported all was well. With a few facetious remarks the burial party left us to our fate.

We conversed quietly for a minute or two checking up on each other's degree of discomfort. Tony had just asked me in a loud voice whether my breathing tube was working when an even louder voice from immediately overhead interrupted him. It was the raucous voice of the guard commander who was performing his usual trick of standing with both feet firmly planted on the top of the hole. As a matter of fact he was standing fairly and squarely on Peter's breathing tube, rendering it useless. We lay like the dead, hoping that he had not heard us. From inside the building I heard Claude Weaver's loud yodel; the church clock struck the quarter; the Italian shouted, and my heart missed a beat. A little trickle of earth ran into my eye as he shifted his position; a clod of earth flopped down with a strange echoing thud by Tony's legs; then complete silence except for our laboured breathing and the pounding of our hearts. An age seemed to pass and then, when I still thought that the guard commander was standing above us, I heard the crash of bolts as he closed the gate into the field.

The passing of time was punctuated by the village clock as it struck the quarters. The time went by quickly and soon it was getting dark outside. Tony and I found breathing easy because as soon as the Italians had gone we managed to force a few small holes at either end of the tunnel which let in some fresh air. In the centre, Peter was not so fortunate for his breathing tube never recovered from the guard commander's heavy feet.

We planned to start leaving the hole at ten o'clock. Tony was to climb out first, taking with him a small bag of food. The route lay across the field and under the first wire, then between the wires to the corner of the field, under the empty sentry box and through the outer wire. We planned to join up under a row of vines a hundred yards from the camp.

Just after ten o'clock I heard a rattle of falling earth followed by what sounded like a minor land subsidence. Tony was heaving his seventeen stone out of the hole. Shortly afterwards I heard him as he scraped over the roof on his way to the wire. Peter departed next and I prepared myself to move by edging down towards the entrance. A quarter of an hour later I started to try to get out. As I had to emerge feet first, my feet appeared, then my unsuspecting body and lastly my head. Apart from anything else it was extremely difficult to emerge at all without waving my legs in the air. After ten minutes I emerged into what at first I took to be a sunny day. Then my eyes focussed and I saw, shining brightly in the moonlight, the sentry boxes forty yards away. There were twenty-five yards of field between me and freedom.

I started to crawl across the field feeling like a fly on an electric light bulb. Every now and then a nightjar let out a noise which made me jump and some marsh bird kept giving long piercing whistles like the guard giving the alarm. The rattle of the main gate as the orderly officer came in sounded exactly like a squad loading Bren guns by numbers.

I reached the wire at last, where I was out of sight of the sentry boxes, and crawled under it without making a sound. The next few minutes were almost pure joy as, knowing I was nearly free, I pulled myself along through dew-wet, sweet-smelling grass until, soaked to the skin, I arrived at the last obstacle, the wire under the sentry box. Climbing through it my shirt got caught in a strand and made a noise. The sound was telegraphed down the fence to the occupied box in the house compound. The sentry, no doubt waking up with a start, uttered a horrid ejaculation. Then, like a dog, he held his head motionless for a full minute listening. I lay still, my head pressed into the grass, half in the camp and half out. Then abruptly the sentry relaxed and resumed his usual heavy gape. I crawled on, blessing his stupidity. When it was discovered that we had gone, he and his friends were given two years' imprisonment.

The time was now midnight and it seemed to be unlikely that the other two would have waited so long at the rendezvous, so even when I went down the second row of trees in which we had planned to meet, I was not surprised to find no one. We had arranged another rendezvous on the road in case of accidents, and so I went on feeling certain I would find them waiting for me there. But when at the second rendezvous there was no sign of them it occurred to me that they might be waiting in another row of trees. I therefore walked down the road as far as the first row of vines and crawled back along it. But I still found no sign of them and began to feel a little worried. I had expected them to wait at the second rendezvous until at least half past twelve because the ten miles into Parma would only take three hours and our train was not due to leave until five fifteen. It was now a quarter past twelve and I decided that I would wait at the rendezvous on the road until one o'clock.

At one o'clock, when there was still no sign of them, I gave up waiting. It looked very much as if they had gone on to the station to wait for me there. In view of the risk of staying in the camp vicinity I decided to set out alone for the station.

It was a wonderful night and I felt so free and full of life that there was little room for gloomy thoughts about my failure to rendezvous with the others.

Before I had gone two hundred yards I met a man coming the other way. I still had battledress over my civilian clothes but he did not notice anything odd about my appearance and merely passed by with a friendly *'Buona sera.'*

The road I had to take went in a circle round the village and finally brought me out on the Parma road about half a mile east of Fontanellato. Once on this road I took off my battledress and buried it in a ditch. While I was taking it off I made a disastrous discovery. Getting through the second wire fence I had torn the back of my blouse and made a great rent in the civilian shirt underneath. It was ripped from the shoulder all the way down one sleeve, and it was now impossible to wear it in daylight. Underneath I was wearing only a vest. The sweater which I was going to wear for the train journey was being used by Tony as a receptacle for our food. There was nothing for it but take the shirt off and wear only the vest, even though this made me look little better than a tramp.

In spite of everything, the night was so fine and warm and I was so thrilled with life that the gravity of the situation did not dawn on me. I would be able to cover the vest with a sweater when I met the others. In the meanwhile, oh purest joy!

The miles floated by unnoticed and I felt tireless. Very soon I came to a level crossing, which I remembered from the map was a few hundred yards from the main road from Parma to Milan. I approached it warily, expecting a night watchman to challenge me. Nothing stirred as I crossed the line, however, and I was soon walking swiftly toward the sound of heavy traffic which proclaimed the *Strada Nazionale*, which was a fine wide road with four lines of traffic and a white kerb-stone on either side.

Between Fontanellato and Parma there flows the Taro River, a broad swift stream with steep banks and a rocky bed. The *strada* crosses the river by a bridge four hundred yards long, to which I soon came. The bridge had been guarded at one time but now the sentry box at the end of it was not occupied. This information had come from someone who went into Parma for medical treatment.

By half past two I was within four miles of Parma and, since I was just then approaching a small village in which I could hear dogs barking, I decided that it would be prudent to make a détour down a small lane leading off to the right. Half a mile further on, feeling thirsty, I stopped to drink from a swift, gurgling irrigation-dyke running by the road side. Then I sat down on a bank and dozed off to sleep, lulled by a restful chorus from thousands of crickets and intermittent solos from frogs. The moon hung like a copper shield in the west; a more mellow and tolerant moon than the one I had cursed three hours before. There was a sweet smell of new hay in the air and the warm impression of a flower garden not so far away. These gave me a feeling that I had never felt before; that I was experiencing beauty, that I was really appreciating it and that this moment would be with me forever.

I woke up at four o'clock and started off toward the station. The little twisting country lane took me past every farm in the district and at each a dog barked.

On the outskirts of Parma I rejoined the main road and was soon walking along grey, sleeping streets disturbed only by the hurrying footsteps of some nocturnal visitor or the swish of a bicycle as a *carabiniere* returned home from night duty. Dark haunts opened off the road and an evil stench was wafted from their depths. Soon I came to Parma River and stood on the bridge sniffing the good fresh smell from the water beneath.

It was still only quarter to five and so I walked as slowly as I dared down the broad avenue which runs between the road and river bridges. When I reached the station there was nearly twenty-five minutes to go and so I sat on a stone seat in some gardens in the square outside. It was cold now and I fell into an uneasy sleep.

Five minutes later I woke up with a start when a pudding-faced *carabiniere* sat down beside me with a bump. I looked up and he eyed me suspiciously, or so I thought.

At ten past five there was still no sign of the others and so foolishly, I went into the station to buy my ticket. I said, 'Third single to Milan,' in my best Italian and was given my ticket with the change by the girl behind the grille without apparently creating the least suspicion. Then I walked past the ticket man at the barrier and stared back at the *carabiniere* lounging beside him unconcerned. This gave me confidence and I began to forget the strange apparel I was wearing.

For the life of me I could not remember the word for 'platform,' and so, rather than give myself away as a foreigner at such an early stage, I walked about the station hoping that I should see a notice telling me the right place to go for the Milan train. Just a moment before a quarter past five a train came into another platform from the south and so I presumed that it was my train and started back towards the subway. Before I had gone ten yards an officious-looking man, dressed in the gorgeous uniform of the Italian train police, tapped me on the shoulder and asked me what I was doing. I told him in broken Italian mixed with Spanish that I was a Spanish workman on my way to Como, and as much more of the story as I could manage with my limited vocabulary. When he saw my pass the swastikas seemed to annoy him and he would not listen to a long story I was telling about pilgrimage to the beautiful city Parma. 'You had better come along with me to explain all this to the *carabinieri,*' he said, and so I was marched along to the station police-post. There I found a junior *carabiniere* officer seated at a desk and I was told to sit down. My papers were placed before him and I began to tell him that I had to get to Milan by the train that was already in the station and since I had authority for the journey he should let me go. He said nothing for a moment or two as he scrutinised my pass. Then he glanced at me and looked at the pass again, obviously comparing the photograph with my appearance. The pass seemed to satisfy him for he put it aside with a grunt and turned his attention to the letter of recommendation. He read it through and again seemed perfectly satisfied for he nodded to the train guard who had brought me in and began to be a little less frigid in his manner. Meanwhile I tried to put over the 'poor Spaniard in a strange country' act in a convincing way for there was still a minute or two before the train was due to leave and an offensive at that stage might have turned the battle in my favour. But the *carabiniere*, although he remained quite amiable, did not seem inclined to let me go. He gave me back my pass and letter, apparently quite satisfied with them, but there still remained in his manner an undercurrent of suspicion due probably to my shabby appearance. The *carabiniere* sergeant had said something to the effect that a man on his way from one job of work to another would be dressed in his best clothes and not a disreputable vest, and this was, I think, the reason why I was not released.

At the end of another ten minutes a *carabiniere* corporal came into the office and the officer asked me for my pass again and showed it to the new arrival. The corporal whistled with excitement when he saw it and said something to the officer which I could not catch. The officer in his turn then became very excited and picked up the telephone and gave a number. A moment later he was talking to someone, a note of urgency in his voice, but he spoke so quickly that I could not understand what he was saying. He put the receiver down with a bang and, rubbing his hands together, leered at me in an unpleasant manner. What all this was about I had no idea but from the general atmosphere of noisy confidence in the office, it appeared as if the noose was tightening about me.

From the subsequent conversation I gathered that the Corporal had shown two people on to the train who had similar passes to mine and, as I had previously denied that there were any others with me, the Italians were naturally suspicious, so had phoned to Piacenza to have the train stopped and the two people in question interrogated. Unhappily there could be no doubt who the two were and it looked as though our little adventure was drifting to its doom through my stupidity in going on to the station platform alone.

A little time later the telephone rang again and from the conversation I gathered that things were going according to plan. At one stage the *carabiniere* read the name 'Gonzalez' from my pass and nodded and smiled when the man at the other end said something in confirmation.

The conversation ended and the officer turned to me with a grin and said, 'Are you English? Do you speak English?' I told him that I had learned a little English in school but could only understand it very slightly.

'Well, I don't believe you,' he said, 'because we have just caught your two friends at Piacenza, and they are both English, of that we are certain.'

'My two friends?' I asked, 'I have not got two friends at Piacenza!'

Everyone in the room laughed at this in a disheartening way and the officer said, 'Come on; It is no good denying it, you are an English prisoner of war.'

There did not seem to be any doubt that the game was up so I played my last card, admitted that I was a prisoner and said that I came from Bari. This would ensure me a good long journey on which there might well be an opportunity to jump the train. They swallowed this at first and even started looking at timetables, but the plan was ruined when a call came from Fontanellato claiming me as one of their prisoners.

In due course I rejoined Tony Roncoroni and Peter Joscelyne and we were taken back to Fontanellato, and thrust into the 'cooler.'

The cooler was a comfortable place with spring beds and plenty of space. The kitchen fed us on rations and so, all in all, it was no punishment. There were three other beds in the room besides our own, one occupied by Beauclair who had tackled the Bed Bug two nights before and the other two labelled 'Day' and 'Ross.' It struck us that the Italians were being over confident in this and we hoped against hope that they would be confounded.

At the end of ten days there was still no sign of Jimmy and Michael, and as we knew that they planned to be over the frontier on the eleventh day, we felt safe in pulling the interpreters' leg about the labels on the beds. It was obvious they were giving up all hope of catching them and when another day passed without any news of them, we became jubilant. But just before dark on the twelfth day there was a bustle outside the door and Jimmy and Michael were pushed into the room, followed by the interpreter. At first they said nothing to us but after the Italian had gone and the door was locked, Jimmy, looking thin and tired, told us the story.

When they had left the camp fourteen days before, they had struck north across country. The going was so difficult, thanks to the irrigation ditches which were hard to cross, that it took them four days to reach the River Po. At that early stage they were two days behind schedule. On the third day, they were walking along a country lane when they noticed five or six young men on bicycles following them. For nearly an hour the men stayed behind until finally they started calling out. Jimmy and Michael were in no mood for argument and so they jumped through a hole in the hedge and ran across country for all they were worth. They managed to shake off their pursuers in a short time and found another lane that took them in the right direction. It was then that Jimmy made the frightful discovery that in the chase he had lost his food belt containing not only half the food that the pair were carrying but also his pass and half their money. This loss, the discovery of which was so similar to that of my own torn shirt, was the indirect cause of their failure.

On the fourth night they reached the River Po and lay up on the bank for a time to wait for an opportunity to cross. During the day, thirteen ducklings swam slowly past within easy reach of them and Jimmy, on the spur of the moment, stretched out his hand and collected the thirteenth as it went by. This he proceeded to pluck in a business-like way but was unable to cook owing to the danger of lighting a fire. For the rest of that day they were plagued by a myriad of small children looking for the thirteenth duckling. They nearly fell victims to the menace of children like so many of their predecessors.

That evening they walked down the river until they found a rowing boat in which, although it had no oars, they decided to cross the river. They intended to use drift-wood to control the boat but as soon as they had cast off they found they had very little control and were rushing headlong down-stream. The boat kept spinning round in the current and it was all they could do to stay afloat. By chance the stream gradually bore them over to the other bank where the current was not so swift and they were able to use their driftwood oars to reach the shore two miles below their starting place.

For two days they were hopelessly lost in the hills. There were only rough tracks and no one of whom to ask the way. When they had wasted a day by going ten miles out of their way they found a peasant who put them on the right track. The full significance of the loss of their food now showed itself, for all this time they had to live on half rations which meant barely half a tin of composite ration each a day. The ration, worked out medically, was sufficiently good to support hard work for three weeks, but only provided a whole tin was eaten each day.

On the evening of the eleventh day they reached the outskirts of Como, still two days behind schedule. The route entailed passing through the town and crossing the main railway line to Switzerland at a point where it ran into a tunnel. This was the only possible place to make the crossing because the line itself was guarded closely. Once over the line they would find themselves in good cover overlooking the actual frontier and by lying up throughout the day they could learn enough to make their attempt on the following night. The question was whether to walk through the town straight away or wait until the next night. The food situation was critical and the sooner it was eased the better. On the other hand they were tired and there was therefore more chance of making a mistake than if they waited until next day when they had rested.

The choice was one which so many escapers had to make. Was it better to submit to the urge to get on or was it wiser to take the last hurdle slowly? It is a question which is answered wrongly by at least one escaper in two. There was the longing to end the mental strain as soon as possible and to get a square meal, and the feeling of confidence which can lead you astray as surely as the lack of it.

Jimmy and Michael went on into the town to try to cross the railway line before light and in so doing made a fatal mistake. They had a sketch-map of the town which showed the road they had to take in order to reach the railway tunnel. There were no incidents on the way through the town and they were soon walking through the outskirts on the far side. According to their map they should have been walking along a road with the railway running on one side of it and a large park with scattered trees in it on the other, but even in darkness they could see that this was not so and they soon came to a place where the road ended in some gates. Cursing the sketch-map which they thought was incorrect, they retraced their footsteps but failed to find the right road even after wandering about for some hours. They had to decide whether to return to their starting-point and wait until the next night or try to find a new lying-up place on that side of town.

They had by now made up their minds that the sketch-map was useless and so they decided to go back through town and find another way across the railway on the following night.

Half-way through the town they were stopped by two *carabinieri* who demanded to see their passes. After showing their one pass they were allowed to proceed. A mile further on a *carabiniere* came up from behind and told them to halt. They recognized him as one of the men who stopped them in the town. He said he was sorry but it was necessary for them to come back with him to the *Carabiniere* station and explain who they were and what they were doing. They told him that they were Germans from Milan who had come out for the day and missed the last train. Unless they got back to Milan in time for work in the morning they would inevitably be punished.

'Nevertheless,' the *carabiniere* said, 'You must come along with me because I believe that you are escaped prisoners of war.'

Since neither of them could speak a word of German and it was therefore quite certain that their story would be discredited when they reached the *Carabiniere* station, Michael tore up his pass and threw it into a ditch.

At the station they were searched and their money found and placed on the table. They were then taken into another room in turn and interrogated. But they were exhausted and were disinclined to make intelligent replies, yet while Michael was in another room Jimmy managed to steal back half the money that was lying unwatched on the table. He did not take it all but left a number of notes of the smaller denominations in the hope that the others would not be noticed. Soon after Michael's return to the room the theft was discovered and he was accused of stealing the money because by this time Jimmy was being questioned. Michael denied having anything to do with it, but they insisted on searching him; he demanded an apology when the search revealed nothing. Three minutes later Michael really did take some money off the table but the *carabinieri* were by this time rather afraid of him and did not dare search him again. Jimmy was searched when he returned, but only half the money that he had stolen was found.

The following day they were taken back to Fontanellato by train and at Milan station they produced the money and offered their guards a meal. The Italians thanked them and together they sat down in the station buffet. The rest of their journey was uneventful and they reached camp at dusk.

Although we had all failed to get out of the country we had learned some useful lessons, the most important of which was the absolute necessity of being well-dressed. Good passes were not enough if the holder of them was dressed like a tramp. The old point of making wrong decisions at the end of a long day had come out once more. Also we had picked up some priceless experience about the working of the Italian mind and the conditions in the country, and if we should ever have to make another bid, we should find the experience of the greatest value.

After our escape, we did not consider trying again because it was apparent that the Italian part in the war was ending. Their defeat in Tunisia was followed by the loss of Sicily in July. Others were not so patient. A remarkable tunnel was dug down between the walls and had begun to make progress when the Armistice came in September. Before that the guards had been made to dig a deep trench near the wire to foil any tunnel attempts. The soil from the tunnel was concealed in the attics and was still there several years later.

Jack Comyn and Hugh Hope, the maker of our dummies, co-operated in the only attempt in the latter weeks. Comyn was made British assistant to a sergeant who looked after clothing confiscated from parcels sent from England. The Italians were meticulous about accounting for everything and Comyn did the paper-work twice a week in the hut outside the camp where the clothing was stored. He soon grasped that he had an ideal opportunity to don some of the clothing and get out of an unlocked window overlooking the road, if the sergeant's attention could be diverted. Comyn cleared the plan with the S.B.O., Colonel De Burgh, and collected maps, food and a compass which he hid in his battledress and put the plan into action.

While Hope engaged the sergeant's attention in one room, Jack Comyn did a quick change in the other, dirtied his face and donned a workman's hat that he had made of paper, picked up a hammer that he had previously found lying about and got out of the window. He wrote, 'I looked round. There seemed to be nobody about. I had to walk along the road past the front of the camp. All went well until the road veered away towards the town. Suddenly a man in uniform stepped from behind a tree in front of me. I knew him well; he was the Brigadier (equivalent to a sergeant) of the *carabiniere* detachment which supplemented the camp guards. *"Dove andate?"* he addressed me. Alas my Italian was not good enough to maintain any pretence of being a building worker, certainly in the face of the *Carabiniere Reali*, one of the best police forces in Europe.

'Within a few minutes I was ushered into the office of the Camp Commandant. This was Colonello Vicedomini. He was of the old school, a perfect gentleman, liked by all. The Brigadier told him I was *Tenente* Comyn, caught while trying to escape. I was still in my disguise, and at first the colonel refused to believe it was me. When convinced, his consternation was amazing. "But *Tenente* Comyn" he exclaimed, "my sentries on the wire might have shot you—and then what would your mother have said?" As I had not expected this question I was uncertain how to reply, but his concern touched me, and I received with equanimity the statutory sentence of twenty eight days solitary confinement which he awarded.'

3: The Armistice

AFTER the surrender of the Axis forces in Tunisia, King Victor Emmanuel was determined to make peace with the Allies. On 25th July 1943, in a decisive move, he ordered the arrest of Mussolini and installed Marshal Badoglio as head of a non-Fascist Government.

When the news of the fall of Mussolini reached Fontanellato it produced great excitement among the Italians. Initially they thought it meant the end of the war for them. The camp soldiery poured out of their huts, jumping up and down with delight, tearing the portraits of *Il Duce* from the walls and treading them underfoot. The Fascist salute was immediately abandoned and all the Fascist symbols on house numbers, kilometre stones, signposts, etc., were torn down or painted out overnight.

Meanwhile, unknown to us, in the succeeding days there was intense diplomatic activity to attempt to end the war in Italy. Richard Lamb, in his book *War in Italy 1943–45—A Cruel Story*, describes how Italy, after the fall of Mussolini, could have been brought into the war on the side of the Allies, and the fighting in the southern half of the country could have been avoided.

There was a suggestion that an anti-Fascist army from Italian prisoners-of-war should be formed. But Anthony Eden, the British Foreign Secretary, insisted on 'unconditional surrender' if any Italian Government wished to make peace. So the opportunity for an unopposed Allied landing in Italy was lost.

On 25th July the Germans had four divisions fighting in Sicily, two divisions in the south and only one incompletely-equipped division in central Italy, whereas the Allies had six divisions in North Africa and Egypt, including the U.S. 82nd Airborne Division, in addition to the two armies engaged in the Sicilian campaign. Although short of landing craft, these would have been largely unnecessary if the landings were unopposed.

When Badoglio assumed power at the head of the new Government he sat back and did nothing. No attempt was made to seal the German—Italian frontier. Germany reacted quickly and sent large forces into northern and central Italy. By the end of August the Germans had seven fully-equipped divisions in Italy.

However, the Italian authorities did take one action which vitally affected the future of every Allied prisoner-of-war in Italy. When the Germans demanded that British prisoners-of-war be handed over and sent to Germany, this was peremptorily refused by the Italian Foreign Minister, Raffaele Guariglia.

Badoglio, fearing arrest by the Germans, did nothing to make contact with the Allies until, prompted by the King, missions were sent to Tangiers and Lisbon with the message that the Italians were ready to change sides. This approach was rebuffed by the British Cabinet led by Eden (Churchill was away *en route* to Quebec), who insisted there could be no negotiations unless the principle of unconditional surrender was accepted. After much time had been lost, General Castellano was authorised to fly to Sicily to inform General Eisenhower that the Italian Government was prepared to accept 'unconditional surrender' provided the Armistice was announced after an Allied landing in 'sufficient strength.' A short surrender document was signed by Castellano on 3rd September. In this it was agreed that the U.S. 82nd Airborne Division would land on the airfields near Rome and thereafter co-operate in operations with the Italian

Motorised Corps of four divisions under General Carboni, whose task was to block all routes leading to the airfields.

In order to co-ordinate plans with the Italians, General Maxwell Taylor, Second-in-Command of 82nd Airborne Division, and Colonel Gardiner arrived in Rome on 7th September. They were dismayed to find that no preparations had been made by the Italian General Staff. It had been agreed they would provide searchlights to illuminate the airfields and also 350 lorries and much heavy equipment for use by the Americans. Badoglio had not ordered any action on Castellano's plan and, in the absence of this, the Italian General Staff did nothing.

General Carboni, the officer responsible for defending Rome, had lost his nerve. He emphasised the large numbers of German troops in the area, and gave a false report on the shortage of petrol and ammunition for the Italian mobile corps. Taylor and Gardiner demanded to see Badoglio to impress on him the necessity of the Italians complying with the commitment made by the Castellano mission. Badoglio rejected this, saying the situation had changed and Castellano had not known all the facts.

In view of the lack of Italian co-operation, General Taylor concluded that the airborne landings were too hazardous. On receipt of his message an irate General Eisenhower cancelled the airborne landings, but would not postpone the date of the Armistice from the 8th to the 12th September as Badoglio wanted. Some American forces had already started and had to be recalled at the last moment. As Richard Lamb says, 'Thus the Italians lost a heaven-sent opportunity to emerge from the fighting side-by-side with U.S. troops against the Germans.'

The S.B.O. (Senior British Officer), Lt.-Col. Hugo De Burgh, D.S.O., M.C., made it his business to establish good relations with the Italian Commandant, Colonello Vicedomini, a veteran of World War 1, who had fought with the British and was almost openly Anglophile. His Second-in-Command was Capitano Camino who was even more friendly towards us. He had an English wife and had been in business in England before the war.

While it was obvious to the prisoners that Italy could not continue to fight the Allies for very much longer, a new anxiety came to the surface. Would the Germans come in and take over the camp? We had long discussions on what would happen if Italy surrendered. Some thought the Germans would withdraw to the line of the River Po or even to the Alps. In hindsight this was not a sensible forecast. On the contrary they were more likely to keep the Allies as far away from Germany for as long as they could.

Every S.B.O. had been given an order by the War Office that, in the event of an Armistice, prisoners should remain in their camps until further orders were received. The thinking behind this must have supposed that the Allies would overrun most of Italy quite quickly; also to avoid the danger of reprisals if there were mass break-outs by prisoners. The wisdom of this order was challenged by G.H.Q. Middle-East in Cairo, but no amending instruction was sent to S.B.Os. in Italy. In contrast, on 6th September the Italian War Office issued an order to Camp Commandants that they had to prevent British P.O.W.s falling into German hands. If camps could not be properly defended the prisoners should be set at liberty. How many Commandants received this order is not known, but it seems likely that Colonello Vicedomini did. He certainly made our exit easier by having a gap cut in the perimeter fence.

The evening of 8th September was hot and sultry. Suddenly there was a great commotion in the courtyard and on the road outside the camp. We went to the windows to see what was happening. In the courtyard and round the guard room the soldiers were shouting, dancing, and throwing their caps in the air. We could hear the words *'pace'* and *'armistizio!'* Presently the Commandant came over to our building from his office;

a few minutes later the word went round to assemble in the main hall. The S.B.O. said he had an unconfirmed report of an armistice. Everyone had to remain calm and dignified, and he would try to keep everyone informed of the latest news. Later it was confirmed that an Armistice between the Allies and Italy had been signed at 7.20 p.m.

We all went to bed in a state of controlled excitement, wondering what the morrow would bring.

4: *The March Out—First Days of Freedom*

ON THURSDAY, 9th September, 1943, as we were dressing, the order was given to parade in the yard at 9.00 a.m., The S.B.O. said there was a danger that the Germans would arrive at any time to take over the camp. The Commandant had arranged for scouts to be sent out to give early warning of any approach by German troops. Therefore all prisoners must be ready to move at five minutes' notice, taking with them only what could be carried in a haversack. The alarm would be the blowing of three 'Gs' on a bugle.

During the morning haversack rations and some food from Red Cross parcels were issued, also a small quantity of lire provided by the Commandant. Nevertheless, there was time for most people to have a last drink of vermouth in the bar which was soon packed. Tommy Pitman and his helpers were kept busy serving drinks as fast as they could. During the morning two JU88s flew low over the camp, but there was no hostile action.

Then the alarm sounded. Memories vary on the actual time of this. Douglas Flowerdew thought it was 10.00 a.m.; Denny Abbott said, 'It was as we were having lunch;' Hugh Jobson and Lt.-Col. De Burgh, who should know, said it was at 12.00 noon. He thought an orderly body marching across country would be less suspicious, rather than a rabble. The Germans might regard our military formation as a friendly one if we were seen.

Everyone was outside within ten minutes. No.2 Company (Lt.-Col. Ted Everett) was first to be ready and marched out in threes through a gap in the wire at the far end of the playing field, guided by Lt.-Col. Hugh Mainwaring and Capt. Camino, who had reconnoitred a lying-up area during the morning. The other Companies quickly followed. An incongruous sight was Eric Newby leaving the camp on horseback. Newby had fallen down the marble stairs on 7th September and broken his ankle. Just outside the wire a cavalry regiment trooper produced a horse which he said, 'Was as quiet as a lamb.' Newby was lifted on to its back and off they went, having been photographed by Ronnie Noble.

Lt.-Col. Denis Gibbs remarked on a marvellous feeling of freedom which came over him as they were marching out and he always thought he would be home by Christmas. Ian English wrote, 'It was grand to be crossing fields again without guards in attendance.'

Everyone seemed, as Newby wrote, 'Irrationally happy, they all could have been recaptured by three armed Germans.'

The leaders kept up a good pace. It was a hot day and soon everyone was sweating profusely. During the march, which was in a north-westerly direction, a German Junkers 52 flew over quite low down. The column must surely have been spotted. The lying up area, which was about five miles from the camp, was the Rovacchia di Paroletta. It became known as the Bund. It was a deep winding riverbed with steep banks covered with scrub, beeches and poplars bordering the River Rovacchia. Here the Companies dispersed, each to its own area pointed out by Hugh Mainwaring.

The orders were to keep under cover; air and ground sentries were to be posted. Adrian Barber remembered being told there should be no talking to the locals! The orders included what was described as firm information that there had been Allied landings at Trieste, Genoa and La Spezia.

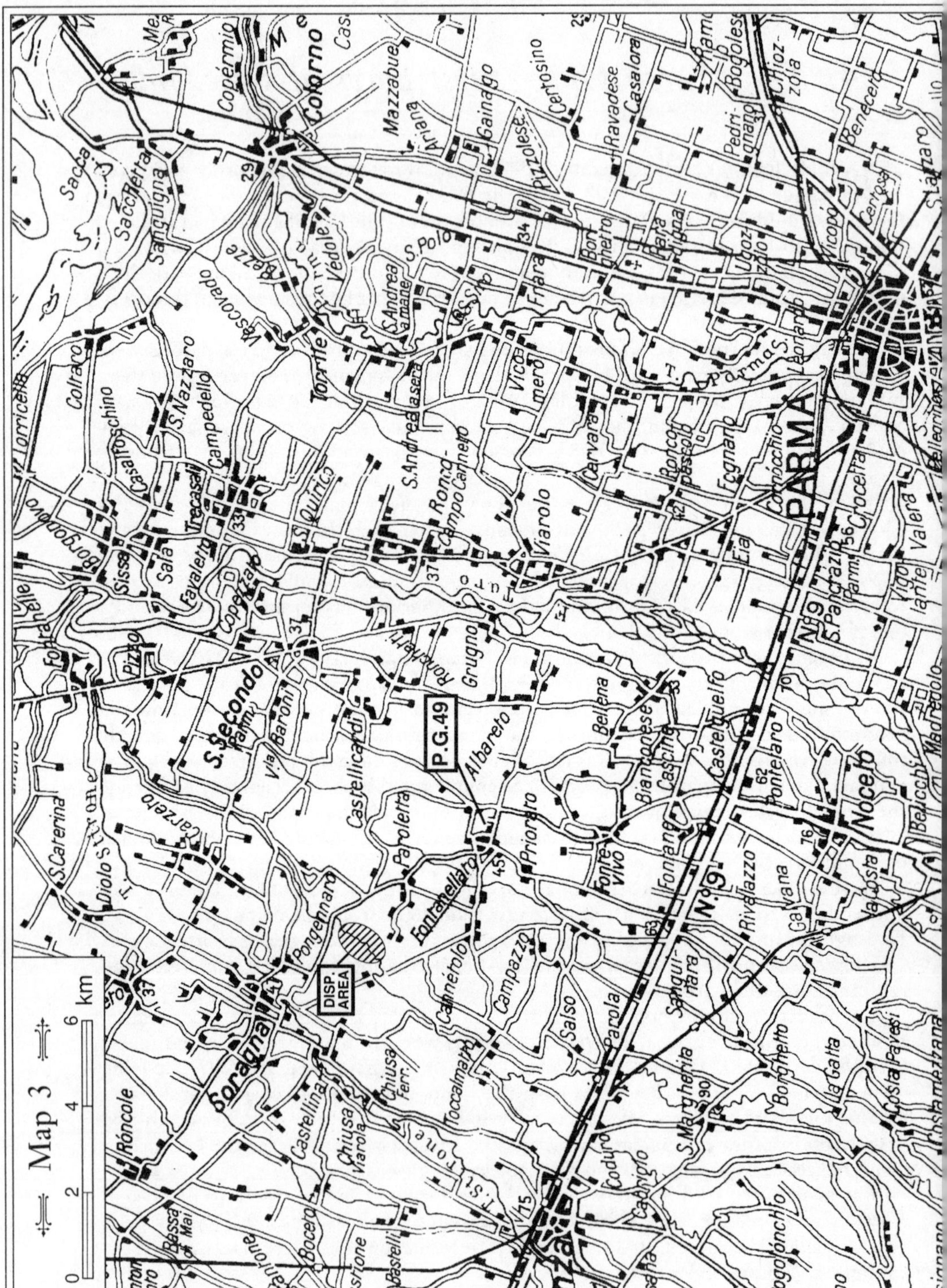
Map 3
0 2 4 6 km
P.G.49
DISP. AREA
PARMA
Colorno
S.Secondo
Soragna
Noceto
Fontanellato
Fontevivo
Castelguelfo
Albareto
Priorato
Pongennaro
Paroletta
Castellina
Chiusa Viarola
Toccalmatto
Campazzo
Salso
Parola
Roncole
Sissa
Trecasali
Viarolo
Vicomero
S.Polo
S.Quirico
Torrile
Vedole
Mezzano
Ravadese
Casalora
Pizzolese
S.Pancrazio
Fognano
Eia
Sanguigna
Sacca
Coltaro
S.Nazzaro
Campedello
Cannetolo
S.Andrea
Baroni
Castellicardi
Grugno
Bellena
Fontana
S.Margherita
Borghetto
La Gatta
Costa Pavesi
Rivalazzo
Pontetaro
Vigolante
Valera
Crocetta
Copezzato
Coduro
Cogolonchio
Sanguinara
Gainago
Mazzabue
Centosino
Pizzo
Fontanelle
Diolo
S.Caterina
Viarolo
Ronco Campo Canneto
Bianconese
Cascina

Notwithstanding the order to stay together and under cover, a few officers were anxious to be on their way. Later in the afternoon of 9th September Johnnie Birkbeck sidled up to Duggie Clark and suggested 'it was time to be off.' So they crept away trying 'to avoid being seen by our own people who were all over the place, in case we ran into a senior officer who might not see eye to eye with us on this point.' When they got clear they changed into civilian shirts and light khaki shorts which they had brought with them and they buried their battledress.

During the afternoon news came through from Italian civilians that the Germans had arrived at the camp in two trucks soon after the prisoners had left. They were furious that the 'birds had flown,' and arrested the Commandant, Colonello Vicedomini. He, poor man, was sent to a concentration camp in Germany. Although he managed to survive the frightful conditions, his health was irreparably impaired and he died soon after his return to Italy at the end of the war. The Germans ransacked the camp and looted everything they wanted and, it was said, became hopelessly drunk on our wine ration. Afterwards the people of Fontanellato went into the camp and salvaged food and clothing, a lot of which was brought out to the prisoners during the next two or three days.

That night the prisoners lay out under the stars trying to sleep. The main discomfort was the swarms of midges and mosquitos which feasted on any exposed skin. As Peter Langrishe wrote, 'We exchanged our relatively comfortable and ordered existence for a rough and uncertain way of life.' Those on sentry duty could hear the noise of heavy traffic on the Via Emilia, the main road from Bologna to Milan. The difficulty was that we could not tell which way the traffic was going. Some thought it meant the Germans were pulling out, others that they were reinforcing Italy as fast as they could. From time to time we could see giant 12-engined German transport planes lumbering over the Lombardy plain. Otherwise there was little air activity.

The morning of the 10th September was fairly quiet. The S.B.O. called a conference at 1.00 p.m. at which he said that there were too many hiding in this fairly small area, so No.3 Company (Lt.-Col. Burne), No.4 Company (Lt.-Col. Ardern) and the Other Ranks Company (Major Fane Hervey) would move off that night to the hills. The remaining two Companies would probably move the next night. He considered he had carried out the War Office order as far as he was able in the prevailing circumstances.

During the day the local Italians came with food and civilian clothing. Many prisoners changed there and then, giving their battledress to the Italians. Others, such as Jack Comyn, kept their battledress jackets, thinking they might be shot as spies without some item of British uniform. For that reason several, including Ian English, Jack Moore, Wilfred White, 'Toots' Williams and Ted Pryke, did not change out of battledress, at least until much later. Bill Bowder and Peter Ellis made the mistake of handing over their army boots as well as their battledress and were given cheap thin shoes in exchange. They lived bitterly to regret this in the coming weeks. Most of the civilian clothes were thin, of poor quality and often a bad fit. In fact, there were some strange sights on the Lombardy Plain as a result of the change of clothes. One of the strangest must have been Douglas Flowerdew; having heard that the Germans were rounding up able-bodied Italian men to work in factories and on defences, he decided he would be safer dressed as a woman. He was fitted up with a blue stockinette dress, a blue kerchief padded out with maize hair on his head and high heeled shoes! Philip Kindersley reckoned that by the evening of the 10th September about two hundred prisoners had been taken to the local farms.

That night the three Companies, less those who had already left, moved off. Major Fane Hervey had reconnoitred down towards the Via Emilia and had been told that the road and railway were patrolled. He had also heard the English news which talked about strong forces landing at Taranto, the Italians were taking up arms against the Germans, but there was no word of landings further north.

At this time prisoners could be seen in small groups earnestly discussing what they should do. Robert Williams summed it up by listing six possible options:—

1. To wait, hopefully for only a short time, for the arrival of the Allied troops;
2. To walk south and cross the lines to rejoin the British Army;
3. To enter Vichy France;
4. To cross into Switzerland and be interned;
5. To go to the coast, find a boatman and sail south or to Corsica;
6. To contact an Allied submarine or gun-boat.

A few opted for Switzerland which was the nearest safe haven, but the near certainty of being interned was a big disadvantage. The option of a boat or naval vessel did not arise until later, but a few did manage to escape that way. But Tom Pitman, Black, Arthur Gilbey, Tom Wheeler, Eric Hopkins and Maurice Goddard with six from 28 Field Regiment, and John Woods on his own set off in the direction of Genoa or La Spezia. Some, perhaps more bold or more far-seeing than their fellows, set off straightaway, or a least within two or three days, to walk south. The majority chose to wait for the arrival of the Allies. This was not mainly because it was the easiest and, perhaps, most comfortable option, but also because of the uncertainty attached to going north, west or south when the information on the battle situation and the whereabouts of the Allies was so vague, even when that could be obtained. 'Let us wait until things are clearer' was the general philosophy. They were no doubt influenced to some extent by the weather remaining fine, mainly sunny and very warm.

A fairly large number of ex-prisoners from Fontanellato elected to stay, for some days at any rate, on farms in the general neighbourhood of the town. Among these were Norman Girling, Dick Booth, Bert Dennis, Bill Ramshaw, Adrian Barber, Lt.-Col. Denis Gibbs, Peter Barshall, Barnard, Whitehead, Hemmings, A. A. Jones, 'Doc' Rogers, Rex Smith, Peter Langrishe, Gervase Nicholls, Geoffrey Phalp, Denis Orme, Jim Thickett, 'Q' Evans, Reggie Beales, Capt. Lowsley-Williams, Dick Kamman, Gordon Beasley, Tom Stuchberry, Peter Holworthy, Garth Ledgard, Greenwood, Marcus Kane-Burman—the South African dentist, Jack Clarke and Jack Paterson.

By day they would come from the various farms to the general area of the Bund which, as Gervase Nicholls said, 'became quite a social centre.' Signora Camino, the Italian interpreter's wife, and some of her friends, used to bring a picnic. Lowsley-Williams went round dressed only in a pair of shorts and a straw hat. Gordon Beasley became a self-appointed billeting officer and Dick Kamman made himself responsible for collecting news bulletins.

Barber describes the beauty of Lombardy Plain in September—'a rich, incredibly fertile expanse of corn and maize, thick undulating grass, tall limes, stunted willows interspersed with vines, and the whole area divided by wide, grassy walks or avenues like the well-kept pleasances in an old-world garden.'

Several offered some unskilled help with farm work, harvesting, muck-spreading, and occasionally treading grapes, stripping maize cobs and the like. Gervase Nicholls and Geoffrey Phalp helped to load a sow into a cart. Nicholls wrote, 'It took four of us, plus the old grannie, who was armed with a broom, to get the animal into the cart. Two of us held her, one by each ear, with Geoffrey in his innocence on her tail. The poor sow must have been very frightened and lost her self-control. As a result, Geoffrey's trousers were a lamentable sight. Elsie, the daughter, laughed until she cried, but she did take his trousers and wash them.' Stuart Hood and Ted Mumford continued to help with farm work when they went up into the hills. They did some ploughing and digging and built up quite a reputation among the locals, so their services were in demand.

In the early morning of 20th September the Germans, knowing full well that there were numerous British prisoners in the general area of Fontanellato, raided several farms, which resulted in thirteen prisoners being recaptured, with more in the next few days. Very unfortunately one officer had kept, against orders, a detailed diary. This contained names of Italians who had helped the prisoners, with tragic consequences. Andrea Baruffini, of Cannetolo, Fontanellato, and another farmer, were captured and sent to Germany. Both died or were killed in Mauthausen. As a result of this and the fact that it became increasingly unlikely that an Allied landing in the north would be launched, many ex-prisoners moved away from the Plain, either towards Switzerland or west to the Apennines.

Noel Burdett and Geoffrey Collins were two who lived in the countryside near Fontanellato, fed by local people. They tunnelled out a shelter to hide in by day. When the Germans raided the area they hid in a field of maize, and through the tall stalks, watched German field boots tramping by. Then a baker, Ferrucio Incerti, persuaded Dr. Guiseppe Sambataro to drive them to his brother Fernando Incerti's flat in Parma. Here they were hidden for seven weeks. One night they were taken to another escapee hideout where they found Ronnie Noble and a companion. On the night of the 18th November, acting on a tip-off, young Fascist *Milizia* arrived to search the flat. Fortunately, Fernando's niece dashed upstairs to warn Burdett and Collins, who climbed out on to the roof where they hid for three hours. Finding nobody and no signs of occupation the *Milizia* left cursing. The escapers would no longer put the Incerti family at risk and left the flat. They came into the hands of *Italia Libra*, a communist network who moved them round several hideouts in Parma.

A fairly large number of prisoners had already moved south or west into the hills, feeling it safer to wait there to see how the situation developed. Those that remained of No.1 Fontanellato Company on 12th September moved as a Company over the railway and the Via Emilia. There was a lot of noise and confusion getting over the wires alongside the line and several people got split up. This party included Philip Kindersley, Ronald Orr-Ewing, Tom Vickers, Peter Watson, Peter Stericker, Gilbert Pearson and Douglas Turnage. Also travelling west into the hills were Pat de Clermont, Charles Hedley, Jack Comyn, Donald Astley-Cooper, Toby Graham, Tony Davies, Michael Gilbert, Anthony Laing, Robert Williams, Terry Philipsz, Ian English, Jack Moore, Jimmy James and Wilfred White, moving in groups of two, three or four.

The favoured area was Bardi, Varsi, the Pessola Valley, Pellegrino and south towards the valley of the River Taro. As it happened this was a district where there were many Italians who had lived in England for a time; a few more had experienced life in America. Ian English tells how he and his three companions were offered lunch by Signor Moliere and this was taken with Waldorf Astoria cutlery.

In the first few days the ex-prisoners did not know what sort of reception they would be given by the Italians but doubts were quickly swept away by the friendliness and hospitality extended to Allied servicemen.

Most officers decided it would be unwise to walk in daylight, also that roads should be avoided. This led to some difficult night marches, in the early days across strange country and in most cases without maps. However, Graham, Davies and Gilbert decided to walk only by day and so make better progress. Jack Donagher, with Tom Wildy, resolved to travel on roads and, if possible, to use public transport.

Pip Gardner, travelling with Percy Gers and Jimmy Gardner, decided to move east from the Fontanellato area, as they thought there would be too many ex-prisoners-of-war in the hills to the west. Bill Bowder and Peter Ellis also thought east was the best direction.

An exception to this general trend was Ronald Mann. He had badly damaged his right eye on 2nd September and was sent to a prison hospital at Piacenza. The Germans took over the hospital soon after the Armistice. However, on 3rd October Mann managed to escape, using a rope made of sheets. The nuns at a mental hospital the other side of town sheltered him for one night. Then, guided by a monk, he made his way south into the hills.

During this time the Germans made a proclamation over the radio and on posters ordering all Italian army personnel to report to the nearest German headquarters. Also it was declared an offence to shelter, offer food or help in any way Allied prisoners-of-war. Those caught doing so would suffer the direst penalties. As an inducement the Germans offered 1,400 lire (about £20), later increased to 2,500 lire, to any Italian providing information which led to the arrest of an Allied serviceman. As Robert Williams said, '£20 was not as much as the price of a pig.' The vast majority of good Italian people simply ignored this proclamation.

Peter Langrishe and his three companions found themselves in the tiny village of Pieve di Bardi, of which the head man, one Agostino Ferrari, had been for some years a chef at the Connaught Rooms in London. This hamlet of about a dozen families was at one time looking after nearly four hundred escapees.

5: *Relations with the Italians*

ROGER Absalom, in his book *A Strange Alliance*, has written the definitive work on this subject. His monumental research, covering a large number of Allied ex-prisoners and nearly an equal number of Italians in Northern and Central Italy, led to a detailed analysis of all aspects of the complex relationship between the Italians and their former enemies, who arrived in their midst in the weeks and months following the Armistice on 8th September, 1943.

It is not the purpose of this chapter to do the same thing, even on a smaller scale, as Absalom has done so capably. The aim is only to describe the experiences, the reactions with, and the help received from the Italians by those former prisoners of PG49 at Fontanellato who have contributed their accounts. However, many of the thoughts in this chapter are inspired by Absalom's work.

Tony Davies expressed the feeling of many ex-prisoners when he wrote, 'We were living on close terms with people whom, in the ordinary course of events, we should never have met, and whose character, philosophy and mode of living would have remained utterly outside our ken. It was an opportunity that comes the way of very few and it was education in its fullest and richest sense. I consider myself lucky to have had a chance to get to know such people; and, starting out as I did with an intense hatred of all things Italian, I very soon learned that the hard-working Italian peasant is a really delightful person. The ones we met on this walk were the salt of the earth.'

Denny Abbott, walking with Noel Durrant and Theo (Steve) Stephenson, were met by boundless kindliness. The Italians had nothing to gain. If they were caught they could be shot, as indeed many were, and their houses burnt down. As a result of his experiences Abbott said, 'I will never again turn a genuine beggar from my door.' He thought he had learnt to spot an impostor. He appreciated new values of things normally taken for granted, for example a meal, a bed or at least some shelter. Peter Watson said that, 'Despite the German patrols and Fascist Militia, which would burn a farm and shoot anyone giving shelter to refugees, the peasants, with very few exceptions and despite the ever-increasing price on our heads, fed us, let us sleep in their barns and kept their silence.'

Dick Carver found that, unless there was *paura* (fear) due to rumours of house searches and arrests, the *contadini* were almost invariably kind and hospitable. Jack Comyn remembered that on the whole of his walk he was refused hospitality only twice. Money was never offered and never requested. They would leave a note asking the Allies to recognise how much their hosts had done for them. Drew Bethel came to a village where all hundred people suffered from trachoma. He said, 'Their ignorance made their kindness positively biblical.'

The section of Italian society the majority of Fontanellato prisoners had most contact with were the *contadini*—the peasant farmers, particularly those in the Apennines. Certainly they came across, and in most cases received considerable help from the better-off members of society; but it was the *contadini* who had the most direct effect on the lives and well-being of the escapers. So what sort of people were they?

Donald Shaw, who was a countryman himself, noticed that, although many of the families were poor, their small-holdings were self-sufficient. Each had a vineyard (in the districts where vines could be grown), and small fields on the mountain sides. Few fields were given over to grazing; they relied instead on upland pastures to which the children drove the cattle and sheep. Oxen were the main motive power, though mules were important in some districts. On the steep stony mountain tracks sledges were preferred to wheels. There was no mechanisation whatever. Sheep provided the wool for spinning and knitting. The pig—every family had one—was an important part of the rural economy, providing enough bacon and *salame* to last a year. Philip Kindersley noted that the average *contadino* had one cow, two oxen, a pig and sundry chickens, and perhaps a vineyard, a field of maize and wheat.

Maize was ground into a flour for making *polenta* which was cooked in a large pot over the open fire. When the housewife judged that it had reached the right consistency, it was taken off and poured on to the table where it ran over the surface like lava. Tomato puree and perhaps some grated cheese would be added, and everyone gathered round to eat this porage-like food.

In the northern Apennines and other areas where they grew well, much use was made of chestnuts. They were eaten roasted or boiled. Also they were ground into flour which was baked into bread or cakes. Many ex-prisoners found these very stodgy, unpalatable and not easily digested.

At the time the prisoners arrived in their midst, the *contadini* were not short of food. In the weeks following the Armistice an active black market developed. The produce of the farms was in strong demand and the peasants enjoyed a period of mild prosperity. The main shortages were clothes, footwear and salt, most of which came from Sicily. It was only later when the winter set in and the strain of feeding long-stay prisoners and refugees began to be felt, that food became scarce.

The nature of the smallholdings demanded constant toil from every member of the family. Work started before dawn and continued till late evening. The menfolk often had to give their labour on the landlord's farm. When the danger of arrest by Germans or Fascists became acute, it was vital for the running of the farm that the man of the house be kept safe. So it was that he often slept in a hut or a cave, while the prisoners were in his barn.

Ronald Mann gave an interesting description of a *contadino's* house at Frascara in Abruzzi where he lived for some weeks, which is probably fairly typical. The living-room was ten feet square. The walls, from which the plaster was flaking off, and the ceiling, were blackened by smoke. The floor was made of red flagstones. The furniture consisted of a table and five cord-seated chairs. On the walls hung two frying-pans, two or three enamel bowls, two army mess tins, an iron and a grating for a fire. The fire itself was in a small brick semi-circle and had only a small chimney. Above it was an iron bar with hooks for holding cooking pots, some of which were copper. The fire was kept low because wood was scarce, which was a common situation in Abruzzi, and was used for cooking and very little else. This was perhaps just as well because it was very smoky. On a shelf was a polished brass water container of a beautiful shape. All the water had to be carried in from outside. In the basement, which was used as a lavatory, was a hen house. Robert Williams wrote in his diary that the houses were often in a complete muddle with no attempt to make the living conditions comfortable.

Many peasants were simply not interested in the war, except when they had a relative who was a prisoner in Egypt, England or America, or was fighting in Russia. A proportion had spent some time between the wars in America or England. They had picked up a little English, even if sometimes it was only 'Goddam son of a bitch!' But many had travelled no farther than the nearest town and were extremely ignorant of the outside world. Some thought England was part of Egypt and, if one lived in England, it must be in London. Mussolini's propaganda told them that in England everyone ate five meals a day. Few newspapers were read, but radio was listened to with rapt attention. They naturally enjoyed being able to tune in to foreign broadcasts, particularly the B.B.C., after long years of Fascist suppression and censorship. Perhaps this was a source of many wild rumours which abounded and confused the escapers; 'I have a friend who spoke to a man whose brother had heard on the wireless ...'

The *contadini* had a long tradition of hospitality to strangers and those they thought were worse off than themselves. But this is not sufficient explanation of the multitude of examples of escapers being given food, shelter and succour, often for many months, of prolonged self-sacrifice and usually at considerable risk to themselves and their families. Roger Absalom has closely examined the motives, conscious or unconscious, of the Italian people, particularly the *contadini*, in helping the Allied escapers. These applied equally to those from Fontanellato. Two cases are recorded of the motive being carefully explained to the British officers.

Jack Comyn, writing about the conversations held in the evenings with the host family—'all too often the subject was the fate of their sons, far away with the Italian divisions in Russia, prisoners-of-war in Britain or Canada, or just missing. Many mothers told us they trusted in the Lord that, if they looked after us, someone would look after their own sons.' Comyn, worried as everyone was about German retribution if their hosts were discovered sheltering Allied prisoners-of-war, always asked to sleep in the cowshed or a barn, but not in the house. They hoped that, if surprised in the byre, they could vow that the farmer had no knowledge of their presence on the farm. On one occasion, after a convivial evening, they were pressed to sleep in beds. Comyn said, 'I carefully explained the reason for refusing and insisted we should sleep in the byre. An hour later we were escorted there and found all the family's finest pillows, linen and blankets laid out on the stone floor behind the cow's tails. I fear that my Italian had not been good enough that evening and that our hosts had concluded, from what I said, only that English preferences were somewhat eccentric.'

Eric Newby, when summoned down to a village and guided by a little boy, found himself in a mediæval house. In the splendid kitchen seated round a massive table were six men, each with a glass of wine in front of him. Newby wrote, 'The effect produced by the whole lot of them looking down the long table towards me where I stood, a ruinous figure by the door, was of some sort of Selection Board ... I was motioned to take a seat and a glass of wine was poured for me. There was no small talk. The Chairman of the Board, for that was obviously what he was, said carefully and very slowly so that I could understand 'We have been talking about you among ourselves for some days. Many of the people in this village and in the farms round about have sons and relatives who are being hunted by the Germans. Three of them were taken the other day. Some of them have sons in Russia, of whom, so far, there is no news and who may never return. They feel you are in a similar condition to that of their sons who, they hope, are being given help wherever they are, and they think it is their duty to help you through the coming winter, which otherwise you will not survive.' They decided to build him a house which no one except those present and their families would ever hear about.

The help given by the peasants had a moral rather than a material basis. They distrusted and had traditionally resisted the 'authorities.' So to make sacrifices and to take risks for those fleeing from the forces of law and order came naturally to them. Their history had been one of exploitation. The escapers were probably the first outsiders who were not automatically seen as exploiters. The *contadini* were looking, whether they consciously realised it or not, for two things—a new freedom in the post-war world, and the achievement of their true identity and the respect of other sections of Italian society. They could contribute to these aims by helping prisoners-of-war. They were in fact playing a more important role in the post-Armistice war effort in support of the Allies than most townspeople, though this thought probably did not occur to them. The escapers were a means to obtain recognition of a moral status previously denied to them in Italian society.

Absalom wrote, 'The Allied escapers and the Italian *contadini* had a common purpose—to survive the war. For the Italians that included the means for their continued existence—their land, the tools to work it and their livestock.' Most were not politically motivated as many partisans were, but they were looking for a new order and a new freedom in which their lives and status would be very different from their experience up to now.

The handling of ex-prisoners-of-war who decided or were persuaded to stay in an area for some time varied. Some peasants looked on their particular prisoner(s) as their private property and did not want their neighbours to interfere. Robert Williams wrote that the Baldini family in Torsana were determined to help him and Terry Philipsz, while at the same time doing everything they could to keep their secret from the neighbours. They did not wish them to come into their house because of fear of reprisals, but their aim was to keep them until finally released by the advance of the Allies into the Torsana district. Similarly Adrian Barber and Dick Booth were not allowed out of their house during the day in case they were seen by neighbours and given away by careless talk. In other villages many of the inhabitants took their share in looking after the escapers.

Italian peasant culture decreed that women occupied a subordinate place. For generations they had been humiliated and oppressed by men. This was often noticed by Fontanellato escapers in the absence of courtesy and the expression of thanks to female members of the household. The women would not sit down till the men had eaten. The ex-prisoners would be pressed to eat more, but did not know how much should be left for the women and girls.

It was noticeable that often it was the woman of the house who decided whether or not to take in the escapers. Maurice Goddard said that their requests for food and overnight shelter in a barn were sometimes refused by the menfolk, 'But invariably they were overruled by the women whose maternal instincts seldom failed us.' When A. A. Jones and Norman Rogers were north of Aquila on 14th October in an area where there had been much retribution by the Germans, including the shooting of an Italian for helping the British, the women were so scared that they refused them shelter, although their sympathy made tears run down their cheeks.

The older women always wore black dresses. One result of the post-Armistice invasion of refugees was that some women began to question their subordination in family and community, and some would readily have gone to England, though knowing nothing of the language or the country. Robert Williams wrote in his diary, 'The girls come up in the evening to knit and talk. This family has an amazing trust in us because they will allow the girls to visit us at all hours, but they wouldn't allow any such confidence from the Italians.'

It was a common experience, remarked on by Philip Kindersley, Gervase Nicholls and Ian English, that the poorest people were often the most hospitable and were more ready to share what little they had. Robert Williams put it the other way; that the richer the household the poorer the hospitality. An example was given by Hugh Jobson when on 23rd September they were refused food and permission to listen to the radio news by a baroness. Pat Gibson, when surveying likely farms for shelter, always chose the poorest in the belief that the richer-looking ones were more likely to belong to Fascists or their sympathisers. Some escapers graded farms according to the number of haystacks in the yard. Five meant the family was too well-to-do and might be fascist in outlook. Only one haystack indicated the family was too poor, though probably friendly. Two haystacks were about right.

Although most of the ex-prisoners' contacts were with the *contadini*, some escapers were given remarkable hospitality by well-to-do Italians. Jack Comyn records how he and Donald Astley-Cooper were taken to the house of Signor Pietro Falconi, a large landowner. They were asked to show their hands. After examining them, he said, 'Ah officers, I see. You are welcome.' They were overwhelmed by kindness during their three days' stay. The night after their arrival Signor Falconi gave a large cocktail party for his friends to meet them. By day they rode with him on well-bred horses over his estate, oblivious of the fact that there was a German post only a quarter-of-a-mile away. Pip and Jimmy Gardner and Percy Gers were taken to the very comfortable and well-appointed house of a bicycle manufacturer. He sent his wife into the town to buy clothes for them. Their host gave them a bicycle each and a wad of lire and sent them on their way.

Tony Davies wrote of the night of 30th September in a village near Firenzuola when they were approached by a man speaking faultless English who invited them to his house. They were offered a bath with plenty of running water, an elegant dinner and interesting conversation over cognac and cigars. The next morning, after a good sleep in comfortable beds, he replaced some of their tattered clothing. Their host then walked with them for two hours to ensure they took the quickest route through the mountains.

A. A. Jones and Norman Rogers visited Count Brasi Foglietti at the castle of Monte Acuto near Florence. They were also given a hot bath, some clothes and a map, followed by ham and eggs. There were four people in the Castle—the count, his wife, his mother and sister. The husband of the count's sister was a prisoner-of-war in India. They were asked to contact Sir Thomas Wilson, late Under-Secretary of State for the Colonies, and Lady Markham Knell of Sloane Square or the Women's Army and Navy Club. After these few hours of civilisation Jones and Rogers were on their way again by 1.00 p.m. with a picnic of rabbit. Jones wrote, 'We didn't go far before we set upon it. It starts to rain and we are miserable, mud to the top of my boots. Heaven knows how Norman manages in his shoes. Thank goodness we hit a good contact.'

Anthony Laing, when he arrived at the village of Santa Brigida just north of Florence, was warmly welcomed and generously treated by Leopoldo Tarchianni, a Florentine silk merchant, and his entire family at their summer home. He writes, 'So much so that at the first sign of Autumn I began to hesitate about moving south.' However, he eventually decided to move on and felt more comfortable on his own. 'A last visit to Florence to the Tarchianni home, where they generously replaced my wardrobe, gave me money and maps, and Leopoldo pressed his Berretta automatic upon me.'

Peter Langrishe remembers, 'At Trevi we were befriended by a man and his family in a comfortable house, well fed and wined. He was a most amusing character who had been driving heavy transport in Cyrenaica. He had been at Sidi Barrani and Tobruk, but had "scarpered" successfully; "he was not going to get caught," he said.'

On the 28th September 'Toots' Williams, Hugh Jobson and Ted Pryke had reached Umbertide. They stopped at a large villa owned by Signor George Bruffani and were given a warm welcome. After a hot wash and shave, they were given a wonderful supper at which whisky was served. Afterwards, a bed each with clean sheets. Signor Bruffani owned the Grand Hotel at Perugia. His mother had been married to a Cockney pub-keeper in London.

Anthony Laing, Jack Clarke and Teddy Mumford received immense help from the Valvona-Buti family. They lived in a large two-storey apartment in the centre of

Florence. In the family were the son Kim, aged eighteen, and a daughter Toy, of about ten, with an Austrian governess, Antonia Pilser. Pam Buti was born of Italian parents in Northamptonshire before the first World War and was very proud of her British nationality.

Anthony Laing writes, 'From the 24th September, only sixteen days after the Armistice, until 1st March when she was arrested, this very brave lady housed fourteen Allied P.O.W.s, including four of us at one time for a month. Throughout this time she was very generously and ably helped by Mario Nappini, thanks to whom we ate remarkably well and never went hungry. He also provided money and other necessities against our notes of hand. The family were delightful and treated us as a family and we passed a memorable and very happy and comfortable Christmas 1943 with them. They did not want us to leave, but Jack Clarke, Teddy Mumford and I thought that they had done more than their share and that for their own safety they should have a rest. Having tried the Lines and Yugoslavia we then thought it prudent to make for Switzerland. We left them on 21st February, but on the 26th we were replaced by two American Rangers and a British private. They were all arrested in Viale Alessandro Volta on the 1st March and that evening, after dark, the Buti apartment was raided by the Republican Secret Police, who found Erland Hindson, a South African P.O.W. who had been housed since November. The story of what happened later to the Valvona-Buti family is told in Appendix 1.

The actions taken and help given by priests appear in many of the accounts. In view of the important position they held in rural communities, this is not surprising. The priest at Contile, when showing Toby Graham, Michael Gilbert and Tony Davies round his church, said, 'You see, Signore, I am not merely the spiritual father of my flock here in Contile; I am also their adviser and father on pretty well everything else. They bring all their problems to me. When they are sick or hurt, I tend them, as there's no doctor within a day's journey of this place. Family quarrels are brought to me for arbitration and disobedient sons and daughters are sent to me for punishment and guidance. I am called Father, and I am their father and they are all my children.'

Robert Williams said that priests were the special target of the Blackshirt Militia, who were more barbarous than the Germans. Several priests were tortured and shot. But Williams and Terry Philipsz received help from several priests. Some gave Williams, who was an Anglican, up as a lost cause, but Philipsz was a Catholic, which helped.

Ian English remarked that, if there seemed to be no one about when they came to a village looking for a night's shelter, or if perhaps they had been refused at one or two houses, they usually went to the priest's house. Very often he passed them on to one of his flock but, before doing so, he usually let them see a map or listen to the radio news.

Anthony Laing contributes this account of the work of Don Egidio Brogi in and around the village of Acone. 'Some ten miles to the north-east of Florence lie the twin villages of Acone, Santa Maria and Sant' Eustachio, Santa Maria lying at the foot of a semi-circle of rolling hills to the west, like the stage of a classical Greek theatre. Across the River Sieve, one mile to the east, there is similar good farmland including the vineyards of Rufina and, five miles to the south, is the industrial town of Pontassieve. Acone was, therefore, from the Italian point of view, an ideal site for a working-camp of some two hundred-plus Allied other ranks. It was said to have been a happy camp. The prisoners worked hard and were generally well liked by the farmers and industrialist for whom they worked.

'When the Armistice came the Italian Army unit guarding the camp abandoned their charges and fled, and the prisoners filtered out into the countryside. Some turned to the farms where they had worked and were supported by them, generally in hiding in the surrounding hills, but those who had worked in adjoining towns had no ready hides and greatly outnumbered the villagers of Acone, who were trying to sustain and shelter them. Although some British men set off south the remainder was sufficient to place an impossible burden on the villagers and, with the approach of winter, to create a very dangerous security situation.

'Don Egidio Brogi, the elderly parish priest of Sant' Eustachio Acone took over the entire situation. Under his direction the P.O.W.s were moved away from the villages and found shelter in outlying areas, often in caves or well-hidden huts. As the villages were unable to feed all the prisoners Don Egidio ceaselessly toured the area in his little old car raising money and collecting and buying food, clothes and necessities for the P.O.W.s. In this he was greatly helped by the support of the Action Party in Florence. By this time there was also a steady stream of escapers passing through and over two hundred of these were re-clothed, had their boots mended and were well fed and rested before being put on their way south with money, maps and much useful information.

'During this time he also had to deal with a Fascist Police spy who, by means of a bogus escape scheme which promised to take them to Rome in small groups, was slowly attracting P.O.W.s and handing them over to the Germans.

'As time went on the P.O.W.s hiding locally grew tired of staying hidden and, over-confident and thoughtless, began to show themselves frequently and openly in the villages in spite of warnings from the local *Carabinieri* and the Fascist chief. This resulted in two round-ups which, due to friendly warnings and other helpful reasons, were unsuccessful.

'Roger Absalom tells of the fate of this brave priest: on 5th May, 1944, Don Egidio came home to find his house surrounded. He was arrested and imprisoned in the Le Murate prison in Florence. He was eventually released, thanks to the efforts of the Cardinal Archbishop of Florence and two senior members of the Fascist secret police who, it is thought, bribed his judges. The Allied Screening Commission, not noted for its generosity, itself recommended the award of the King's Medal for Courage but, like everyone else, this brave kindly man received only an Alexander Certificate!'

Some escapers, either by accident or design, came to monasteries in the hills. Philip Kindersley and Ronald Orr-Ewing, after an exhausting walk across mountains, reached the monastery at La Verna. They were given lunch by the Franciscan friars. One told them they had given meals to over four hundred British servicemen. Jack Comyn and Donald Astley-Cooper made the same monastery their goal, as all their *contadini* hosts had told them they would receive help from the monks, which they did. Comyn wrote, 'The monastery stands at 3,700 feet and was visible from afar as we gradually ascended to it up mule tracks from a wide valley to its north. Although from that side it looked lovely and remote, indeed unchanged since the Middle Ages, we found when we got there that on its south side, up which ran a road, it was a hive of activity, thronged with escapers, deserters and refugees from the bombing of Rome.' They were told they would be given a meal but they could not stay the night. Apparently the Germans knew that the monks were offering hospitality to a large number of people. The monks pleaded that it was a rule of their Order, ordained by St. Francis himself, that assistance should never be denied to any supplicant. The Germans accepted this, provided no one was allowed to spend a night at the monastery. In addition to the meal Comyn had his boots repaired by a cobbler monk. Graham, Gilbert and Davies also visited this monastery and also the monastery of Eremo.

Tony Davies has given a vivid description of his and his companion's arrival at the monastery on Monte Catria, a very high mountain with a huge cross on its summit. 'I shall remember vividly all my life that walk down into the shadowed valley. Behind us the cross stood silhouetted against the clouds scudding across the face of the moon ... gradually we became aware of organ music floating up from the depths below and for some minutes we stood spellbound. I have never heard anything so beautiful; it is impossible to imagine a more perfect setting for those majestic chords. The music grew louder as we continued downwards and presently we turned a corner and saw ... the lights of the monastery.' They were welcomed with grave dignity by a monk and then offered wine and a very good meal. After, Davies and Toby Graham sat before a magnificent open fire while Michael Gilbert had an interview with the Father Superior. A great part of this was conducted in Latin. One wonders how many other British ex-prisoners could make themselves understood in Latin. The Father Superior was most pleasant and indicated that they could stay in the monastery for as long as they liked—until the Allies arrived, if necessary. Afterwards Gilbert said,'This place had much to recommend it. Some time spent in meditation in these surroundings would suit me admirably.' The others expostulated that they might be stuck there for months.

For a number of reasons some ex-prisoners stayed in one place and sometimes with one family for several weeks. This naturally led to a closer relationship than if one was on a 'bed and breakfast' basis, moving on after one night, or two or three at the most.

Adrian Barber and Dick Booth stayed for six weeks with the Bandi family, three sons, three daughters, a daughter-in-law and a grandchild. They slept in the loft, were called down for breakfast, and then spent the day in a bedroom apart from a short period for lunch downstairs. They played patience and read Italian newspapers. They were permitted a short period outside for exercise at dusk. There was no oven in the house and the food was cooked on raked-out ashes, which led to meat being usually over-cooked. They noticed they were given better meals than the family had themselves. The arrival of visitors always caused alarm in case the Englishmen should be spotted. This existence was brought to an end by increased Fascist activity in the village and rumours of the imminent arrival of Germans in San Michele.

Philip Kindersley and Ronald Orr-Ewing had been joined by Tom Vickers. Apart from some days in October when Vickers went off to look for a bungalow near Rapallo which belonged to his aunt, they lived with three separate families in the Monastero and Noceto area from mid-September to the end of October. At that time they were largely unaffected by the war. The main shortages were clothes, footwear and salt. They stayed with, or on the farms of Giacomo Restighini, Celerte Pesca and Guiseppe Negri. Giacomo's aunt Zia Luiga was a 'tough old battleaxe' of seventy-three, who had a heart of gold and with no fear of the Germans or the Fascists. Gradually the situation in Monastero became more difficult; many Yugoslav, Greek and Russian refugees arrived in the area. These, with the British, made food supplies more precarious. The people became afraid of spies and Germans. So on 31st October Tom Vickers decided to head for Switzerland and Orr-Ewing and Kindersley set off south.

Pat de Clermont, Jack Comyn, Charles Hedley and Donald Astley-Cooper, all of the 8th Hussars, lived in the foothills of the Apennines with the Regalo family from mid-September to mid-October. Hugh Hope and Derek Hornby were not far away. The supply and maintenance of these and other ex-prisoners was organised by the landowner, Signor Palumbo. As Comyn wrote, 'Every now and then Palumbo would send up to the farm a horse and cart carrying flour, salami, ham, cheese and wine, and sometimes a chicken. His generosity was amazing.' The people were more worried about betrayal by a *spia*—a local with Fascist or German sympathies—than they were of the Germans. The latter appeared occasionally in ones or twos looking for fresh fruit and vegetables and wine.

Signor Palumbo put them in touch with Manlio Carloni and his wife, a charming young couple who lived in a modern flat just outside Fidenza. By mid-October Comyn and Astley-Cooper thought they should move south. De Clermont was against it. He and Hedley stayed where they were all that winter and in the spring moved south to near Florence. They were freed by the Allies in June, 1944.

Staying in one place was often forced on escapers because of severe weather or the numbers of Germans in the area. Those who failed to get through the lines by early winter often had to sit out the winter until spring came. In other cases they were strongly influenced against going on by Italians or by Allied servicemen who had tried it and failed.

Ronald Mann, having reached the Gran Sasso area early in December, was told about a British paratrooper who was collecting together Allied ex-prisoners to take them through the lines. He never found him, but met a miner named Vittorio Massara, who took him to his little house above the village of Frascara. Massara made a grotto in the hillside for Mann and his companion. After two months heavy snow fell and it became impossible for them to continue living in the grotto. So the Massara family invited them to move into a back room of their house, where they remained for another month. There was no road to Frascara and only fifteen families living there. They all kept the secret of Mann and his companion's presence amongst them.

Denny Abbott, Noel Durrant and Theo Stephenson were in a similar position to Ronald Mann. They crossed the River Pescara on 7th November, having been told it was madness to try to cross the river as all the bridges were guarded. The three Indian Army officers crossed the river on a railway bridge near Popoli by night. The weather turned very cold, their clothes were thin and their boots in a bad state. They were told that the Germans were in all the villages, there were frequent ski patrols in the hills, and it was much too cold to attempt to cross the mountains.

A shepherd guided them to a small house or, more accurately, a hovel by the side of a stream. The house was full of people, but they were welcomed by a woman called Annina, who was the dominant character in the household. After a day or two they moved into a cave. Annina organised food for them in the village of San Tommaso, but this proved to be haphazard. As winter advanced food became scarcer, as did firewood, which was jealously guarded by the Italians. On the night of 31st December two or three feet of snow fell, with deep drifts. The three officers staggered down to Annina's house on New Year's Day. This increased the pressure on Annina, coupled with the news that the Germans caught a woman who had sheltered prisoners-of-war near Caramanico and shot her and her daughter. She showed them a new cave about two miles away up in the mountains, and she brought food up to them through the snow in her thin slippers as often as she could. They were there till March, 1944.

After Robert Smyth and Stafford Tolley had been recaptured on 21st November by unavoidably walking into a German gun emplacement they were eventually taken to Frosinone Transit Camp where they found Jack Clarke, Anthony Laing, Hugh Fane Hervey, Donald Macaulay and Bob Smyth. These ex-PG49 escapers jumped the train taking them to Germany—of which more later. This was near Orte. From there Smyth moved to Montebuono near Rieti, where the Brunetti family took them in and let them stay until March, 1944. After a second escape, the Trucco family, living near Montenero, looked after Smyth for ten days at the end of May.

A few Fontanellato escapers were sometimes somewhat critical of the Italians. Denis Gibbs made a comparison between Tuscans and Umbrians. On 13th October Norman Girling, Rex Smith and Sgt. Turner crossed from Tuscany into Umbria. After a day or two he remarked that they found the Umbrians more cheerful and happy, whereas the people they had encountered in Tuscany were inclined to be indolent, selfish and over-inclined to whine about their problems. A. A. Jones wrote in his diary for 19th October, 'A cold morning, but we warm up by the fire, whilst sharing breakfast with our kind hosts. We all ate out of the common dish.' Later that day he and Norman Rogers had to circle round Scanno as there were Germans in the town. Then he wrote, 'The helpless way in which Italians of all ages act is maddening. They are quite useless and openly expect the Allies to liberate them without any effort on the part of Italy itself.' What prompted these very critical remarks is not clear.

Readers of Roger Absalom's *A Strange Alliance*, Chapter Six, who have no experience of the life of ex-prisoners-of-war and their Italian helpers in 1943 and 1944, may conclude that Robert Williams adopted a high-minded, almost colonial attitude to the people of Torsana, with whom he and Terry Philipsz lived for a long period. Absalom made considerable use of Williams' diary which he (Williams) freely admits he should not have kept. Perhaps he failed to realise quite a number of British prisoners-of-war disliked and despised Italians before the Armistice and the exit from the camp. This was because of the way they had treated some British prisoners-of-war, and because at Capua they had shot two escapers in cold blood. But, as Williams says, 'They redeemed themselves after we got out.' When he wrote in his diary, 'How like wogs these people are in appearance, customs and manners ... spitting everywhere ... always discussing either money or local chat, etc., etc.,' Williams was using his diary as an outlet for his frustrations at his circumscribed life when, more often than not, he was tired, hungry, wet or not well. He would not have written in that way after a period of reflection.

Surely the most happy and successful inter-relationship among ex-prisoners from Fontanellato and their helpers was Eric Newby and Wanda Skof, the daughter of a school teacher near the town. They met the day after the march out of the camp. She helped Newby in various ways, not least by starting to teach him Italian. Her father was imprisoned by the Germans for a time. They fell in love and were married in the spring of 1946, in spite of the opposition of the then Head of the Allied Screening Commission, who had been the Senior British Officer at Fontanellato, Lt.-Col. Hugo De Burgh. They have since enjoyed fifty years of married life.

On the subject of the relationship between the Allied ex-prisoners and the Italians, let Anthony Laing have the last word.

Lest We Forget

There must be very few of the 50,000 Allied P.O.W.s who enjoyed freedom, for however short a period, in Italy in 1943/4 who do not freely acknowledge a great debt of gratitude to the Italians who helped us in so many ways to find and maintain our liberty. There were many one-night stops that we cannot remember. Their similarity and anonymity unfortunately does not help us to recall them. But most of us will not forget the poor *contadini* families, their elders huddled by the fireside, who killed the fatted calf for their unheralded foreign visitors and risked their homes and lives to shelter them. Because of our failing memories and their anonymity, most of them may never have been thanked as we would have liked. We can only hope that they escaped punishment and did not suffer for helping us.

6: Health and Morale

FALLING ill, or having an accident, was a constant, if unspoken, worry of escaping ex-prisoners-of-war. They well knew that the chance of receiving trained medical help in the remote rural or mountainous parts of Italy was slender indeed. In fact, it was British or Dominion ex-prisoner doctors who brought help to the *contadini* when they encountered illness when walking through the country. Jimmy James examined Signora Moliere who had severe stomach pains, and another woman with a bad foot, both near Pellegrino. Marcus Kane-Burman, while walking south, on at least two occasions relieved severe pain suffered by hill-farming families by extracting teeth. Needless to say this had to be done without anaesthetics, while the family and Jack Clarke and A. B. MacLean had to listen to the screams and groans of the patients.

Anthony Laing, who was walking with Donald Macaulay, R.A.M.C., wrote, 'We spent the night in a poor and remote Abruzzi farmhouse much against the wish of a very disagreeable husband. After a generous supper they enquired why the wife's wrist was bandaged and she replied that she had fallen on it while working on the farm. Macaulay said that he was a doctor and that, if it would be helpful, he would happily examine it for her. 'Her wrist's all right, the Priest has seen it,' snapped the husband. We said that we were very grateful for his hospitality which we would like to repay as best we could and that Donald was a *grande professore medico*.

He agreed very reluctantly and, as Macaulay carefully removed the Priest's skimpy and dirty bandage, he watched uneasily as though Donald was undressing her. After various painful flexings and careful examination Donald said that the bandage was useless, that the wrist had been broken and had not been set properly, and that, unless it was re-set soon, she would be handicapped for life. We attempted to translate this without provoking the husband's wrath or undermining their obvious faith in the efficacy of their Church.

The following morning she gave us a very good breakfast and we thanked her warmly and said our goodbyes. With her husband out of earshot we again emphasised the urgency of getting her wrist re-set. She looked at us with a pensive, yet grateful, smile and gently said, 'But there is so much to do before the snow comes. Perhaps I will go then.'

The first British patient was Eric Newby who had broken his ankle on 7th September. He was taken from a farm near the Bund to the hospital in Fontanellato. Fortunately his ankle seemed to mend quickly and it was not long before he could move about a bit.

During the last few days in the camp Michael Gilbert had been suffering from a large carbuncle in his armpit. It was very painful for the first few days, particularly in the hot weather, but he never complained and did his utmost to keep up with Toby Graham and Tony Davies. The latter boiled pieces of shirt to poultice the suppurating boil and then dressed it with Germolene ointment which Davies carried with him. Conscious of the beneficial effects of sunlight, he and Graham strapped Gilbert's arm up so the carbuncle could be exposed to the sun for two hours a day. This did it good, but it was an uncomfortable position for walking long distances.

Foot care was obviously a vital requirement. In the early stages several escapers suffered from blisters, including Dick Booth, Ted Pryke and Hugh Jobson. The latter strained his Achilles tendon on 27th September and it was extremely painful for the next ten days. Those who had exchanged their army boots for Italian civilian shoes invariably developed sore feet. Peter Ellis, Bill Bowder, Duggie Clarke and John Birkbeck all suffered badly, as did Colonel De Burgh and Reggie Phillips. Toby Graham had cut his boots down to look like shoes to help him appear inconspicuous for his escape attempt before the Armistice; this made them uncomfortable to walk in and he developed painful blisters. Noel Durrant suffered a septic foot when he and his companions were hiding during the winter. Probably as a result of the repeated soakings in late October and November, Erik Hampson one morning found his legs seized by a form of rheumatism and was unable to move them. Fortunately a day's rest largely put the trouble right. Drew Bethel, walking alone, scrambling down a slope, fell and sprained a knee. He lay in an outbuilding away from the village from 10th to 12th October. He wrote, 'The good Samaritans of Aragno fed me, bandaged and poulticed my horribly-swollen knee, got the cobbler to repair my boots, all the while in constant terror of German and Fascist retribution.' Similarly, Douglas Flowerdew sprained an ankle. It was poulticed with nearly boiling water by an old woman living in a very poor cabin. The treatment was painful but effective and next day he was able to continue.

There were several cases of illness. Diarrhoea and dysentery were perhaps the commonest. John Woods was a chronic case and it never really cleared up from September until he rejoined the British in May, 1944. Walking with Woods was Peter Gunter who had sores on both his feet and face. Norman Girling developed diarrhoea, having been walking for three weeks. During the last stages of Stuart Hood's adventures, when he was in Siena and the Germans were withdrawing towards Florence, he went down with fever and dysentery and was out of action for several days. Geoffrey Phalp developed diarrhoea towards the end of October. Gervase Nicholls described how they used the pages of *A Tale of Two Cities* as toilet paper. He had brought the book from the camp for something to read. He found he had to read quickly to stay ahead of Phalp's requirements!

Theo Stephenson developed bronchitis during the winter of 1943–44. No medicines were available. A German deserter came to his help by getting hold of some quinine and aspirin through his Italian fiancée who lived in the village of San Tommaso. Peter Stericker, walking with Peter Watson, fell ill on the journey, probably brought on by the frequent wet, cold nights and lack of proper food and clothing. A poor couple in a leaky hovel nursed him devotedly, if crudely, for a few days. The first day he could get to his feet a German patrol arrived and they had to spend the day on a cold, wet hillside. Similarly, Toby Graham had one feverish night and was put to bed. He was well enough to go on the next day. Ronald Orr-Ewing, travelling with Philip Kindersley, went down with jaundice on 6th November, so they stayed at an inn. He was too ill to move on the next day and it was not until the 9th that he felt just about able to leave the inn. By the 10th he was feeling much better and they did twenty miles that day. But the next day he was examined by an Italian doctor who said he was taking a risk and should rest for a few days. They did not move on again until the 15th November.

Eric Newby describes how, when he arrived at Abramo's house well up in the hills, the Italian looked at him and said, 'You don't look too good.' Soon he was given a very strong drink made from grain and juniper berries and put to bed. Abramo gave him an immensely thick shirt. Sweating profusely from the fever, the shirt was changed repeatedly. He was also given a disagreeable bitter infusion made with moss. Newby said, 'Abramo was one of the gentlest men I have ever met, in spite of his horny hands, and being nursed by him I felt as if I was one of his lambs.' By the third day he was cured. Abramo said it was the shirts which saved him. They had belonged to his great-grandfather. Abramo's father lived to eighty-seven and his grandfather to over ninety.

Newby calculated that these shirts must have been made in the latter half of the eighteenth century.

Jack Clarke, in his very short and abbreviated notes, said he was held up by illness from 10th to 15th November. He gave no details. Tommy Pitman was caught in a terrible blizzard one night in the mountains above Armatrice. He was wading through snow four to five feet deep trying to find a mountain hut where he knew other escapers were sheltering. Eventually they heard his shouts and went out to pull him in. As a result of that ordeal Pitman lost all the skin off the back of his hands. However, he said they healed fairly quickly.

Pat Davis, when he left the vicinity of the Camp, travelled with Donald Futrell up into the hills. Being undecided on a definite plan, they moved from farm to farm, gradually getting nearer to Genoa. Pat was a very good linguist. He spoke German and Italian and soon picked up the Genoese dialect.

In a sweep by the enemy Davis and Futrell became separated, but Davis stumbled into a small house where six girls were sitting round the kitchen stove. One said, 'I will take you to a family who will help you.' This was the Pesce family. Gianni Pesce, who was the employer of the girl who brought Pat to him, had several hat shops in Genoa and also owned a small estate in Olba San Pietro. Pat Davis fell ill there and was in a serious condition both physically and mentally. He was nursed by Signora Pesce and her mother Ninetta, though at great risk to themselves. He remained there for several months until the Allies occupied the area.

In the fugitive existence lived by the ex-prisoners-of-war, morale was as important as health. Perhaps naturally this varied from the very high to the depth of depression.

When Ronald Mann had escaped from the prison hospital at Piacenza and got out into the country he describes his sensation of being free. 'The sound of running water, the scent of the trees and mountain air, and, above all, the fact that after ... months in prison camps, I was free. It was breathtaking. I felt the same kind of excitement I did as a child ... I was surprised by joy. It did not matter that I was still in occupied territory and might be hunted down, recaptured, even shot. What mattered was that I was free and able to make my own decisions.'

Tony Davies wrote how well he remembered the glorious feeling of freedom on the first week's walking. 'It was not only freedom from captivity that brought such elation, but the freedom from all the cares of the world. We carried all our possessions in our pockets; we were beholden to no man and were responsible only to ourselves,' and also, 'Our natural enjoyment at exploring little-known parts of a foreign country, without a penny in our pockets and depending for food and shelter on our own resourcefulness, was sharpened by the added spice of danger which was never far away.' Later, having had their first bath since leaving Fontanellato, in the River Parma, 'We lay sunning ourselves on the warm stones and let the beauty of the place envelop us. The grandeur of the mountains, the rippling of the water and, above all, the riot of colour from the deep blue of the sky to the golden peaks in the distance was a spectacle to refresh mind and body. It was with a feeling of inner elation and happiness that we set out again on our journey.' However, by mid-October the strain was beginning to tell. The tension rose; Davies became irritable and morose with outbursts of temper. Toby Graham said as they were approaching Aquila he became tired and irritable and there were arguments. In the last half of October, Davies, Graham and Gilbert were driving themselves on. Davies admitted that his optimism had gone. The filthy food, the lice and the vagrant life depressed him. Similarly, Denis Gibbs became very fed up with being treated like a tramp. He sometimes despaired of the long distance they had to walk to reach the Allies.

Maurice Goddard and Erik Hampson kept their aim of being home by Christmas constantly before them. This helped them to keep going in bad weather when their spirits flagged and stamina and nerves were over-stretched. Their daily thoughts were on the enemy, on food and sleep.

When Douglas Flowerdew was recaptured he spent three days in a small hovel with forty other recaptured escapers. It was about the worst experience he can remember and his morale was very low. It made him absolutely determined to try to escape again. John Woods quite naturally became very depressed after the partisan camp in which he had been living was raided and Arthur Hall was recaptured. Peter Gunter had been retaken earlier, so he was now on his own. Also his attempts to get through the line had failed.

When Stuart Hood was living in a house at Migliana, he developed and had fits of black depression. He was keeping under cover which led to a feeling of claustrophobia. Then followed a German sweep of the area and he determined to set out on his own. But this led, as he puts it, to 'a nightmare of loneliness' and he seemed to lose his sense of direction. It was this fear of loneliness which prevented Ian English from going on his own when he became frustrated at the slow progress he, Jack Moore and Wilfred White were making.

Eric Newby tells how very depressed he became when forced to leave Pian del Sotto. The future seemed bleak. When the winter came he could no longer hide in the woods and he thought he would probably be retaken. Whereas before he had been part of a stable way of life when he lived with the Agata family—'I lost an essential part of whatever courage and willpower I possessed previously and the capacity to make decisions, qualities which were essential if I was to survive.' Later, when he and Donald Shaw were in the cave which the Italians had built for them, Shaw said they must stick it out through the winter for the sake of all the sacrifices made on their behalf by the *contadini*. It crossed Newby's mind that the best thing they could do was to give themselves up and be no more trouble to the local people.

Adrian Barber is quite candid about his morale in his account of the time after leaving Fontanellato. When he and Dick Booth were forced to move from the farm where they had lived for some time because the Germans arrived in nearby San Michele, they had a wet, tiring and muddy walk when Barber said he could hardly keep up with their guide, Luigi. They were quite exhausted by evening and he admits to being in a very low state. On 3rd December they had four refusals of shelter. The weather had broken, their boots were in a bad state and Barber had a severe cold. He and Booth discussed the situation and thought of the advantages of being a prisoner-of-war. They would have companionship, the probability of Red Cross parcels, a certain minimum degree of comfort, a supply of cigarettes and communication, albeit very slowly, with their families. They concluded that the lesser of two evils would be to be back 'in the bag.' So they decided to walk on main roads. If they evaded capture, all well and good; if they were re-arrested, they would be more relieved than upset.

In contrast, the depth of depression suffered by others who were recaptured is very easy to understand. Denny Abbott, having survived the winter in a remote hut in the mountains, when rounded up in the cemetery at Guardiagrele within a short distance of the British lines, was overcome by a black depression such as he had not known before or since.

Tony Davies, who hurtled down a steep bank straight into a German trench and was promptly shot in the ankle, wrote, 'I lay and listened to his (the German's) raving and gradually the sickening truth hit me hard between the ribs. After the months of trudging and hoping and the amazing freedom of our long trek through the heart of Italy, it was all over. I had failed at the very end and I was back exactly where I had started—a prisoner-of-war ... at that moment I grew up. All I knew was an unendurable sense of disappointment, rage and frustration, an annihilating sense of failure. The desolation and misery were more profound than anything I had ever felt before or, indeed, have ever felt since.'

Religious faith and a belief in the power of prayer was for some people a support on which they leant. Ronald Mann mentioned several times how he prayed for guidance as to what his next move should be. Eric Newby wrote that Donald Shaw was a conventional Christian. He went to services every Sunday in the prison camp, just as he had before the war. 'It was not just lip service to the established religion. He believed in God and the efficacy of prayer.' Newby also believed in God, but in a different way from Shaw. He said, 'At one time I had prayed that a bomb would not fall on the people in England I loved; but it seemed almost impertinent—better, if anything, to pray that bombs would cease to fall on anyone.'

Denis Gibbs was a strong believer in God and wrote that on his very long journey to rejoin the British he prayed frequently, particularly at the end, for strength to carry on. When Hugo De Burgh, with Reggie Phillips, was climbing Monte Rosa to get into Switzerland he wrote, 'But mostly we plodded on praying; at least, I did. I prayed all the time—"God give my knees strength to go ten yards more" and each time I looked up the top was farther off.'

Maurice Goddard and Erik Hampson found themselves separated from five German soldiers by a river torrent thirty feet across. 'We watched them for some time, unable to believe we had not yet been seen ... we crouched and ran along the narrow track towards a bend, expecting every moment to hear and feel shots, but none came. To this day I believe the hand of Providence guided us that day, lowering a curtain between us and the enemy.'

After Ian English and his companions got through the lines, he reflected on how fortunate they had been. They could just as easily have taken a wrong turning and run into Germans. Hence his firm belief that they had been guided by the hand of God.

7: Getting to Switzerland

OF THE various options open to the ex-prisoners from Fontanellato once they had marched out of the camp, going to Switzerland was one of the most attractive. It was by far the nearest destination where one could be certain of escaping from the jurisdiction of the Germans. Genoa, La Spezia or even Livorno were nearer, but whether one could meet Allied forces in those areas was uncertain in September 1943 and, as the weeks passed, became more and more unlikely. To walk south to meet the advancing Allied armies meant a journey, in September, of at least six hundred miles. The main disadvantage of going to Switzerland was that one would be interned for the remainder of the war. In the event, it was not quite as long as this. Once the American army, which landed in the south of France in August, 1944, had liberated the country bordering the Swiss frontier, the Swiss authorities allowed the internees to leave. Most were flown from Annemasse to Northolt in Dakotas by the Americans.

Perhaps it was the likelihood of internment which resulted in only a small number of Fontanellato prisoners making for Switzerland.

The first to decide to go that way and the first to succeed were Douglas Clarke and John Birkbeck. As early as the afternoon of 9th September they had come to the conclusion that six hundred prisoners hiding in a relatively small area of the Bund were extremely vulnerable and they were determined not to be retaken. Therefore they surreptitiously, because the order to disperse had not been given, left the main body and hid themselves in bushes some distance away. Having changed into some sort of civilian clothing, they moved off to the north and came to the village of Soragna. They met a woman who could speak English and who said she could provide them with a pair of trousers each. These arrived the next morning, whereupon Clarke and Birkbeck moved off in a westerly direction. They had been told that the Germans had taken over the prisoner-of-war camp at Bussetto, 15 kilometres north-west of Fontanellato. The news decided them to cross the River Po and make for Switzerland and, as Clarke wrote, 'Thinking rather stupidly that, once we got there, we should be able to get home to England after a month or so.'

On the second day they walked to the banks of the Po and along it till they came to a small 'port' with a dozen rowing boats. Two boys offered to row them across the river. In the evening they rode into the village of Copella on the handlebars of bicycles ridden by two small boys. Their host that evening, a smuggler with one arm, gave Clarke a hat as he said his fair hair was too conspicuous. Next morning he showed them across the main Cremona to Mantova road on which some German traffic was passing. Keeping to by-roads and paths, they came to the River Oglio which they swam, with their clothes tied on their heads. That night was spent in a barn of a farm in the village of Cignano, with several tame rabbits running over them. This thoroughly upset John Birkbeck who disliked rabbits, much to Duggie Clarke's amusement.

On 12th September they had to do a détour round Rovato where there were Germans. In the small village of Torbisto, which is a little to the south of Lake d'Iseo, a man told them they would do well to get a boat part of the way up the lake. Having no money, Birkbeck offered the man a pair of gold cuff-links. So it was arranged that the man would take them to Clusane and get a boat for them. Leaving at 5.00 a.m., everything worked as planned. They were rowed up the lake for two hours and were then put on shore a little north of Tavernola. Although not very far, it did save several hours' walking. They then took to the hills and walked on and on. Duggie Clarke, who was wearing an old pair of Italian shoes, developed several painful blisters on his feet. He could struggle on only by walking on the sides of his feet. Their route took them over the Giogo della Cantoniera pass. On the way up they met a carrier with a mule cart. He could not give them a lift up, but once they had reached the top he let them sit on top of his load and took them to an inn in the village of Costello. The days were very hot and they became extremely thirsty. They drank from every conceivable source—pumps, streams where cattle bathed and women washed their clothes, rivers, lakes and even puddles. They could not get enough water.

An early start on 14th September got them to Bargesto, where they fell in with an English woman who had married an Italian. In her house was Gunner Metcalfe who had reached that point by train and bus. The woman suggested they should catch up with two Italians who had just left to cross the mountains, as they would guide them. Johnny Birkbeck set off as fast as he could and caught them, while Clarke and Metcalfe hobbled along behind. They eventually reached the top of the Passo del Venerocolo. Over the other side they found Birkbeck waiting for them, having had the route to Tirano, their final objective, pointed out to him by the Italians who had gone on. When they reached the river, Birkbeck thought it much too dangerous to use the bridge. Metcalfe could not swim, so Birkbeck undressed, tied his clothes to his head and waded in; halfway across he was swept away by the current. However, he struck out and managed to reach the far bank. Clarke and Metcalfe struggled up the river side, found the bridge and crossed it. When they eventually met again they walked along the main road to Villa di Tirano, a village a few miles west of Tirano itself. At the inn, after a good meal, they started the search for a guide. After a lot of persuasion two young men offered their services. Clarke wrote, 'Tremendous bartering took place and at last terms were agreed. We offered all we had; my gold watch, Johnny's wrist watch, signet ring and gold pin.' They each slept in a bed that night and Metcalfe provided the cash for the bill.

Their guides arrived at 5.00 a.m. the next morning, 15th September. They climbed straight up the mountain. Their guides were like mountain goats, but for the escapers it was a stiff climb, particularly as they were lame. At the frequent rests the guides produced flasks of wine, which they passed round with the words *'Corraggio! Corraggio!'* Then they could see the Italian frontier guard-post. The guides then demanded better payment and refused to take them any further. An argument ensued; Clarke and Birkbeck had nothing more to offer. They had handed over their valuables and the Italians had to accept it. When, soon after, they could see the red and white frontier posts they said good-bye to their guides. They had nearly covered the last few hundred yards when suddenly a soldier stepped out from behind a tree and challenged them. This was a shock, as they were not certain whether they had crossed the frontier or not. The sentry might be a German. However, he was Swiss and shook them warmly by the hand.

Clarke and Birkbeck had taken five and a half days to travel the approximate one-hundred-and-twenty miles from Fontanellato. They were the first, by a large margin, from that camp to escape from the part of Italy occupied by the Germans.

Three R.A.F. officers, Derek Iles, Bill Rainford and Peter Bragg, set off for Switzerland after one night in the Bund. They had the idea of making for Como until they met some gipsies who, when told of this plan, just laughed and said, 'You can't go there. We have heard on the B.B.C. that the escaping prisoners-of-war are making for Como and the Germans, who no doubt have heard the same broadcast, will be waiting for them there.' The gipsies were very helpful, telling them where to cross the Po and the route to take thereafter. They advised them to try to cross the frontier north of Bergamo, some way east of Como. They walked for ten days and only on the last day had the benefit of a guide in the shape of a smuggler who knew every inch of the country. They crossed over Monte Fiernina and reached Switzerland about the 20th or 21st September.

Lt.-Col. Dick Wheeler, with Colonel De Burgh and Reggie Phillips, was taken to Milan and eventually up to the valley of Aosta. Here they decided that three travelling together might cause difficulties, so Wheeler went off on his own and did a lone crossing of the frontier, arriving in Switzerland on 23rd September.

Undoubtedly the most gallant and the most dramatic escape into Switzerland, and the one that came nearest to disaster, was that effected by Lt.-Col. Hugo De Burgh and Capt. Reggie Phillips. To attempt to summarise it is not to do the story full justice, so it appears as Appendix 3, as it was printed in the November 1945 number of *Blackwood's Magazine* under the title 'Smuggler's Way.'

It is understood that De Burgh, after recovering from his horrendous experiences, returned to Italy, more or less by the same route, to help other ex-prisoners make good their escapes. At the end of the war he was put in charge of the Allied Screening Commission, a body set up to assess the thousands of claims made by Italians who had helped Allied prisoners-of-war, and to administer the (paltry) sums of money disbursed in settlement of their claims.

Francis Lowsley-Williams had been the S.B.O. at Montalbo and continued as such when that camp was moved to Fontanellato, until the arrival of Lt.-Col. De Burgh. Following the Armistice he remained in the Fontanellato area for a time, then moved north and crossed into Switzerland on 3rd October.

Tom Vickers arrived in Como on the 10th November on the workers' train from Monza. A fortnight earlier he had been told by an old peasant that he had a friend called Gerardo Mazza who had a seed merchants' business at 7 Via Milano in Como. Mazza rather reluctantly agreed to give Vickers a billet, and he spent five days and nights sharing the family bedroom with the Mazzas and their small daughter. He was confined to the kitchen by day.

On 16th November the first of his three guides, dressed in the uniform of the Excise Service, arrived with two bicycles. In spite of one being too small for Vickers and having a defective dynamo lamp, they rode safely through Como and up into the hills. They hid the bicycles and continued on foot to the cottage of a large villa. The second guide was a sinister-looking man in a heavy black cloak and he took Tom Vickers further on to another cottage. The first guide had refused payment, but Vickers paid the second a thousand lire.

After dark on 18th November he met his third guide who soon turned out to be a disagreeable character. He was not satisfied with the thousand lire which was all Vickers had left and demanded, almost with menaces, two thousand lire. In the end he had to settle for the thousand.

Vickers wrote, 'Just after midnight we made the final approach. There was snow on the frozen ground, the strong chain-link fence was over ten feet high and alarm bells rang as I crawled, as flat on the ground as possible, underneath the wire and into Switzerland and safety! A minute's silent prayer of gratitude and I walked down quickly to the lighted houses in the Swiss valley below.'

Noel Burdett and Geoffrey Collins came into the hands of *Italia Libra* in Parma. They found them a place on a loaded furniture lorry going to Milan. At the outskirts the lorry halted and, as Burdett wrote, 'The driver opened up the back and an armed *carabinieri* officer searched it. Geoffrey was feigning sleep on a sofa and I was on the floor; the officer did not give us a second glance. Another bit of luck and a very blessed one.'

The 1st to the 3rd December was spent in a caretaker's hut on a Milan building site. They particularly enjoyed his tasty rabbit stew; that is, until he told them it had been cat! On the 3rd they met twenty-five Other Rank escapees in a warehouse and were joined by a guide. The plan was for them to be divided into groups of two or three; one person in each group had to be known to one person in the group behind. They had to keep fifty yards between groups.

They were taken to a tram stop nearby; tickets to the Central Station were provided. Then a train journey to Caslino d'Erba, tickets again provided. They were told to follow the group in front; no watches to be visible or book or newspaper carried. The train was blacked out so they should pretend to sleep. When Caslino was reached they followed the guide on foot through the darkness to Lake Como. Then into small boats which were found in unoccupied lakeside villas. They landed on the west shore and were then faced with a very steep climb up to the snows of the frontier zone. Here, at about 3.00 a.m., they said good-bye to their guide.

The party of escapers still had about fifteen kilometres to go, through deep snow. They lost their way and circled round vainly for about four hours. But as dawn was breaking they realised they were near the frontier. Suddenly in front of them appeared the eight-foot barbed wire fence with a Swiss soldier patrolling on the other side of it. Burdett called to him in French, then in German, while they hid at the edge of a forest. The sentry quickly realised who they were and urged them to hurry as Italian frontier guards were soon due to appear on their dawn patrol. A mile further on they came to a reception centre in the Ticinese village of Brusella.

Captains J. G. Canning and A. J. Green remained on the plain near San Secondo for nearly two months. They were looked after by Paolo Rossetti at Corticelli farm. Gino Cantoni, Ernesto Rastelli and the family Frazzi also helped. Having heard they could be repatriated from Switzerland, they decided to go there. They went from Castelguelfo to Luino by train accompanied and guided by a lady they knew as Dulcina. Changing trains they reached Valdomino where they found that the priest and about two hundred inhabitants had that morning been taken away by the Germans. By chance they met a Snr. Bertoli who was a guide. They paid him two thousand lire, and leaving at 9.00 p.m. they reached Swiss territory at 6.00 a.m. on 9th December.

John De Bendern and Captain A. P. Mitchell had first gone to Montalbo where they had been imprisoned before being moved to Fontanellato. But there were too many Germans in that area, so they moved to Parma where Noel Burdett saw them. Perhaps helped by *Italia Libra*, they were guided over the mountains by smugglers.

Peter Barshall had led a party south-west up into the hills with the idea of reaching La Spezia. After several weeks with no news of a landing, Barshall and three companions decided to make for Milan, as Barshall's father had had a business partner in Milan. They went by train from Cusignano to Fidenza where a railway worker bought the tickets for Milan. In spite of air raids and security checks, they reached Milan safely. Having spent the night in an air raid shelter, they took another train to Como. Here they met a guide by arrangement, who accompanied them in a taxi to the east bank of the lake. There they were helped by two smugglers who took them in a rowing boat as far as Brienno The last stage was a westerly climb over the mountains to cross the frontier east of Cabbio.

Captain Reginald Benson was one of several escapers who first went south or south-west into the hills before finally deciding to make for Switzerland. Benson went to Bardi and stayed there till 9th December. An escape organisation contacted him and he left for Piacenza. Here he took a train for Milan where he stayed for five days in a house near his guide. They then went by train to near the frontier which he crossed on 16th December with the help of smugglers.

Charles Castle, who for a time was with Captain K. Frazer, went from Fidenza to the River Taro beyond Bardi. Stories of arrests of prisoners by Fascists and Germans caused him to return on foot to Fidenza. Castle wrote, 'Luigi Bertorelli who had already been paid in advance, promised to put us in touch with an organisation who would assist us to get to Switzerland.' Bertorelli accompanied him to Milan, then Castle bought a single ticket on a bus for Ponte Chiasso which is near the frontier. 'I was shown a place where the border fence had collapsed due to a landslide, and decided we could get through there. There was no time to lose because it was nearly 10.00 p.m., the time of the curfew which was strictly enforced.'

Eric Cutler, who used to play a vigorous game of rugger at scrum half on the camp playground before the Armistice, stayed with three companions in the countryside near Fontanellato as guests of Professor Negri Avanzini of Cannetolo di Fontanellato and then with Andrea Baruffini's family. After about five weeks they moved to near Medesano where they were helped by the Grandi, Fossi, Foglia and Albertini families.

The four escapers decided on a change of plan. They returned to the plain and went to Parma hoping to contact an organisation which would get them to Switzerland. Here they were helped by the Bertoli and Azzali families. Thanks to the initiative of Gianni Grannello of Castelguelfo who procured food, money and cigarettes, they reached Milan by train. Here they stayed for some time assisted by a group of students who belonged to an organisation, perhaps *Italia Libra*. The organisation 'Davis' commanded by Lieut. 'Arca' who had already transferred two hundred and fifty Allied ex-prisoners into Switzerland, decided to arrange for the four escapers to cross the frontier by an experimental route of Intragna, Socraggio, Cavaglio and Brissago.

Two other ex-prisoners from Fontanellato who went to Medesano and who were also helped by Albi Albertini, and who later moved back to Parma, were Harold C. Carver and a companion. They remained in Parma until the end of January 1944, staying in the house of Nando Ferri and also being helped by the Meli family. During their last week they had to hide in a wood store. Guided by Jack Comino they then left for Lake Maggiore and crossed the frontier on 8th February without anyone asking for or receiving money from them.

Extremely worried by the danger in which they were putting the Buti family in Florence, Jack Clarke, Ted Mumford and Anthony Laing set off for Milan, accompanied by their guide, Angelo Salvatore. They spent the night of 22nd February, 1944, in Milan and the following morning got the train to Laveno on Lake Maggiore, where they said good-bye to Salvatore. They then took the boat to Cannero, then a bus to Cannobio, where the café proprietor suggested suitable guides, and finally, as evening fell, they walked up the valley to Socraggio, where they met their guides. These were *contrabandieri*, or smugglers.

In Laing's account the last day sounded like an anti-climax, after the many adventures and dangers of his Italian journeyings; being re-caught when near the Allied lines, jumping from a train which was taking them to Germany, some weeks in Florence in civilised surroundings, a train journey to Venice and Padova and back to Florence. He wrote, 'The following morning we left at dawn and, like all good Italian businessmen, in gents' natty city suits and shoes and carrying briefcases, we slipped and slithered our way up to a col, which we were assured was the Swiss frontier, and where we said good-bye to our guides. We descended similarly on the other side and, having just reached the tree line, were happily and carelessly talking when a voice behind us called "*Alt.*"

Turning, I saw a German soldier in the usual field grey uniform. My heart sank; had we failed again? But no, he was a Swiss soldier.'

Two couples of escapers had very similar routes and experiences before they reached Switzerland. These were Lieuts. Richard N. Brooke and J. W. Younger and Lieuts. J. W. Burman and W. Benzie. A few days after leaving the camp they, separately, moved to Mariano di Pellegrino, a locality which like Bardi was very welcoming to ex-prisoners. Brooke and Younger lived there for nearly seven months, being looked after by Ida Papisca and Lazzaro Bazzoni. They came in contact with partisan bands, but found them ineffective. Brooke wrote, 'Near Pellegrino we made contact with an organisation called *Partito d'Azione* who gave us a guide to take us by train from Fidenza to Milan and on to Varese, then towards a little village hardly a mile from the border. From there we walked to the frontier which was marked by a steel wire. We passed under it where ran a little drain, crossed a river and reached Pontetresa in Switzerland.' In contrast to many routes, this was very easy and practical.

Similarly Lieuts. Burman and Benzie spent several months in the Pellegrino, Salsomaggiore, Varano di Marchesi and Vernasca area. Benzie wrote that Lazzaro Bazzoni of Casa Masaschi near Pellegrino showed himself to be inexhaustible in helping British prisoners of war. They were taken by car to Fidenza where they took the train to Milan and from there to Laveno on Lake Maggiore. They crossed the lake to Intra and then, accompanied by guides, two men and a woman, they walked to Brissago in Switzerland.

8: *Why Walk?*

THE GREAT majority of Allied prisoners tried to follow strict security rules. At first many thought it would not be safe to walk by day. This led to difficult night marches. Others thought it would be highly dangerous to walk along main roads; that it would be better to go across country or sometimes along minor rural roads. There was a lot of truth in this and many escapers could produce evidence that these precautions were justified.

A few others, perhaps bolder or more imaginative, took the view that the quickest way to reach their objective was to go by public transport. While accepting that, in spite of their civilian clothes, they would be recognised as foreigners, they were confident they would not be given away by their fellow travellers. Also in the first few weeks restrictions on travel could well be ignored.

We have seen in the last chapter how several ex-prisoners from Fontanellato who decided to make for Switzerland, travelled from Fidenza or Piacenza at least as far as Milan, and sometimes nearly up to the frontier by train. They were often guided by Italians; in other cases tickets were bought for them by local people.

Ronald Mann was a fairly early train traveller. Having escaped from the prison hospital at Piacenza on 3rd October, he went to a mental hospital the other side of the town. He had been there previously to visit a British soldier who was a patient there. This hospital was run by nuns, who allowed him to stay for one night. The next morning he and a soldier from a Guards regiment were guided by a Franciscan monk across the town to the railway station. Germans seemed to be everywhere. However, the three boarded a train without mishap and arrived at Bettola. Here their guide left them and the two escapers started their walk into the hills.

G. F. Spooner went down with malaria in August, 1943, and was taken to a hospital at a monastery at Alberone. Soon after the Armistice the guards fled and Spooner was able to get away after filing through a padlock on the main gate. The next day he met an Italian who said he was hiding several prisoners and offered to take more; so he returned to the hospital to collect others. No sooner had he got there than the Germans arrived and started to move the prisoners out of the hospital.

Spooner hid under some mattresses and was not discovered. The monks sheltered him for five days, gave him civilian clothes and then took him to the railway station, buying him a ticket for Florence. There he contacted another monk who gave him a ticket for Grottammare. On the train he met an Italian who took him to Bojano and sheltered him for six weeks. During the last ten days of this period they were shelled and bombed by the Allies. However, on 23rd October, 1943, Spooner met Canadian troops at Bojano.

Jack Donagher and Tom Wildy made an early decision to go on roads and, where possible, to use transport. Wildy's knowledge of Italian was very limited, so he pretended to be deaf when they were on buses, and Donagher did the talking. As they were approaching Florence, two ladies who knew what they were caught up with them. One was Anna Biagini, who took them to her mother's holiday home in a village. Anna told them that, if she could get them to Florence, it could be arranged for them to be taken off by an M.T.B. from the Adriatic coast. They got to the outskirts of Florence by bus, then on the floor of a vegetable cart. They were kitted out in Bond Street outfits by

Anna's friends. They stayed there for ten days. Colonnello Rigatelli, an ex-*carabiniere*, who Donagher describes as a 'great guy,' made arrangements for them to travel to Ancona by train. The Colonel accompanied them to Bologna where they had to change trains. There was no difficulty about this, as the Colonel had 'fixed' the officials.

Jack Comyn, having decided against going with Colonel Mainwaring, did have a train journey later on. Having walked down the Tiber valley and electing not to go into Rome, they left the river at Todi and turned south. Just outside Todi they stayed at a house where the host's daughter persuaded them there was no danger in their travelling by train to Terni, thirty miles to the south. She often did this journey and knew there were no document checks on the line. Comyn wrote, 'She would take us to the station at Todi and buy our tickets for us. So this gallant girl did. Donald (Astley-Cooper) and I sat silently on the train. At one station we saw Germans on the platform. However, nothing happened and we arrived safely at Terni. From Terni we had not far to walk into the Sabine Hills.'

Lt.-Col. De Burgh in his account 'Smuggler's Way' in *Blackwood's Magazine* wrote that he, Reggie Phillips and Dick Wheeler, 'After many adventures by road and rail, arrived in a small town situated in the valley of Aosta.' But he gave no further details. On 6th October at Scurano Jack Clarke met K. A. Frazer and H. D. Pyman who had just arrived from Fontanellato by car.

Anthony Laing, in the course of his many and lengthy peregrinations down and up Italy, said that he and Jack Clarke had lost the taste for walking and, with Christmas so near, got a train from Arezzo to the outskirts of Florence. Later, having been supplied with genuine identity cards by Signora Amendola, and guided by Angelo Salvatore, he, Jack Clarke and Teddy Mumford set out for Venice by train on 2nd January. Their first objective was to get to Yugoslavia. If this was not possible, they had heard in Florence of the Navy taking people off the beaches in the area. They booked late at night into the Albergo Rialto, on the Grand Canal, for two nights. The next morning, for breakfast, they were shown to the last remaining table at the far end of the dining-room. Happily very little notice was taken of them, for the whole of the remaining forty or so guests were German General Staff Officers! They stayed the second night, thinking that they might be safer there and unlikely to be denounced.

Their intention was to get to Yugoslavia, but this proved impossible, so they took the train to Padova, where they spent two nights in a *pensione*. Their contacts could offer no further help, so they decided to return to Florence. Laing wrote, 'But our train arrived late at Bologna station after the curfew. With the lines disorganised by Allied bombing we were forced, with train-loads of others, to spend the night on the darkened and crowded platforms, during which our identity cards were checked twice.' Later, on 21st February, they took the train to Milan, arriving the following day. They then headed for Switzerland.

Eric Newby was taken from a hiding-place near the River Po in a small Fiat car driven by the local doctor, up into the hills south-west of Fontanellato. When they came to the Via Emilia they found their way blocked by a German motor cyclist who was controlling the traffic. They then passed a long convoy of tanks and trucks of the Sixteenth Panzer Division and on into the centre of Parma, where the little car broke down, under the eyes of the statue of Garibaldi. The doctor managed to re-start the engine and the rest of their journey was uneventful.

Tom Vickers, after a journey west from Monastero to Camogli in the middle of October to find the villa which belonged to his aunt, decided to head north for Switzerland. On 9th November, having been given an official white identity card with the name of Conini Pietro of Caurso, he was taken by two Italians by car across the River

Po and as far as the outskirts of Milan. Next day Agnese Mongucci of Monza took Vickers to the railway station, bought him a third class ticket to Como, and sat with him on a platform bench while they waited for the train, with German military police and Blackshirts walking up and down just in front of them. As Vickers said, 'That half-hour wait for the 7.30 a.m workers' train was pretty scary. I climbed into a half-empty cattle truck. One of the militia men got in and stood at my end, but paid me no attention. Fortunately there was no control of I.D. cards at the barrier, and I walked out into the main square of Como unchallenged.'

'Taffy' Wilcox, travelling with John Strange and Colin Leslie, decided to risk going by train to Rome because Wilcox had leg troubles. Strange, who spoke Italian well, bought three tickets from Fidenza to Rome on 4th November. They got through with only a few scares. In Rome they lived in the British Embassy for a short time, in various hide-outs, with civilians and finally in part of the Vatican Territorial Property, dressed in priests' clothing.

Pip and Jim Gardner and Percy Gers were given generous hospitality by a bicycle manufacturer. He gave them a wad of lire and a bicycle each. They made good progress and cycled straight through Florence. Soon after, Jim Gardner had an accident with his bicycle, which ran away on a hill.

However, he had the wheel repaired in a bicycle shop and the man refused payment. On another day they were overtaken by a German lorry, the driver of which ran out a rope by which he pulled them up the hill! When they got into the hills they found the bicycles were of less use and also more conspicuous, so they exchanged the bikes for walking boots.

In late October they met a group of Partisans near Bacugno. About a fortnight later a partisan arrived with a note from Major Sam Derry suggesting they move to Rome. The partisans would escort them there, but would take only one at a time. Derry suggested Pip Gardner should go first. The next day they boarded a bus. His cover was that he was a cousin of the partisan escorting him. He was going to Rome to have an operation on his throat and he must not speak on the journey under any circumstances. There were several Fascist Militia on the bus. They were attacked by a low-flying American fighter. The bus lurched to a stop and everyone rushed out and lay in the ditch. When the bus stopped at the outskirts of Rome they boarded a local train which took them to the city centre. Gardner then came under the control of Derry's Rome organisation.

Rather surprisingly, no records have been received of mishaps when ex-prisoners were travelling on public transport. In retrospect one wonders why more did not travel that way.

The courtyard and front of the Orfanotrofio, site of Campo P.G.49, Fontanellato

Plaque erected by the people of Fontanellato in 1983 in commemoration of the Allied prisoners of war and the many Italians who helped them

Lieut. Colonel Hugo De Burgh, D.S.O., O.B.E., M.C., Senior British Officer, Campo P.G.49 (taken in 1946)

La Verna Monastery near Chiusi, visited by several escapers from P.G.49. The monks gave food to many Allied prisoners of war

(Standing) Tony Davies (third from left), Toby Graham (fifth from left) and Michael Gilbert (on the right) with a group of ex-Alpini partisans near the summit of Monte Cimone, October 1943

Scontrone. The river Sangro flows through the trees in the foreground

View from Frattura towards the Lines. Monte Greco is the tallest feature in the distance

Monte Greco, 7,625ft, in winter. The route from Frattura over Monte Greco was followed by several ex-prisoners.

9: *With the Partisans*

THE PARTISAN resistance to the German occupation flickered sporadically from fairly soon after the Armistice.

Many escaping prisoners-of-war heard rumours of bands, and some met members of these gangs. Except perhaps in the north of the country most partisan groups were largely ineffective, due to a lack of arms, discipline and organisation. In 1944 and 1945, succoured by air drops of weapons and supplies and, in some cases, Allied soldiers to lead them, the bands became more effective and were at least an irritant to the Germans' defensive effort. Wehrmacht replies were usually savage reprisals often carried out by formations 'resting' out of the line.

Several ex-prisoners from Fontanellato encountered partisan bands to a greater or lesser extent, with varied experiences. Jack Moore, Wilfred White and Ian English met a lawyer at Pieve who described himself as the leader of a band and invited them to join him. They had little faith in the Italians as resistance fighters and, in any case, wished to move on south.

Maurice Goddard and Erik Hampson reached the Gran Sasso area in early November. Here they met a group of partisans who took them to their hideout which was bristling with small arms. They seemed very disorganised and Goddard and Hampson had no desire to stay with them. Anthony Laing, when he reached Monte Morello, north of Florence, made the short comment that he spent ten ineffective days with some partisans. His abiding memories are of the seeming impossibility of the Communist and *Partito d'Azione* members ever being able to agree on anything and of the glowering hatred between the Yugoslavs of Michailovitch and Tito.

Robert Smyth on 19th May, 1944, having crossed the River Po two days before on his way north, met some freedom fighters, but they were only interested in getting even with the Fascists, and not with attacking Germans, so he left them after a few days.

Peter Stericker and Peter Watson, who had been joined by two R.A.F. officers who had been shot down over Sicily, came to Massa, a village above the Ancona to Foligno road. In Watson's words, 'In a dilapidated house on the outskirts we met the Resistance! ... The Massa gang were not exactly the shock troops of the Resistance, being ill-disciplined and idle. Supporting them was a distant and shadowy "Committee," which provided the rations and arms. There was also a delightful resident Communist, who struggled to instill some political ideas into the young men ... The Germans moved a headquarters into the town and the Fascist Militia moved into Pieve Torina with the intention of sorting out the gang. So, on the advice of the Committee, we left.'

Bill Monteith, an R.A.F. fighter pilot, was with a partisan group in the Bardi—Borgo val di Taro area for some time. He describes it as 'routine and pretty useless partisan stuff ... enjoyable in a way.'

When Eric Newby and Donald Shaw were living in the part-hut, part-cave built for them by some of the villagers they were approached by three men, only one of whom was known to Newby. This was disturbing as it meant that the secrecy of their hideout had been compromised. The spokesman had been a corporal in the *Alpini*. All three were armed with rusty weapons. The *Alpini's* proposal was that the three of them, plus another two who were hiding close by, were going to attack and blow up a German petrol dump on the Via Emilia about seven miles west of Parma. They had heard that Newby and Shaw were officers and therefore their military knowledge would be very useful.

When examined in detail it was obviously a ridiculous scheme. They had only Italian hand grenades, no proper explosives. Newby reckoned the Germans would lose a few gallons of petrol, at most. In return they would shoot a number of hostages, burn some villages, and carry out raids into the surrounding country, in which they would round up young Italians and pack them off to forced labour. In Newby's words, 'At this time it was as pointless as the Charge of the Light Brigade.' But the two British officers decided they had no choice but to go with them. They went to the rendezvous the next night, waited in the pouring rain for four hours. But the Italians never turned up; nor were they ever seen again by Newby and Shaw. Perhaps it was just as well.

In late October the R.T.R. trio of Pip and Jim Gardner and Percy Gers were arrested by two men with a shout of *'Mani in alto.'* They turned out to be partisans. They had a plan to attack a German convoy, which, however, came to nothing. The three ex-prisoners spent two nights in Bacugno and in the next village they met more partisans, who were living in a large communal room, with bunks on the walls. One night, the three British officers were alone in the room. Their sleep was disturbed by the entry of a young Italian couple who, oblivious or unaware that they were not alone, made love in front of the fire. There were some sheepish faces the next morning!

Because of the dangers to the people of the village, the partisans suggested they move to a shepherd's hut in the mountains above the tree line. Snow was already on the ground. Food was brought up by the partisans who occasionally had fairly accurate news of the state of the fighting. At this hut they met two South Africans and a New Zealander. They kept the fire going, essential at that height, by cutting down trees with an axe loaned by the partisans. It was now mid-November and they did not want to move on, despite the snow.

Stuart Hood and Ted Mumford, after having a fortnight to consider the matter, made contact with a partisan group on Monte Morello, north of Florence. This was probably the group Anthony Laing had lived with for ten days. It was made up of about fifteen men, including two Russians, two Yugoslavs and a number of young Italians unwilling to be conscripted into the Fascist Republican Army. It was led by a brave but reckless ex-Sergeant-Major from the Italian Army. Weeks passed with little activity.

Ted Mumford was sent off on a mission and he and Hood did not meet again in Italy. His guide was a man called Toto and with them was a gay and irresponsible partisan named Baffo.

Their task was to find a cache of mortar bombs, remove the explosive from them and send it down to the Committee of Liberation in Florence. Mumford was glad to have something definite to do, after weeks of sitting about listening to interminable arguments. After a long climb they came to an upland farmhouse where they spent the night.

Next morning they unearthed the box of small red mortar bombs. Mumford wrote amusingly of his struggles to dismantle the bombs and how Baffo would slip away when he thought things were getting dangerous. He was sent to get a clamp and a wrench and did not return for some hours, having fortified his courage with *grappa*. Eventually Mumford managed to unscrew the casing and remove the small explosive charge. He soon had a haversack full. Next day, when they were waiting to move off to rejoin the rest of the band, a boy came in with news of a *rastrellamento*—a round-up, in which the band had been ambushed.

After waiting several days for more definite information, they learned that several members of the band had been killed, though Stuart Hood had got away. In due course Mumford decided to go to Florence and later to make for Switzerland.

Stuart Hood was to have a much longer time with the partisans. They were ordered to move up into the hills to a ridge known as Monte di Calvana, north of Prato. Early one morning the barn which was their hideout was attacked by Fascist Militia. After a prolonged fire-fight many of the band were killed, but Hood managed to get away and made for Migliana.

After being hidden for some weeks in Migliana, Hood made his escape. The Germans started clearing the country of partisan groups prior to building the Gothic Line above Migliana. Hood walked south alone. Just north of Siena in Chianti country he was picked up by a resistance network run by three Italian officers. They did not trust him, suspecting he might be a spy. How could he prove he was speaking the truth? Hood told them to send a messenger to Campi where he would find the widow of the butcher Lancillotto—the leader of the partisan group on Monte Morello. She would vouch for him. Ten days later the Italian Major came with the news that it was all right; his story had been verified. He said, 'It's just as well. Otherwise we would have had to shoot you.'

Thereafter Hood worked with the Major, who was a landowner, and liaised with a Communist group. A number of South African ex-prisoners who had been in a police battalion were in the area. They were rather undisciplined, difficult to deal with and took the law into their own hands. In Hood's words, 'South Africans with the deep inferiority complex of the men who had surrendered at Tobruk. They were narrow, tough, ignorant. They ate at the peasants' tables, slept with their daughters and scoffed at them in Afrikaans.'

After several weeks in which Hood came to know the area and the people who lived in it intimately, the Italian Major made contact with an Allied submarine on the Tuscan coast, and they were promised an arms drop. The coded message would come over the radio. Hood moved round the area alerting all those he could trust. One May evening they heard the message, 'The cigarettes have arrived.'

At the dropping zone they found one man too many—a stranger who could not explain his identity or presence. After questioning him and getting no satisfactory answers, Hood had to decide what was to be done with him. He had seen the people involved in the operation and the location of the dropping zone. He knew too much. Stuart Hood decided he had to be shot. The drop itself was bungled. They received only sten guns and ammunition, grenades, boots and socks, but no light machine-guns or mortars, no gadgets for sabotage. The peasants grabbed most of the boots, socks, cigarettes and chocolate. Later they sabotaged communications and attacked a German convoy. The Germans burnt every house within a couple of miles of the ambush and killed the menfolk.

As the Allies drew nearer, Hood was ordered to go into Siena and make contact with the Free French. Once again he had difficulty in establishing his identity and finished up in a cage full of German prisoners, before eventually he was taken in hand by the American Army. In 1989 Stuart Hood was made an honorary citizen of Campi Bisenzio and a member of the National Association of Italian Partisans.

Early in 1944 Robert Williams and Terry Philipsz moved into Tuscany and came to the village of Torsana. Here they were looked after by the extended family of Pietro Baldini. The latter took a proprietorial interest in the two British officers, and kept secret the help given to them by his family. In March an ex-member of the Italian navy called Domenico Azzari came to see them. He had been dropped by parachute some miles away and was in command of Special Force No. 1 'Rutland Mission.' He was in radio contact with a base in the south and also with I.S.9. Their names were sent to the Allies on the S.O.E. radio link, but their parents never received news of them.

The Allies dropped arms, clothing and food to a group collecting in the hills. There were rumours that Azzari was selling the arms dropped to him. Though the truth of this was never established, it was soon evident that Azzari was unreliable. Williams resolved to play a more active role in organising resistance. But to quote Roger Absalom, 'To his horror Williams discovered that arms and ammunition dropped by the Allies were being freely distributed to any local youths prepared to volunteer for service, whose idea of guerilla warfare was to get drunk and discharge their weapons at the nearby landscape.' In trying to influence the organisation of the partisans, Williams found that many of the local boys refused to take any offensive action, but only to keep their arms for self-defence. At the camp in the hills were an Eastern Russian and an American Air Force Colonel who was re-captured soon afterwards. Williams found his task very difficult and tiring. The partisans were arrogant and often bullied and extorted money and food from the villagers.

It became clear to him that most of the bands were largely ineffective. One band which did useful work was run by Major Oldham, an escaped prisoner-of-war, and made up of Russians.

About this time the German Hermann Goering Division, which was 'resting' out of the line, and a Fascist Blackshirt Brigade raided the area, surrounded the camp, shot many men and women, and took large numbers away for questioning. Williams wrote, 'By some freak of fortune we escaped and travelled almost without stopping for two days and nights, climbing the highest snow-clad mountains to do so.'

Although radios were scarce they listened whenever they could to keep abreast with news of the war. Also the B.B.C. broadcast coded messages in Italian for agents every night after the news. He said, 'To hear your own positive message was a warning that the drop asked for by an S.O.E. officer would be made that night, all things being equal.' By July, 1944, the band he had organised received one drop. But it did not contain arms which they badly needed, as they had only a few old Italian rifles, a pistol and a Besa light machine-gun.

By August, 1944, Williams and Philipsz, physically exhausted by miles of walking in rough mountain country in their efforts to organise resistance bands, and finding that the members were loth to hunt for food and did not want to leave their farms for more than a few days, disbanded their group. Antipathy between one band and another and between the bands and the local people was building up. So the British officers went into 'semi-retirement.' But the cumulative effect of Allied help was beginning to be felt. An English major with a radio operator was parachuted into a neighbouring province. He started to organise resistance, and they heard reports of mortar and artillery duels, towns raided, traffic ambushed and bridges blown. Resistance was growing and becoming a thorn in the enemy's side.

As John Woods and Arthur Hall were approaching the River Pescara at the end of November, 1943, they were frequently warned of the great dangers of attempting to cross the river. The Germans were everywhere, they were told. These warnings were often accompanied by offers of shelter until the Allies arrived, which the locals expected to be quite soon. But the two British officers realised they were getting fairly near the lines and were determined to press on.

A farmer offered to take them to a man of substance who was an active anti-fascist and was now in hiding. Woods and Hall had been wary of guides, but now sensed they would need one to get across the Pescara and around Popoli. The man they were introduced to was clearly well-educated and questioned them closely in order to satisfy himself they were not German spies. He then said he could provide guides to take them across the river, and through Popoli to the partisans in the mountains on the far side.

So it was that they were guided across the river by a bridge and, separately, through Popoli where there were many Germans, several of them the worse for drink. Though they passed within a few yards of them they were ignored. They slept in a cottage on the outskirts of the village. Next morning, guided by the owner of the cottage carrying an old rifle which he kept firing into the air to demonstrate his disdain for the Germans, they climbed up to near the top of Monte Morrone. Here they came to a large camp where they were welcomed by about a hundred Italian partisans, and a dozen or so Allied other ranks who had been prisoners at Sulmona until the Armistice.

After a few days' rest, Woods and Hall attempted to get through the lines, but were fired on at Cansano. So they returned to the partisan camp. They were surprised at the size of this. It was centred round a log cabin and a number of timber and stone outbuildings with corrugated iron roofs. The band was made up of Italian army officers as well as other ranks, plus some local young men. Some of the wives were also there with a few children. Woods thought they came up only in the day to bring supplies. Provisioning was clearly a problem, but this was sheep country and they fed off mutton and potatoes. Many of the Allied other ranks were Indian and they took a full part in helping to run the camp. There seemed to be a good quantity of rifles and hand guns in the camp.

The next evening Woods was invited to go down to Popoli to hear the Allied radio broadcast in the house of a communist family. The following morning as he and his guide were climbing up to the partisan camp they saw it come under intense German mortar fire, backed up by fire from infantry which surrounded the camp. They then closed in from all sides. Woods and his guide were fired on but they managed to run off and get into hiding. From there they saw Arthur Hall, the British and Indian other ranks and most of the Italian partisans being rounded up and marched down the mountain under heavy escort.

Fortunately for the partisans, the Germans needed labour to keep the roads clear of snow, so the Italians were not shot or transported to Germany. But they were savagely beaten to get them to reveal who were their leaders. Not one of them was betrayed, such was their bravery. New leaders arose, including Salvatore, Guiseppe and Lorenzo. Woods rejoined them there. But the camp was a dangerous place. The Germans could see by the smoke from fires that it was being re-occupied. The area was constantly patrolled, though, because of the weather, these patrols were fairly easy to avoid. It meant sleeping in a different place each night. So John Woods set to work to construct his own hideout in the mountains by digging a trench on a fairly steep slope, covering it with an iron sheet, making a door from timber retrieved from the camp and camouflaging it with soil, turf and bracken. It snowed every day and it was so cold that he could not stand more than two or three nights at a time in the hide. Some nights he would return to the camp where it was warmer, and occasionally go down to Popoli to his friends, the Ciccarellis, the communist family, or their next-door neighbours, the Cipriani's, who were Fascists. Though they were diametrically opposed to each other politically, these two families were united in wishing to protect John Woods.

In late January, 1944, Woods was in Popoli when it suffered a low-level and a high-level saturation bombing attack. These raids became a daily occurrence. Popoli was on the direct route from Pescara to Rome and the Allies were trying to prevent the Germans transferring troops from the east to the west end of the Gustav Line, and cut off reinforcements to the German defences round the Anzio beach-head. Woods had acquired a blank identity card from a bombed printing works in Popoli and, using forgery skills he had learnt in the prison camp, he filled it in, calling himself Giovanni Boschi. But to the partisans he remained *'Capitano Inglesi.'* He now spoke fluent Italian in the broad Abruzzi dialect. He also studied and adopted the Italian gestures and mannerisms. However, this did not prevent him being arrested by a German traffic controller. He was taken to a hut and his British Army identity tags were removed. His Beretta, supplied by the partisans, had not yet been discovered. As the German was using a wall telephone to summon assistance, Woods lashed out with his bare fists and ran from the room. The German fired and missed, as did another who was outside the hut. Zig-zagging as he ran, he remained unscathed until he fell into some bomb debris, smashing his nose and suffering severe cuts on his legs, face and hands. The Popoli doctor patched him up, but his wounds turned septic.

The Germans thought Woods was an agent sent to organise the partisans and was in touch with the Allies. Some older Italians even taunted the Germans with the thought, so the Germans increased their efforts to capture John Woods and offered a large reward.

After these scares he spent more time in the mountains with the partisans. He was living, or existing, from day to day, in intolerable conditions. The Italians were a happy-go-lucky, friendly group with a love of life but, at the same time, brave. In order to avoid savage reprisals, much of the sabotage carried out by the partisans, mainly the destruction of communications, was done during air raids, which occurred almost daily. Alternatively, the sabotage was made to appear as if it was air raid damage. This ruse was effective so the Popoli area did not suffer the mass shootings and burning of houses which was inflicted by the Germans in many other areas. The men seized were put to work in forced labour gangs. This was very severe, but quite a number succeeded in escaping to fight another day,

John Younger spent four months living with Italians in the Pellegrino area. In January, 1944, he and two others joined a partisan band which could not do very much for lack of arms. So, after a month, he formed an organisation for sending escapers to Switzerland which resulted in eighteen officers reaching safety. Soon after, Younger was instructed by partisan leaders to organise a scheme for evacuation by sea. This proved a failure, as did a similar scheme in the Complano area. So, back at Pellegrino working with partisans and ex-prisoners, he collected useful military information which was passed to agents for onward transmission to Allied forces. He commanded a partisan group for a month, carrying out acts of sabotage. Early in October, 1944, he joined a party of escapers who were guided to an American unit at Seravenza.

Another officer who was active with partisans was Jack Baddeley. He had several weeks in the Pellegrino area until German activity increased in May, 1944. Then for two months he served with partisans at Monte Barigazzo, participating in the occupation of Bardi. After the Germans re-took Bardi, Baddeley moved to Borgo Taro where for two-and-a-half months he led bands sabotaging railway bridges, lines and trains. On 18th October he joined a party of ex-prisoners who were guided to Antona. He and an Italian met Allied troops near Pietra Santa on 25th October.

John Ballantyne had a short period with a rebel band near Bedonia, but as they were very ineffective, he left them and moved back to Cereseto. In January, 1944, he led three Other Ranks in a move to the north, but became snowed up at Selva. Moving back to the Bardi area, which in May, 1944, came to be controlled by partisans, he was appointed liaison officer with a partisan band. The area was raided by Germans and Ballantyne and another ex-prisoner had to go into hiding for nine days. He now formed a new band whose sole task was to collect military information. This was a considerable help to the Allied forces in the area. John Ballantyne, having led this intelligence-gathering band for some weeks, was guided back to Allied troops at Ruosina at the end of October, 1944.

10: Walking South

THOSE ex-prisoners who had elected not to make for Switzerland, or to remain in a secure and reasonably comfortable hideout, decided sooner or later to begin the long walk south towards the slowly-advancing Allied armies.

A few made this decision very early when still in the Plain of Lombardy and in the vicinity of Fontanellato. Very few recognised the time and distance that would be involved or, as they set off under the warm autumn sun, that two or three months later they would be clambering about, ill-clad, in the snow.

About the earliest was the 'Toots' Williams, Hugh Jobson, Ted Pryke and Ian Shaw party. They had listened to the B.B.C. on 10th September from a place in the foothills and decided on the 11th to set off walking without more delay. A group of ten officers, including Lt.-Col. Denis Gibbs, moved away from the Bund on the night of the 14th September. A. A. Jones and 'Doc' Rogers set off south on the 16th, while Gibbs, Norman Girling and Rex Smith, having been walking at night, made the final decision to head south on 18th September. Maurice Goddard and Erik Hampson set off from the Bardi area in the third week of September. Peter Langrishe, John Eadie, Bunny Buist and David Buchanan left a farm at Toccalmatta on 30th September at the beginning of their long journey. It was on the same day that Gervase Nicholls and Geoffrey Phalp left a farm a few kilometres away from Fontanellato and headed south.

Jack Moore, Wilfred White and Ian English decided to start walking on 3rd October, but agreed to wait a week in case Jimmy James had managed to get away from the Germans at Valmozzola Station where he had taken a sick English soldier to put him on a train for Parma; so they did not leave until 10th October. Ronald Mann, who had himself been in hospital at Piacenza, escaped and went into the hills, made the decision on 17th October not to wait for the arrival of the Allies, but to try to get through the lines. Perhaps the last to face this choice and opt for walking were Philip Kindersley and Ronald Orr-Ewing who left Noceto on 1st November.

The optimum size of party was another item for decision and it is interesting how different groups, starting from the same general area and with the same objective in mind, arrived at different solutions. Anthony Laing, John Woods at first (though he later joined up with Peter Gunter and Arthur Hall), and later Drew Bethel chose to be on their own, maintaining they could get on faster that way, and perhaps preferring to be independent and beholden to no one. It was easier to make decisions on one's own and harder to find help and accommodation in a group. After Fano, when David Buchanan dropped out because of the very bad state of his feet, Peter Langrishe then went on on his own.

Many others, such as Goddard and Hampson, Stericker and Watson, Nicholls and Phalp, 'Dean' MacDonnell and Dick Carver, Eric Hopkins with Tom Wheeler, Lt.-Col. Burne and Gerald Churchill, Bill Bowder and Peter Ellis, A A. Jones and 'Doc' Rogers, thought that two was the right number. Binks Forster, Henry Armstrong and Bill Reid were together until early November. They met Rex Ord who had been on his own and he joined them. But after a few days they found that four together was too many, particularly for the peasant families to provide food for them. So they split up—Armstrong and Reid, and Forster with Ord.

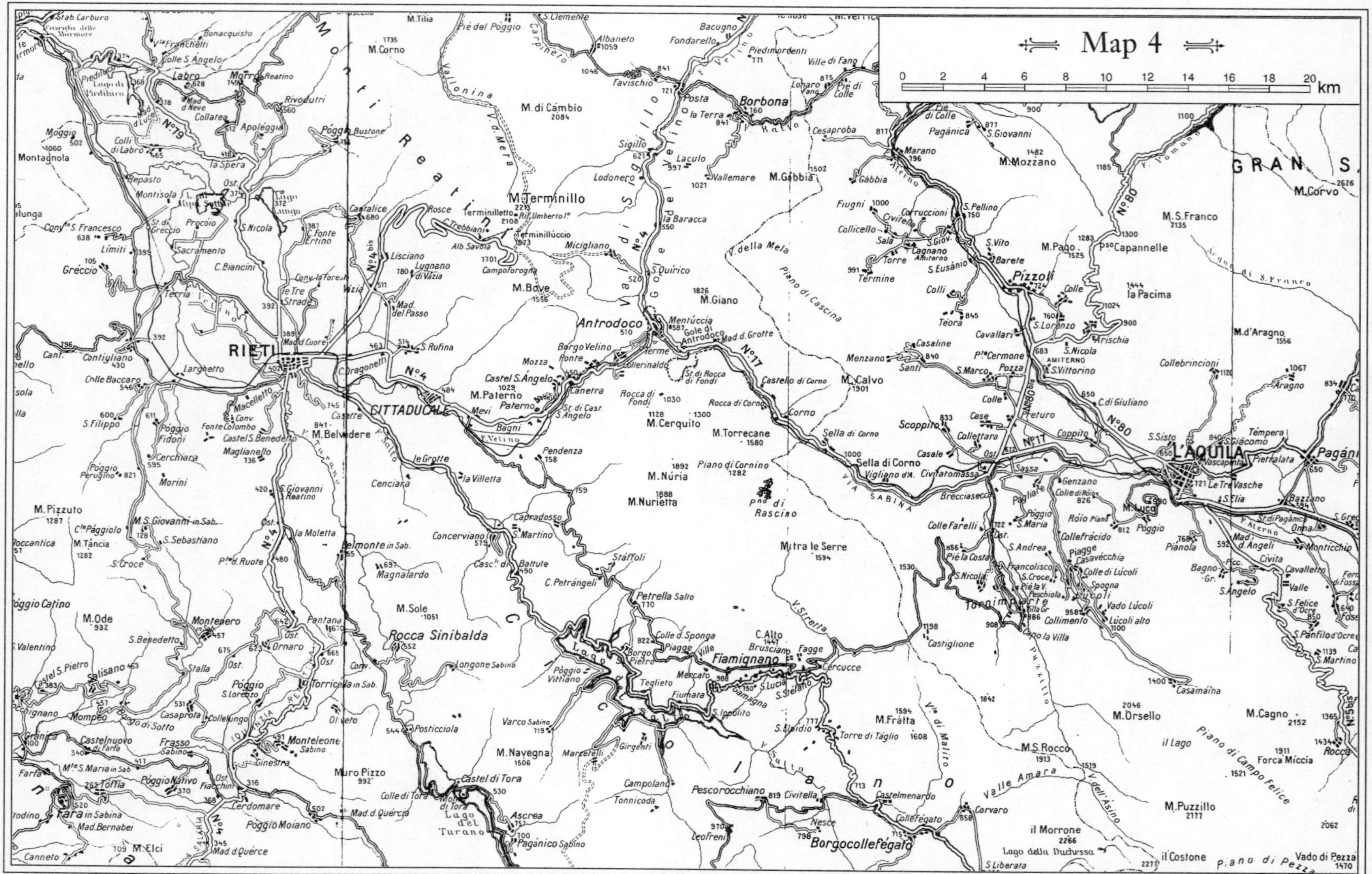

Map 4
0
2
4
6
8
10
12
14
16
18
20
km
RIETI
L'AQUILA
CITTADUCALE
Antrodoco
Borbona
Pizzoli
Fiamignano
Borgocollefegato
Rocca Sinibalda
Monti Reatini
Val di Sigillo
Gole del Velino
Cicolano
Lago del Salto
Lago del Turano
GRAN S
M.Terminillo
2213
M.di Cambio
2084
M.Giano
M.Nuria
M.Nurietta
M.Calvo
M.Cerquito
M.Torrecane
Sella di Corno
Piano di Cornino
Pno di Rascino
Mtra le Serre
M.Corvo
M.S.Franco
M.Mozzano
M.Gabbia
M.Pago
Pso Capannelle
la Pacima
M.d'Aragno
M.Orsello
M.Cagno
M.S.Rocco
M.Puzzillo
il Morrone
Lago della Duchessa
Piano di Campo Felice
Piano di Pezza
M.Fratta
M.Navegna
M.Sole
M.Ode
M.Pizzuto
M.Corno
M.Tilia
M.Bove
M.Belvedere
M.Paterno
Castel S.Angelo
Borgo Velino
Posta
Montereale
Paganica
Sassa
Preturo
Civitaromassa
Tornimparte
Lucoli
Petrella Salto
Pescorocchiano
Castel di Tora
Ascrea
Paganico Sabino
Monteleone Sabino
Poggio Moiano
Montenero
Greccio
Contigliano
Labro
Morro Reatino
Rivodutri
Cantalice
Lisciano
Poggio Bustone
Apoleggia
Cerchiara
Morini
Concerviano
Magnalardo
Belmonte in Sab.
Varco Sabino
Longone Sabino
Torricella in Sab.
Posticciola
Muro Pizzo
Colle di Tora
Casaprota
Frasso Sabino
Castelnuovo di Farfa
Mompeo
Salisano
Fara in Sabina
Toffia
Poggio Nativo
M.Elci
Canneto
N°4
N°17
N°80
N°79
N°4 bis
N°5 bis
VIA SALARIA
VIA SABINA

Parties of three were common. Toby Graham, Michael Gilbert and Tony Davies; Pip and Jim Gardner and Percy Gers; Jack Kempton, Tom Craig and 'Tubby' Wilson; Denny Abbott, Noel Durrant and Theo Stephenson (all Garhwali officers); and Ian English, Jack Moore and Wilfred White were examples.

That four escapers travelling together could be successful was demonstrated by three D.C.L.I. officers—'Toots' Williams, Hugh Jobson and Ted Pryke, who were joined by Ian Shaw of the Green Howards. They did one of the longest walks. Another four who walked a long way were Denis Gibbs, Norman Girling, and Rex Smith, who were joined by Sgt. Turner on 27th September.

Every-day decisions, whether minor or important, had to be made; which of two paths to take, whether to press on for a few more miles at the end of a day, and which house to try for food and shelter. More fundamental questions had to be settled, such as whether to stop and lie up till the Allies arrived or to press on; and which route to take when getting near the lines. Most of these decisions were reached after generally amicable, though often lengthy discussions. Tony Davies wrote that he, Michael Gilbert and Toby Graham agreed a system whereby they took it in turns for one of them to have the decisive vote for each day. This worked well for the first few weeks. But when the weather deteriorated and they were often wet and cold, they became irritable and very tired due to the long distances they were covering, and not unnaturally arguments occurred. Finally one day, being unable to agree, Graham decided to go off on his own. He was quite confident in this step, being basically an individualist, and he had enough stamina and a good sense of direction. Jack Comyn described how at first in his 8th Hussar party of Pat de Clermont, Charles Hedley, Donald Astley-Cooper and himself, the decisions were made by the senior officer, which was de Clermont. By mid-October, Comyn and Astley-Cooper thought they should start walking south. De Clermont disagreed and there was an acrimonious discussion. Comyn and Astley-Cooper decided no longer to defer to the senior officer present and they split up. As luck would have it, the two officers who stayed were home several months before the other two. In 'Toots' Williams' party they agreed he should be the leader, Jobson the navigator, Pryke the quarter-master in charge of the food they were carrying, and Shaw the interpreter. This worked pretty well.

Having once decided to walk south, the daily routine was much the same for everybody. An early start, soon after dawn, was made with or without breakfast, which, for most *contadini*, was simply acorn coffee and dry bread—sometimes even without the bread. If the escapers met Italians who offered them some food in the middle of the day, this would of course be accepted, leading to a stop for an hour or two. They would then walk till the late afternoon or early evening when they would look out for a suitable house or farm where they could ask for food and shelter. Nor were the British the only persons making demands on these poor friendly and hospitable people for, in mid-September, there were many deserting Italian soldiers walking home.

Peter Langrishe wrote, 'We developed a technique for finding reasonably safe lodgings at the end of each day's march. This involved approaching someone working in the fields with a request for help—an approach which almost never failed, as we reasoned that no neo-Fascist would demean himself with manual labour.' Dick Carver made it a rule never to stay in one place more than one night. This was sensible from the security point of view, but it was not always possible to stick to because of bad weather or minor illness. On the other hand, when the circumstances demanded it, some continued walking after dark; 'Doc' Rogers with A. A. Jones and the Gibbs party were examples.

A common experience after a day's march was the conversation with the family in the evening. Not only the family; villagers would come into the house in numbers to ask questions, or merely to stare at the ex-prisoners as if they were zoo animals. The conversations usually took the same form, of close questioning of the visitors—'Where have you come from? Where are you going?' When told, the *contadini* would often say 'Don't go there; there are too many Germans and Fascists. Very dangerous. *Molto pericoloso!*' Then they would ask about families—were they married? If so, how many children did they have? If a married officer had no children they wanted to know why. Philip Kindersley amazed his hosts when he said he had five children, the youngest of whom he had never seen. Some escapers carried a photograph of wife or children. When produced, this was always a 'conversation stopper' as it was passed round the room.

Then the talk switched to the war. 'Why were the Allies taking so long to come up to Northern Italy?' Those with Communist sympathies, and there were many, often said the British and Americans were no good and were only playing at war. It was only the Russians who were doing any fighting. All the Allies did was bomb towns and kill civilians. Others were highly impressed when told that their guests had been in the 8th Army. The Fascist government propaganda had stressed the idea that to beat the glorious Italian army the 8th Army was quite extraordinarily efficient, the like of which had never been seen previously. Many of the *contadini* families had sons or nephews who were prisoners-of-war in Egypt or England, or were in Russia and of whom there had been no news for months.

Peter Watson aptly termed the route taken by ex-prisoners walking south as 'the Mountain Highway.' The left of this was the north and east side of the Apennine watershed on the general line of Fornovo—Corniglio—Ramiseto—Castiglione—Firenzuola—Bagno—Sestino—Sassoferrato. This general route was taken by White, Moore and English; Davies, Gilbert and Graham and Watson and Stericker. Some favoured the watershed between Emilia and Tuscany, walking from one mountain along the shoulders to the next—the Alpe de San Benedetto. Perhaps the majority crossed over the mountains into Tuscany, going round the north of Florence, crossing the River Sieve and the upper reaches of the Tiber, and then on the general line of Poppi—Bibbiena—Citta di Castello—Umbertide—Todi—Leonessa. This was the right of the 'Highway.'

On reaching Abruzzi province most parties went west of the Gran Sasso, and had the choice of going east or west of Aquila. Among those going west of that important town were Denis Gibbs' party, Anthony Laing with Donald Macaulay who had joined him near Leonessa, Peter Langrishe, Gervase Nicholls with Geoffrey Phalp, and Robert Smyth with Stafford Tolley, whereas the D.C.L.I. team of Williams, Jobson, Pryke and Shaw, and English, Moore and White chose the hills to the east going by Poggio Cancelli or Campo Tosto—Assergi—Barisciano and down to the River Pescara, east of Popoli. Those taking the westerly line were almost bound to go by, or west of Avezzano—Sulmona and west of the Maiella to the River Sangro, west of Castel di Sangro. Jack Kempton, the English, Moore and White team, Tony Davies and Michael Gilbert moved east of the Maiella.

Keeping direction proved to be a smaller problem than many escapers thought it to be. Several found they could look at a good map at a priest's house, for example, and make a note of the main places on the general route they were following. They could then ask for directions between these places. The places noted down were usually towns which, of course, were avoided whenever possible. Many ex-prisoners were given maps of varying quality. Maurice Goddard and Peter Langrishe had a map of Italy torn out of a school atlas. Denny Abbott had a sketch-map taken from a guide-book, with an approximate scale of a quarter-inch to a mile. Dick Carver had to rely on a rough map and a small compass made in the prison camp. Ian English was given a very detailed map of Parma province and a small compass by an Italian army lieutenant on 12th September; later he was given a similar map of Mugello, the area north and north-east of Florence. Finally, he acquired a large-scale Italian army map of the rivers Pescara and Sangro area. It was so detailed that it was not easy to read, but proved useful nevertheless.

They were well on their way before Denis Gibbs was given a good map on 5th October. This covered the country as far south as Pescara. Jack Comyn met a lady from Rome at La Verna Monastery, who gave him a motoring map on quite a large scale which was invaluable. Peter Langrishe met Fernando Lausi in the hill village of Tripozzo above the Nera valley. Besides providing an excellent meal and shelter, Lausi pressed upon Langrishe a large-scale map of his own area around Arrone, on which he had marked a German Army headquarters and which Langrishe was able to hand over after he reached the Allied lines. Peter Watson and Peter Stericker met two S.A.S. soldiers who gave them a silk map and a button compass which were to prove invaluable. The S.A.S. men had just blown up the Taro valley railway bridge.

The distances travelled in a day depended partly on the weather, partly on who they met to delay the walkers and partly on the nature of the country and the obstacles encountered. Inevitably the journeys were made across the grain of the country. Those on the left of the 'Mountain Highway' had to cross numerous rivers running north or north-east into the River Po or east into the Adriatic. So it meant a climb up to a ridge and a walk down to the next valley repeated again and again. Tony Davies likened it to advancing over a vast sheet of corrugated iron. Pip Gardner and his companions were doing at least ten miles a day. Douglas Flowerdew and Drew Bethel, together and separately, were covering twenty to thirty kilometres a day. Peter Langrishe wrote, 'And so we progressed … at a steady twenty to twenty-five miles a day, sometimes wet, sometimes dry, always hungry.' Michael Gilbert reckoned they averaged at least fifteen kilometres a day. Hugh Jobson and Ted Pryke, who kept diaries and recorded each day's distance, averaged nearly eighteen kilometres a day for the thirty-three days from 10th September to 13th October. A. A. Jones wrote that, 'On the 12th October I and "Doc" Rogers pushed ourselves hard until 0400 hours, when luckily we found a straw barn in which we slept for three hours. Estimated distance of the walk over sixty kilometres in twenty hours.'

Of course, the distances covered depended also on how strong was the motivation to keep going. If one arrived at a 'good billet' with friendly confident hosts who urged one to stay for a few days, it needed a strong will to resist the temptation and push on. This applied especially when one's feet were blistered and boots in disrepair and the weather was wet. In such situations Maurice Goddard kept his aim of being home by Christmas in the front of his mind. This was his motive for keeping walking. Ian English wrote, 'On these wet days it was difficult to know what to do. We were reluctant to go on in pouring rain, but equally we did not want to overstay our welcome. I became very frustrated by these delays. I seemed to have a physiological urge to push on, rather like some birds who get the migratory urge in autumn and spring.' John Woods said he was always for moving on as soon as possible. Tony Davies remembered, 'I had one obsession and that was to be home for Christmas; but we were all equally in a fever of impatience. Each day we drove ourselves to cover more ground; if we had been capable of it, I believe we would have gone at the double, so great was our longing to get the whole business over once and for all.'

The main obstacles to progress were the crossing of main roads and rivers. Most escapers adopted the technique of finding a concealed position from which the road could be watched. The frequency of German traffic was then assessed and a plan made for

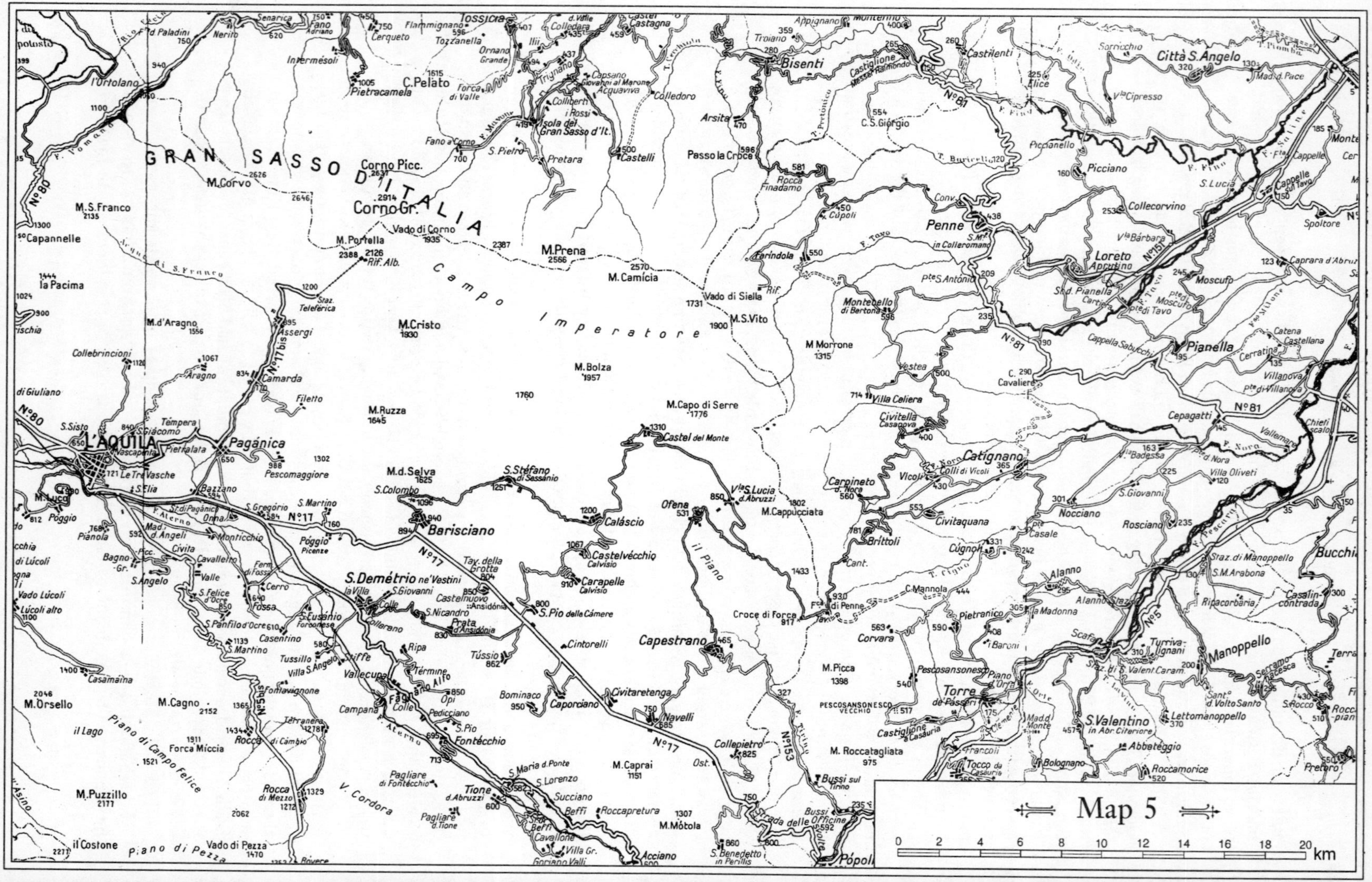
Map 5
0 2 4 6 8 10 12 14 16 18 20 km
GRAN SASSO D'ITALIA
Campo Imperatore
L'AQUILA
Pagánica
Assergi
Camarda
Paganica
Barisciano
S. Demétrio ne' Vestini
Capestrano
Ofena
Calàscio
Castel del Monte
Navelli
Tossicia
Isola del Gran Sasso d'It.
Castelli
Bisenti
Penne
Loreto Aprutino
Pianella
Catignano
Città S. Angelo
Manoppello
Torre de' Pàsseri
S. Valentino in Abr. Citeriore
Pópoli
Bussi sul Tirino
Corno Gr.
Corno Picc.
M. Prena
M. Camícia
M. Cristo
M. Bolza
M. Ruzza
M. Capo di Serre
Vado di Corno
Vado di Siella
Passo la Croce
Fontécchio
Tione d. Abruzzi
Acciano
Rocca di Mezzo
Piano di Campo Felice
Piano di Pezza
N°17
N°80
N°81
N°153
N°5

crossing. When crossing railways, it was sometimes possible to find a culvert under the railway, as Denis Gibbs' party did on 6th October. Ian English wrote that as he, Jack Moore and Wilfred White approached a main road and the River Tronto, they were met by an old woman jabbering hysterically. It was very difficult to understand what she was saying, but they gathered that a German convoy had halted in the village of Tresungo which was on the main road and at which they had intended crossing the river. They retired to a hut on the hillside to wait till the German trucks moved on. Presently they saw the old woman carrying up a large meal of *minestra*, several loaves and a bottle of wine, and she pressed them to stay the night in the hut. So they were very grateful to the old woman for both warning them of danger and providing an excellent meal.

With care it was usually possible to find a place to cross the rivers unobserved, but it was more difficult to find a bridge by which to cross. Either it meant a long détour or the bridge was in a town or village which it was risky to go into. So it meant either scrambling across boulders or wading. Many escapers speak of wading in water varying in depth from a few inches to two or three feet. Adrian Barber told of his crossing of the River Secchio with Dick Booth, when they were having great difficulty in a rapid swirling current. They were rescued by a small boy who ran out into the stream, took their hands and guided them across. Philip Kindersley and Ronald Orr-Ewing fared better on 24th November when they were rowed across the River Sieve by a miller.

Jack Kempton and Tom Craig encountered great difficulty in crossing the River Metauro. They had heard the Germans were building a defensive line based on the river and had put guards on all the bridges. Eventually they found a crossing consisting of two ropes stretched across the river. They attempted to cross on a very windy afternoon, Craig leading the way. He got a quarter of the way over, then a gust of wind caught him and he nearly fell into the swollen river. Kempton tried, but after a few yards he was nearly blown off, turning upside down. But he was able to scramble back. While they were considering what to do, a young girl riding a bicycle and carrying a baby and a shopping bag prepared to cross. She tucked the bicycle over one arm, the baby under the other and with no fuss crossed the rope bridge. The two officers thought if the girl can do it, they could. The trick seemed to be to put both feet wide apart on the lower rope and tuck the upper rope under one arm. They tried again with near disastrous results, but succeeded at the third attempt.

Another difficulty on the long walk was boots. Boots were virtually unobtainable in the Italian countryside in 1943 and almost every escaper's boots gradually disintegrated on the journey. This naturally led to blisters and sore feet. Some, like David Buchanan, had to stop walking because their feet were in such a bad state. A. A. Jones' diary for 14th October records, 'Norman cannot go very much further, his shoes are in tatters and his feet obviously very painful. We walk very slowly. I have to keep waiting for him to catch me up. It depresses me to see the painful way he limps along.' But his feet improved during the next few days and Jones remarked that Doc's feet seem much better 'He's as nimble as a mountain goat.'

Bill Bowder had made the mistake of exchanging his Army boots for cheap civilian shoes on the grounds that boots were too conspicuous. The shoes soon gave out, so he and Peter Ellis went to the San Marino Republic, thinking that they might obtain boots there, by barter if necessary. He wrote, 'Our stay in the town was brief because it was being visited by German officers. We only had time to exchange my valuable watch for two pairs of boots in the open market. The next few days was to see the end of this footwear as we trudged up the steep slopes and into the deep valleys of the Abruzzi. Our bare feet, instead of hardening, became blistered and painful, especially Peter's.' Ian English remembered that in the village of Forgo there was a cobbler's shop which seemed to be the central meeting-place of the village. His boots were in a very bad state, with the sole of one coming away from the upper and a large crack in the upper of the other. The cobbler took one look at them and said they were not worth repairing.

Both Jack Comyn and Denis Gibbs were more fortunate, as both had their boots repaired at the Monastery of La Verna. Comyn wrote, 'I asked our host whether there was any possibility of having my boots repaired and in no time a cobbler monk appeared, took them away and brought them back rejuvenated.' The state of one's footwear was of paramount importance if the long walk south was to be undertaken, and Peter Langrishe found that his army boots just lasted out his 500-mile trek. At one overnight stop in the Tiber valley, not only had he and David Buchanan been given five-star treatment as to food and sleeping accommodation, but they found in the morning that their host had gone to the trouble of anointing their boots with some precious lard.

With the Italians' fear of the Germans and the Fascist militia, escapers were often told of the great dangers of walking any further. These dangers were, more often than not, greatly exaggerated. Gervase Nicholls, walking with Geoffrey Phalp, wrote that, when they got south of Aquila, they began to meet people moving north—mainly Italians, Yugoslavs, and a few British Other Ranks. They said it was quite impossible to get through, there were Germans in all the villages and all the river crossings were guarded. But as they had met no returning British officers or N.C.Os. they decided to push on. In the event they experienced no difficulty for the next few days. Similarly Ian English met a Yugoslav officer in the village of Forgo, who said he had been further south and every road and track was blocked by pro-German Fascist militia who were looking especially for prisoners-of-war. Jack Moore was quite impressed with the man and thought they should stop until the Allies arrived. However, after an argument they went on and did not run into trouble till much later. In late November, John Woods and Arthur Hall were approaching the Pescara River. They were constantly warned of the perils of crossing the river or of passing anywhere nearby. The Moore, White and English party had exactly the same experience.

Another hindrance on the long walk south was the possibility of encountering parties of German or Fascist militia. Of course, one expected them when getting near the front lines, but further back it was less likely, though always a danger to be on the lookout for. Also the attitude of the *carabinieri* was unclear to start with. Generally they seemed to adopt a neutral position and some were actually helpful. One who was not was encountered by Anthony Laing near Val di Nera who tried to detain Laing. He wrote, 'Fortunately he did not bother to search me and, being armed, (Laing had been given a Berretta pistol) I was later able to disarm him and slope off into the night.'

On the pass carrying the main Bologna to Florence road Comyn and Astley-Cooper had to walk a short distance on the road in order to cross it. They were overtaken by a German lorry and they feared the worst. But the German was lost and asked where he was. He seemed satisfied with Comyn's reply in crude Italian. Drew Bethel had a similar experience when he encountered two Germans on a forest path. One asked a question in German, and then pulled out a map. Bethel pretended to be a simple Italian peasant who could not read a map. The Germans seemed to be satisfied. Then Bethel found himself in a German reserve position and escaped only by leaping into a waterfall.

Maurice Goddard and Erik Hampson were approaching the Futa Pass on the Florence to Bologna road when they saw a German training exercise in progress. There was a lot of German army traffic on the main highway. Goddard wrote, 'When all appeared clear, we slid down a bank on to the road and down a slope the other side into some undergrowth. Hardly were we concealed than vehicles screeched to a halt on the road above and troops dismounted and spread out all around us, calling to each other as they searched. It seemed to us that we were their target. After what seemed an age, they remounted and moved off, we remained paralysed for at least an hour until our nerves were steady.'

Philip Kindersley on 18th November was near Pistoia which was full of Germans. He and Ronald Orr-Ewing almost ran into a German working-party near a main road into the town. An Italian woman showed them across this road which was busy with German traffic. Peter Langrishe and David Buchanan had a very close call from being recaptured at Ferentillo in the Nera valley, where they found the town swarming with Germans. To try to look less like escaping prisoners, Langrishe persuaded Buchanan to throw away his walking stick! Ted Pryke, Hugh Jobson, 'Toots' Williams and Ian Shaw ran into a Fascist guard on 30th September. They were in battledress and the guard took them for Germans. They were directed to a German headquarters at Torre di Monte Farco. On 9th October in the Sangro valley when they were crossing a ploughed field they were seen by Germans in two lorries and a motor-cycle, but the latter took no notice.

A rather unusual encounter was experienced by Gervase Nicholls and Geoffrey Phalp on 3rd November, when they were approaching the Velino River and the main Ascoli to Rome road. They met a stranger speaking Italian who asked if they were British ex-prisoners. He took them to meet a friend. They went about a mile through a wood to a cave. Here they were introduced to Generals Neame and O'Connor, a Brigadier and two Colonels. They had a couple of A.D.Cs. out scouting for ex-prisoners to hear their news and give them encouragement. General O'Connor told them that if he had been a few years younger he would set out himself.

Similarly, Peter Stericker and Peter Watson reached the village of Seccotina on 15th October. At a smart villa on the outskirts of the village a woman eyeing them suspiciously asked a number of questions. They then spoke to a well-dressed Italian who seemed to be concealing a revolver. He also questioned them, first in Italian and then in quite good English. A second man came up and he kept them covered with a gun in his hand. Stericker and Watson apparently satisfied the two men because they invited them into the house for breakfast, which included the unusual luxury of bread and honey. A few minutes later an officer wearing major's crowns introduced himself as Brigadier Vaughan. Peter Stericker wrote, 'Two other British officers then appeared and watched us silently as the Brigadier questioned us about where we had been captured, our regiment, and the name of the camp we had come from. One of the other two officers then introduced himself as General O'Connor and his companion as General Neame ... Both generals knew Peter's father ... and both had known my father at the staff college. Neither general wore anything to indicate his rank and they passed in the immediate neighbourhood as Lt.-Colonels ... we reckoned their security was pretty good as no mention had been made in the previous village of San Paolo of there being Englishmen at Seccotina ... the initial excitement we both experienced that there might be the opening of an escape route for ourselves soon vanished. Both generals had as little information as we did about the possible future course of events.' Before leaving, they asked the generals' advice and were recommended to keep on the Adriatic side of the mountains and to lie up about a hundred kilometres further south, which they thought would be well south of the next defensive line after the fall of Rome. Their morale was raised by having their original intention confirmed by their high-powered advisers.

Thirty-five years later Stericker met an ex-Commando who had taken part in an operation to take the generals off by boat. The first attempt failed, but the second attempt rescued them and brought them home. General O'Connor later took part in the battle for Normandy as Commander of 8 Corps.

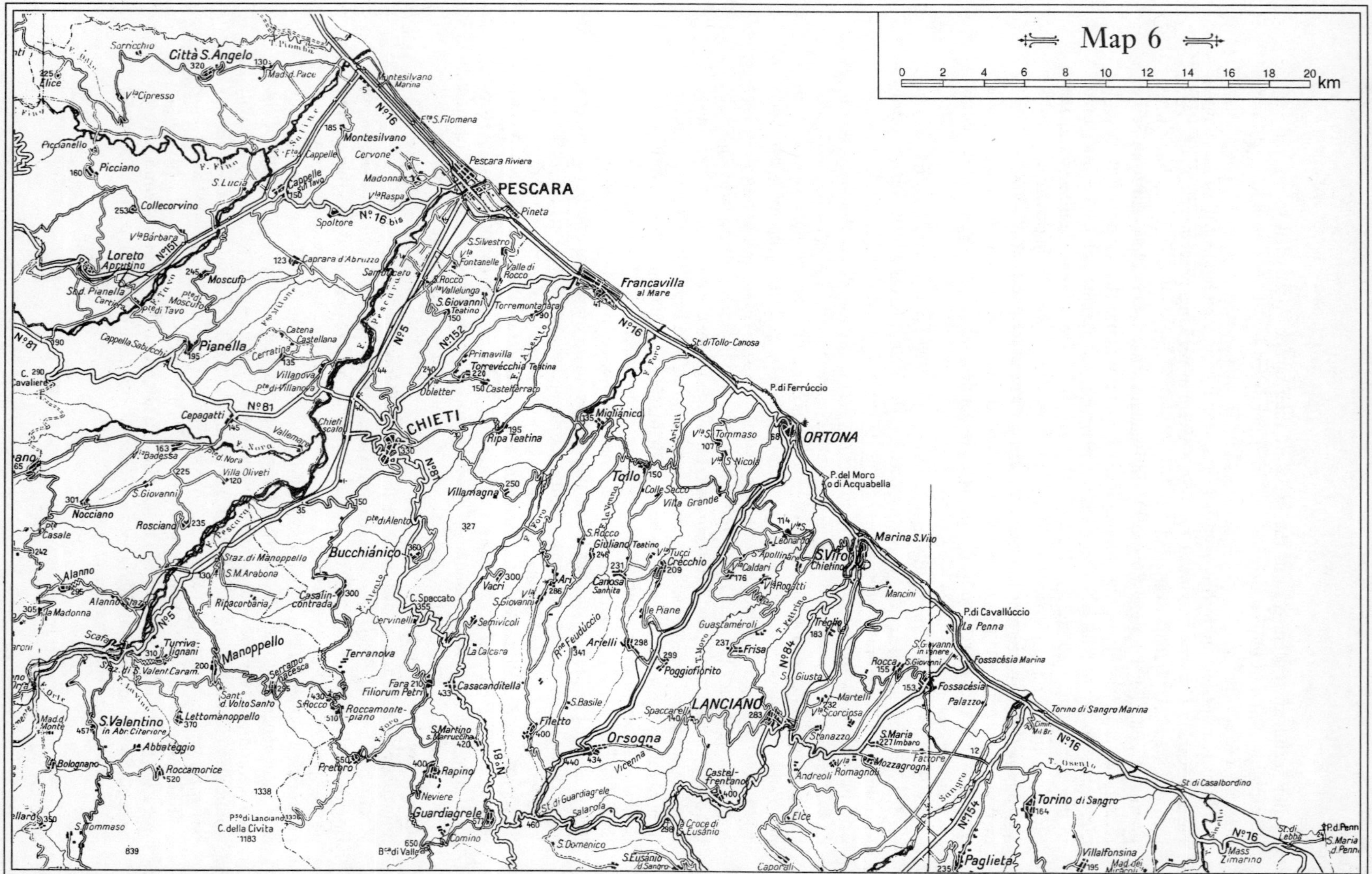

Map 6
0 2 4 6 8 10 12 14 16 18 20 km
PESCARA
Pescara Riviera
Pineta
Montesilvano Marina
Montesilvano
Città S.Angelo
Francavilla al Mare
CHIETI
Chieti scalo
ORTONA
Marina S.Vito
LANCIANO
Orsogna
Guardiagrele
Tollo
Miglianico
Ripa Teatina
Villamagna
Bucchiánico
Manoppello
S.Valentino in Abr. Citeriore
Pianella
Loreto Aprutino
Collecorvino
Picciano
Moscufo
Spoltore
Cepagatti
Nocciano
Rosciano
Alanno
Scafa
Fossacésia
Fossacésia Marina
Torino di Sangro
Torino di Sangro Marina
Paglieta
Frisa
Treglio
Mozzagrogna
Castel-frentano
Rapino
Pretoro
Fara Filiorum Petri
Casacanditella
Filetto
Arielli
Poggiofiorito
Crecchio
Canosa Sannita
Giuliano Teatino
Ari
Vacri
Abbateggio
Roccamorice
Lettomanoppello
Turrivalignani
Serramonacesca
Roccamontepiano
Terranova
Casalincontrada
Villalfonsina
St. di Casalbordino
P.di Ferrúccio
P.del Moro o di Acquabella
P.di Cavallúccio
La Penna
St.di Tollo-Canosa
N°16
N°16 bis
N°5
N°81
N°87
N°151
N°152
N°84
N°154
F. Pescara
F. Foro
T. Osento
Sangro
C.della Civita 1183

11: Recaptured and Jumping off Trains

REGRETTABLY, many of the eighty thousand Allied prisoners in the hands of the Italians on 8th September 1943, the day the Armistice was signed, were recaptured. Roger Absalom calculated that, of this number, only about four thousand succeeded in getting out of Italy by positive means and being repatriated before the war ended. Approximately fifty thousand left their camps and a large proportion were re-caught at various times between 9th September and the end of the fighting in May, 1945. All prisoners at PG49, Fontanellato, got away, but quite a large number fell into the hands of the Germans during the next twelve months.

Some of the first were those recaptured on farms only a few miles from Fontanellato within about a fortnight of getting out of the camp. These included A. N. Evans, Reg Beales and Tom Stuchberry. Eric Newby was told by Wanda that thirteen had been retaken, along with many of the farmers who had sheltered them. When they met later in the mountains she said about eighty prisoners from Fontanellato had been recaptured.

One of the most unfortunate of the early recaptures was Jimmy James, a doctor. Ian English had invited him to join his little group. On 3rd October in the village of Bruschi they were told there was an English soldier who was very ill at Costa d'Arsino. When they got there James examined the soldier, Private Burdett, 51 years old, and diagnosed a perforated appendix, which meant he had to have an operation within twenty-four hours. There was no alternative but to take Burdett down to Valmozzola station on the main Parma to La Spezia line, where he could be put on a train to Parma. Burdett begged Jimmy James not to leave him. As the station was manned by three Germans, it meant that James had to say who he was if he was to ensure that Burdett was transferred quickly to hospital in Parma. So he again became a prisoner-of-war, but Burdett survived. A selfless action, fully in keeping with the highest standards of the medical profession.

Tony Davies and Michael Gilbert had unexpectedly joined up again with Toby Graham. With the latter was a South African called Hal Becker. Towards the end of October 1943 they reached a ridge from which they could look down on a five-mile stretch of the Sangro River and they could see Castel di Sangro and half a dozen villages all packed with German troops. Five hundred feet below them they watched men digging fortifications. They spent the night in an empty cottage up in the mountains. They left the cottage early and set off through the thick mist, the damp cold chilling them to the marrow. They moved to the left for two or three hours, aiming to pass east of Castel di Sangro. They stood on a level plateau, looking across to a tree-clad slope which fell away to the valley. There was no sign of life and all was silent. They decided to attempt it in pairs, Gilbert and Graham going first, and to meet again in the woods. Davies and Becker watched the other two disappear into the woods before they set out. When they were about halfway across the open ground they heard the sharp crack of a rifle, followed by two more. They started to run and then saw a German with a rifle shouting at them. It was a race for shelter. The German knelt down and took deliberate aim. Davies wrote, 'As we reached the trees I heard two shots. One round went whining through the trees, the other hit Hal Becker and over my shoulder I saw him stumble and crash. I was running full tilt down a steep slope and ahead of me, over the lip of a crest, was what looked like some good dead ground. I hurtled downhill and leapt straight over it. There was a sheer drop of ten feet and at the bottom a German working party was digging a weapon pit. I landed literally in their laps. One of them raised a rifle and fired at point-blank range. I saw the movement and heard the shot, but felt nothing. Only when I tried to get up, I found my right foot would not respond ... I realised I had failed at the very end and was back where I started—a prisoner-of-war.' He was only a few miles from the Allied lines.

Private Christiaan Botha had walked south from Fontanellato to Foligno. Here he was recaptured by Fascists and handed over to the Germans. He and others were put on a train heading for Germany, but on 4th November near Perugia some of his colleagues had managed to open the door of the truck. Botha jumped off successfully and walked to Capistrello where he hid awaiting the arrival of the Allied forces in the following summer.

John Measures, whose original party included M. A. 'Pat' Callaghan, John McKinlay and J. Pat Playford, was seen by Gervase Nicholls and Geoffrey Phalp at Santa Maria in company with 'Mac' MacLean. When Nicholls and Phalp moved off from there, MacLean decided to stay and wait for Measures who had gone to a nearby village to try to get his boots repaired.

The 25th November was a miserable day with snow, hail, sleet, and a heavy thunderstorm. In the middle of a snowstorm they met some Italian refugees who told them the Germans had withdrawn, and they were now only on the north side of the River Sangro. Measures and MacLean passed two German gun positions tucked into the hillside, and made their way towards the river two-and-a-half miles away. After passing within a few feet of German positions, they crawled under a large railway viaduct with sentries on top.

Suddenly they stumbled on a notice which said *'Achtung Minen.'* They realised that for a hundred yards they had been walking over mines. John Measures wrote, 'I nearly collapsed with fright! However, we went on and half an hour later met our Waterloo.' MacLean was leading the way down the side of a wood and caught his foot in a trip wire, Ten yards to his left an anti-personnel mine exploded. This made a great hole in his thigh and knocked out his left eye. Two companions dived into the wood for cover and set off another trip wire; both were wounded in the face, wrist and back.

They lay there till dawn in the pouring rain. MacLean was in a serious condition. One companion went to a German position to get help, The Germans acted very promptly and efficiently. They brought a stretcher for MacLean and bandages for the others. They gave the escapers food and cigarettes and dried their clothes. They were taken to a dressing station at Roccaraso. The Germans told them that when the accident happened they were only a kilometre from the Sangro, there were no more German troops ahead of them and the British lines were only three kilometres to the south, When they discovered the escapers were paratroops they made a fuss of them and said what bad luck they had had. Perhaps it was the same minefield which Nicholls and Phalp encountered on 20th November.

Jack Comyn and Donald Astley-Cooper had made good progress and on 29th November had reached Opi twelve miles south of Villavallelonga. As they knew they were near the lines they continued walking through the night in snow two feet deep. They came across three Sikhs sitting in the snow who had given up hope and, as they said, were waiting for death. When urged by Comyn to move, one said, 'Sahib, it is no good. I am too old, too far from home. I shall wait here till death comes.' After a long night came a grey, misty dawn and they realised they did not know where they were. They were dead-tired after twenty-four hours on their feet, chilled and wet from the snow. As the light grew, they saw a stone hut from which emerged a British soldier. So, seeing smoke from a fire, they went over and found two British soldiers and one of another nationality. Comyn and Astley-Cooper took off their shoes and socks to warm their feet. Presently the three Sikhs arrived at the hut. Suddenly they heard the rattle of automatic fire. The British soldiers dashed out of the hut and ran off up the hillside into the forest. The Indians fatalistically remained where they were. The two British officers decided not to go out without their boots on, but retreated into a store-room at the back of the hut. The Germans rounded up the three men and the Indians. A man in Fascist uniform came in and appeared, or chose, not to see them. After some delay the Germans came back and smashed in a boarded-up window opening in their hiding-place. A bespectacled German face looked in and said *'raus.'* In the misery of that moment a large Feldwebel, who was disposed to be friendly, fell them in and they started on a long exhausting march to a prisoner-of-war cage. Comyn and Astley-Cooper had been on their feet for thirty hours with hardly a respite.

Reg Dickinson was recaptured by Germans near Villa Santa Lucia, Abruzzi. Peter Gunter was with John Woods and Arthur Hall. They came to the Aquila—Teramo road on which was a lot of German traffic. Their system was to cross singly and wait for each other at an agreed place under cover. Woods and Hall crossed successfully, but Gunter never arrived at the rendezvous. They waited for hours and searched the area in a heavy blizzard. A few days later Arthur Hall himself was re-captured when the Germans attacked a partisan camp south of Popoli. Fortunately Woods was away from the camp at that time.

Philip Kindersley and Ronald Orr-Ewing had reached the Gubbio area by 3rd December. They were walking down a road crossing a plain when a civilian on a motor-cycle passed slowly by, looking at them with interest. They asked the way to Monte Luiano and were pointed up a mule track, but later a woman said a by-road was easier. At this time the Germans were offering a reward of three thousand lire for the recapture of Allied prisoners. The man on the motor-cycle passed them again. Then Kindersley and Orr-Ewing were met by a man in a black coat who asked them where they were going. He followed them and, though the escapers increased their pace, he kept up. Then they heard a motor-cycle and a car coming from Gubbio. They ran off across the fields, but were pursued by the Fascist militia. They took cover in a deep ravine. The six militia officers shouted at them to come out and fired into the undergrowth very near their hiding-place. They had no alternative but to surrender. They were marched across the field with their hands in the air. They had walked for thirty-three days covering about four hundred miles. No doubt the civilian on the motor-cycle collected his reward.

Gunner Angus Butler, of the South African Artillery, left the Fontanellato area and walked to Sulmona, but on 7th December, 1943, he was re-captured by a German patrol. He was put on a train at Aquila bound for Germany. Again the R.A.F. came to his rescue by bombing the train and Butler escaped in the confusion. He made his way south to the Maiella mountain where he was again apprehended. Butler was taken by lorry from Aquila, making for Spoleto. He was in the rear of the convoy, so he seized an opportunity to jump while the guards' attention was diverted by Canadian prisoners. He moved towards Monte Assisi where he joined a partisan band before it was dispersed by German harassment. With two companions he walked south to San Severino where he was wounded when taking part in guerilla activities. Finally he met Polish troops on 26th June, 1944, at Ascoli Piceno.

Adrian Barber and Dick Booth had become totally disenchanted with everything to do with being escaped prisoners-of-war in the early Italian winter. Often wet and cold, with their clothes and boots in a bad state, not knowing where they would find their next meal and spending nights in draughty barns, they decided on 3rd December to accept the risk of walking on main roads. At least they would travel more quickly that

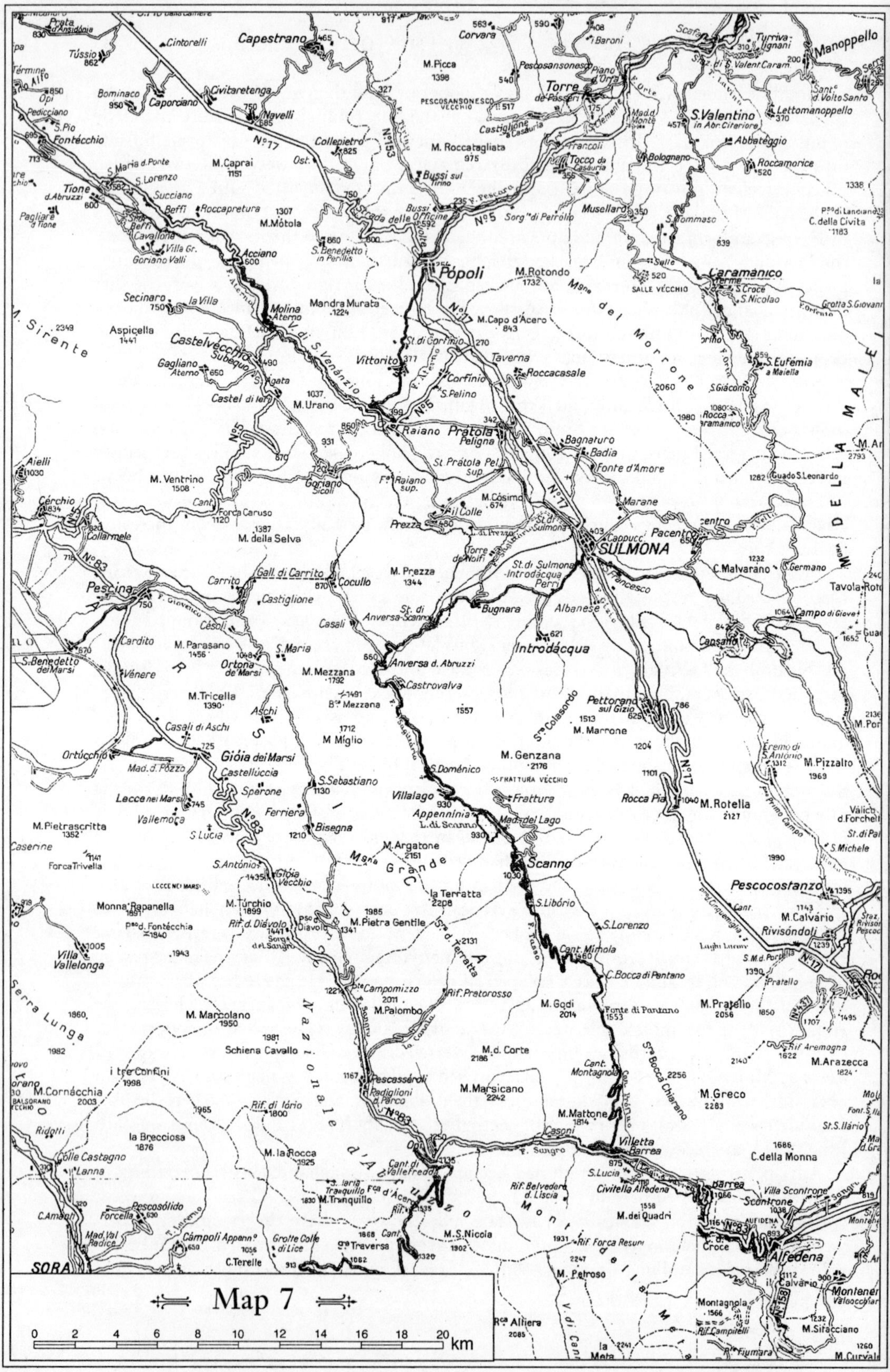

Map 7

0 2 4 6 8 10 12 14 16 18 20 km

way. On 7th December they came to a town in the Penaro valley. Not wanting to walk right through the middle of the town, they turned off on a by-road leading down to a bridge spanning a small river. On the bridge was a youth of fifteen or sixteen dressed in Italian army uniform and with a rifle slung over his shoulder. He appeared to be taking no notice of anything. But when Barber and Booth reached the bridge he straightened himself up and walked towards them. Although appearing to be very embarrassed about the whole situation, he commanded them to halt and asked to what class they belonged. Barber's reply did not satisfy the young sentry and he unslung his rifle, pointing it at Barber's stomach and told them to walk in front of him. Barber wrote, 'I suppose we should have hit him with something or thrown him over the bridge ... as it was we were so tired of the life we had been leading for the previous three months ... that the thought of resistance never occurred to us and we accepted the position with feelings of resignation.'

Eric Newby and Donald Shaw had been living in a hut or cave made for them by some of the village men. But in December they had to move because the hut had been compromised and the Fascist militia were coming to the village that night. They came to a small two-storeyed barn. Here they were helped by a blind man, his two children and two men from the village who constructed beds for them in the lower part of the barn. They were invited to spend Christmas Eve and Christmas Day with various families in the village, and were even given a hot bath. For good measure they listened to King George VI deliver his Christmas message from Sandringham. In this he said, 'Wherever you may be your thoughts will be in distant places and your hearts with those you love.' This brought tears to the eyes of the two British officers. On 29th December Newby was at the door of the barn when he heard a voice commanding him *'Mani in alto,'* and he saw there were a dozen very nasty-looking Fascist militia all armed to the teeth. Shaw, who had gone for a walk, was also captured. The officer-in-charge told them they had been given away by someone in the village, but who had made the condition that no harm would come to the village or its people. The officer said, 'Personally, I am sorry. I would have much pleasure in burning the place to the ground and shooting the lot of them. I don't like traitors and neither do my men.'

In December Pip Gardner was escorted by a partisan to Rome where he came under the protection of the Rome Organisation led by Major Sam Derry, whose idea it was that Gardner should come to Rome. He was given accommodation in a flat owned by Signor Nebulante. He and another English officer, Robert Wilson, went about openly in Rome, including going to the opera, as did many other Allied ex-prisoners. But the German grip was tightening. Early in the New Year, 1944, Signor Nebulante's brother-in-law was arrested and beaten up. On 8th January two plain-clothed Gestapo men came with six S.S. soldiers and arrested them. They were taken to the dreaded Regina Coeli prison.

Denis Gibbs in his book *Apennine Journey* said that C. J. Barnard was walking with him, Norman Girling and Rex Smith. On 19th September Barnard was so far behind that they lost him. Gibbs wrote that Barnard was recaptured in January, 1944. Donald Nott, with two companions from Fontanellato, spent seven weeks in a deserted cabin trying to acquire a boat on the Adriatic coast. Having successfully concluded the complicated negotiations to obtain a boat, they moved down to the shore. But they were betrayed and re-captured at the water's edge on 10th February, 1944.

A similar misfortune befell Peter Watson and Peter Stericker. Having survived in the Gran Sasso for two months, in early March they decided to move to the coast to find a boat. They had to skirt German troop positions and encountered a stream of refugees evicted from their coastal homes. Watson wrote, 'We found a possible boat and its owner, who agreed to let us have oars and sails, provided we stole them. Unfortunately his brother got to hear about it and gave us away. That night, as we gathered in a farmyard, lights sprang out, snarling dogs lunged at us; *"Mani in alto."* Six months after leaving Fontanellato we were taken by the Waffen-S.S.'

Ian Bain travelled to Montefortino from Fontanellato with two other officers. There they stayed till 16th January, 1944, mainly because one of his companions was ill. They then joined a party of ex-prisoners to walk south. But on 10th February they were betrayed and re-captured. They were sent to the old PG53 at Macerata. Later they were being moved to Rome, when Bain jumped off the lorry and rushed to a bombed building where he hid beneath debris so successfully that his escort failed to find him.

One of the most dramatic and courageous escapes before final re-capture was that of Eric Hopkins. After two weeks in the Assisi area he and Tom Wheeler had to wade across a foul-smelling drainage ditch before coming to a main road on which was a fair amount of German traffic. They went to a farmhouse to wash the evil-smelling mud from their legs. They were offered water and towels. They had nearly finished when three armed Germans burst in and took them off for interrogation. They found themselves in a small camp which previously had been an other ranks prisoners' working camp. Among the recaptured British was a mechanic doing maintenance work. Hopkins asked him if he could purloin a pair of pliers. They were told to be ready for early departure to Germany the next day. The compound was surrounded by two barbed wire fences about six feet apart with a third higher fence about thirty feet away. The mechanic cut a hole in the first fence with Hopkins and Wheeler following closely. He did the same in the second fence. As he was crawling through, Hopkins heard the sound of approaching feet. He remembers, 'The guards were being changed, they passing within three feet of my prone figure. When safe to move, I crawled to the outside fence with Tom Wheeler on my heels. It was so dark we could not find the recently-cut hole, so we climbed the fence and bolted. Shortly after there were bursts of machine gun fire and shouts in German, so I reckon we were extremely lucky.'

Hopkins and Wheeler walked south for the next five weeks and by early November were approaching the front line. Having had to lie up in a barn because of foul weather, Eric Hopkins decided to go on alone, leaving Wheeler with two ex-Commandos from Camp 5 whom they had met. He had to abandon his effort because of darkness and deep snow and eventually he reached a small village where he was taken in by a *contadino* family. Here his battledress was dyed blue and he was given an old coat. Early in January, 1944, he was told that, because there were so many Germans in the area, it was no longer safe to look after him. He was taken to a cave near Pescasseroli where there was another British man. This was Freddie Swann. They spent the next seven to eight weeks in the cave with a constant fire in order to survive. Towards the middle of March they were told the danger of them being fed was too great and they had to move. They were taken by a guide to a barn and the door bolted behind them. A few moments later they heard German voices outside. The door was smashed in and they were marched off to headquarters.

Hopkins and Swann were tied together by rope. One of the young soldiers drew his thumb across his throat. They were taken out to a covered lorry and made to sit on the floor with a guard opposite them. When they moved off Hopkins tried to undo the knots and managed to free his right hand, followed by his left; Swann did the same. They agreed to disarm the guard and jump over the tailboard. Hopkins wrote, 'I lunged across to grab the sub-machine-gun, but unfortunately was unable to gain possession. The guard bellowed and the driver applied the brakes. I told my companion to bale out and I followed without delay, rolling over and over. The guard opened fire from above, the tracer bullets ricocheting off the roadway and passing either side … we ran like mad in the opposite direction. Fortunately we had five or six hours of darkness in our favour and were well clear by dawn.' They crossed a range of hills to another valley and, after a week or so, they met an American parachutist in a large cave who told them of a safe route through the front line. They set off next morning, but the route led them into a large concentration of Germans and they were recaptured. This time there was no escape.

Denny Abbott, Noel Durrant and Theo Stephenson, all of the Royal Garhwal Rifles, had crossed the River Pescara on a railway bridge near Popoli on the night of 7th November and come to the village of San Tommaso, where they were fed by Annina and her family. They lived in a cave and, after the New Year and the arrival of the snow and increased danger from Germans, in another cave further up the mountains. They were joined by Sgt. Holland, a tough, self-reliant Cockney who was a breath of fresh air.

In March, as the weather improved, they met a fair-haired Italian called Angelo who said he knew a way through the lines. Twelve men assembled at a house in Scagnano after dark. The journey was in three stages. They did the first two successfully, but the guide for the third stage was late. They heard of a message from a British paratroopist saying that no Allied prisoners were to attempt to go through the line, as there were too many Germans. They ran into two N.C.Os. who became suspicious of a private in the Durham Light Infantry and took him off. The others scattered. They stayed that night in a village with a German Engineer Unit nearby. By this time Stephenson was walking virtually barefoot, and they were all very, very tired. Angelo's plan was to get through the line at Guardiagrele where he had been before. They moved off at dawn, then lay in hiding in a spinney before moving again at dusk. They came to the guide's house where there were two other Englishmen and a South African. The guide was suspicious of the South African and Abbott was asked to question him. He thought he was all right. They waited for the moon to rise at 3.00 a.m. and then moved off in single file. It took an hour to reach Guardiagrele cemetery. Suddenly a figure leapt out of the darkness and fired a pistol shot. There were shouts in German as more of them appeared. The party was rounded up. Angelo had been shot in the thigh and he died later. It was obvious that the 'South African' was a German.

Tommy Pitman, having spent most of the miserable winter of 1943–44 hiding in the mountains in the Armatrice area, was also re-captured.

Jack Kempton and Tom Craig decided to cross the River Tronto by the bridge at Castel di Lama very early one morning. Unfortunately it was guarded by Germans. When half-way across, they were ordered to halt. Speaking bad Italian which the German could not understand, they were put in a guard room to await an interpreter. Presently they were joined by an American parachutist. When the Guard changed at 8.00 a.m. the American stood up and looked out of the window and said, 'I guess this is where I take off.' Whereupon he opened the window and dived into the river. Kempton wrote, 'Tom and I followed and we swam downstream. There was shouting from the bridge and we swam into the shallows on the far bank. Unfortunately we got separated. However, Tom and I met up half-an-hour later, but what happened to the American we never found out. … We were very glad we had met him and shared the benefit of his initiative.'

Douglas Flowerdew, walking alone, had reached the village of Castel Mauro between the rivers Trigno and Bifurno by the 19th October. On the next day a very shifty, disreputable old tramp agreed to guide Flowerdew, saying he knew where the German positions were. They moved off at 4.30 a.m. Having gone only a little way, as they were walking down a path, they heard the ominous order *'Halte.'* When he was searched some Egyptian money was found and the German thought Flowerdew was a spy. He took his watch, but later gave him four hundred lire for it. Down at the post he had to admit who he was. The German soldiers' attitude changed in an instant 'Bravo Tommy! 'ave a tsigarette?' They were most amused at him getting so close; the line was just below them, across the river. He was then given a huge meal. At the German Battalion headquarters he met a British Signals officer and two Other Ranks.

The prisoners were later driven through the night, arriving at about 3.00 a.m. at a three-roomed hovel where there were about forty other Allied prisoners. Flowerdew said that the three days he spent in that hovel were the worst in all his adventures. Then the prisoners were put into an old Italian lorry and driven to Castillione where they were allowed out for an hour. On the next stage to Sulmona, which was a transit camp for Germany, Flowerdew realised there was a possibility of escape by jumping off the truck. After a short halt near the top of the pass near a place called Rocca, the truck was just moving off; Flowerdew saw his chance, put his legs over the tailboard and jumped. He walked quietly away into the trees and then, expecting an alarm, he ran and stumbled up a hill.

Robert Smyth, walking with Stafford Tolley, had passed Aquila, the dried-up lake at Avezzano and Castel di Sangro, and by 21st November had reached San Biagio, near Isernia. There were many German troops in the area. They crossed a road with high banks and walked straight into a gun emplacement. Their Italian was not good enough to deceive the Germans for long. They were taken to Sora and then to Frosinone Transit Camp. In due course they met other prisoners from Fontanellato.

Jack Clarke, with Marcus Kane-Burman and R. G. H. MacLean, made good progress south and by 18th November had reached Frattura. But the next day they were caught by a German patrol near the line. They were taken via Villetta Barrea and Sora to Frosinone Transit Camp.

Anthony Laing and Donald Macaulay also came to Frattura and headed for Monte Greco. There was more snow than they expected and in the afternoon they got lost in a blizzard and subsequently in darkness. Then they saw the most extraordinary yellow-orange light whose shape and brightness seemed to vary continuously. They made for the light and discovered it to be a camp fire within a large tent in which were seated two shepherds who offered them some mutton stew made from their last sheep, the Germans having stolen the rest. Towards dawn they were awakened by shouts of *'Raus! Raus!'* and they stumbled out while a German patrol searched the tent. The Germans left them as suddenly as they had arrived without asking a question or searching them.

In the evening of the next day, they were descending a path in pitch darkness and could hear the sound of German voices on either side. All went well until a cry of *'Halte!'* just prevented Laing from stepping on a German in a fox hole on the banks of the River Sangro. They were searched and the pistol Laing was carrying was discovered. Laing wrote, 'The following morning we were taken to a local headquarters at Villetta Barrea, where followed prolonged interrogation. It was entirely due to Donald's stalwart support and evidence and, I believe, sympathetic treatment from a rather nice German officer ... that I was not dealt with summarily.' After two days at Sora they were taken to Frosinone Transit Camp.

So at this Camp were Smyth, Tolley, Clarke, MacLean and Laing, also Hugh Fane Hervey, all from Fontanellato. They were confined in a first-floor dormitory with a high ceiling in one of several two-storey barrack buildings. By piling tables and chairs Hugh Fane Hervey was able to get through a hatch on to the flat roof. The adjoining building also had a flat roof and was some eight or nine feet away. It also had an external staircase leading down to the ground which offered an escape route. He took a running jump and thankfully landed on the other roof but the noise attracted attention, so he jumped back amid rifle shots and the chairs and tables were hurriedly restored to their former position before the arrival of the guards, who were unable to identify the culprit.

On 30th November they were put on a train to take them to Germany. Fane Hervey concealed an axe smuggled from the kitchen on his person. Smyth said an R.A.F. raid scared the guards into a very sketchy search. The train stopped in Rome for a day with thirty prisoners cooped up in a cattle truck. On 3rd December they cut a hole with the axe in the end of the truck. When the train slowed down near Orte they jumped out. For a fuller account of this escape see Appendix 4. Laing found Clarke in the dark and they made their way to a nearby monastery where they were wonderfully looked after by the Franciscan monks. They had several nights there 'getting over injuries.' Fed, restored, re-clothed and given money by the kind monks, they set off for Arezzo. Tired of walking, they then took a train to the outskirts of Florence.

Robert Smyth and Stafford Tolley were the last two to get out of the train before it stopped completely. In Smyth's words, 'Then all hell broke out. I think fourteen of us got away. Several others escaped from other trucks.' The two got separated but by a strange coincidence met again in a farmhouse the next evening. They moved to the Rieti area where the Brunetti family looked after them during the bad weather. In March, 1944, they moved east towards the Adriatic, but then changed direction to Sulmona. Here they met a guide who would take them over the mountains to the coast. With them were twelve others of various nationalities. About midnight on 6th April they were suddenly surrounded by a German ski patrol and taken back to Sulmona Gaol. By 13th May they were in a transit camp at Mantova. Smyth went with about sixty others to be de-loused. Twenty went in at a time, while the others waited in a courtyard surrounded by a privet hedge and a chain-link fence. Using a smuggled Commando knife-cum-wirecutter, a hole was soon made in the fence. Smyth and six others got out and he then went on his own. After moving towards Genoa he crossed the River Po on 17th May and made for Montovana where the Trucco family looked after him for ten days. Finally, on 8th June he and another Fontanellato officer were recaptured near Bobbio by the Italians. He thought they were going to be shot out of hand, but they survived.

Dermot Chichester (Lord Donegall) walked south with Delmé Seymour-Evans. They stumbled on to a German anti-aircraft gun position, and were recaptured. They were put on a train for Germany. The train was bombed at Colleferro by the American Air Force. Chichester wrote, 'The Germans let us out of the cattle trucks. The whole place was covered in dust and smoke; visibility was nil, so it seemed to me that it was a good time to make a run for it. One of the few really sensible decisions I have made in my life.' Afterwards he was looked after by Italians at Arenazo Romano until June, 1944, when the Allied advance overran the area.

John Philip was on the same train as Dermot Chichester. After leaving the Fontanellato area he, Dmitri Derozhinsky, and another reached Opi. Here they separated before attempting to cross the lines. Philip was re-captured on 31st October near Isernia and taken to Frosinone. Philip's account said it was an R.A.F. raid which caused the confusion on the train near Colleferro enabling them to get away. Afterwards he and a companion reached Rome.

Dmitri Derozhinsky, after separating from John Philip and his companion, remained near San Donato until 22nd November when he joined a party trying to cross the lines. The attempt failed because of deep snow and on 28th November the party was re-captured by a German patrol.

Derozhinsky and another officer may have been put on the same train as Anthony Laing, Hugh Fane Hervey, Jack Clarke, Robert Smyth and Stafford Tolley, because the account says he was entrained for Germany on 4th December, but escaped through a hole they had made in the door of a truck when the train was near Perugia.

12: Getting Round or Through the Lines

IN THEORY, the long coastlines of Italy are ideal for amphibious activities and many expected the Allies would launch several landings to seize important ports such as Livorno, La Spezia, Genoa or Ancona. As has been told, strong rumours soon after the Armistice that these had taken or were about to take place confused and delayed the escaping prisoners-of-war. What had not been taken into account by the 'amateur' strategists was, first, the necessity of air cover for such an operation and the consequent important factor of distance from base of fighter aircraft; second, was the shortage of landing craft which imposed severe limitations on Allied strategy throughout the war.

The other side of the coin was the opportunity given by the long coastline to evacuate prisoners, and to land agents and small raiding parties. The Germans were fully aware of these possibilities and maintained a close vigil on the coasts, and succeeded in disrupting several attempts by the Royal Navy to evacuate prisoners.

Bill Bowder and Peter Ellis met a troop of American parachutists in the Ancona area who told them to make for the mouth of the River Foro where on certain dates the boats were coming in to pick up prisoners. Three days later Bowder and Ellis made contact with a small group of British Commandos whose instructions were to round up as many ex-prisoners as possible and conduct them to the beach. On two successive nights they and numerous other escapers made their way down to the beach, but no boats came. This was an example of the difficulties of such a complicated operation. So many things could go wrong, and often did, and the result was that the number of prisoners taken off to safety in this way was fairly small. Ellis and Bowder became very concerned at the security risks involved in scores of would-be escapers concentrated in a small area near the beaches, thinking that the Germans, who were using the main coast road to supply their forces further south, must get wind of it sooner or later. So they decided to make their own way.

The British authorities did eventually succeed in rescuing the highest-ranking prisoners. Generals Neame and O'Connor and some other senior officers were taken off by sea. Another two were Jack Donagher and 'Tubby' Wilson. Wilson had earlier been walking with Tom Craig and Jack Kempton. Donagher told how he had heard about the sea taxi service from Giacomo Peretti. The operation was organised by some British parachutists. They were taken to the beach no less than five times. On the last time a motor torpedo boat arrived and took them off to Termoli.

Bill Bowder and Peter Ellis left the large collection of ex-prisoners and resumed their walk south, and in a few days reached the outskirts of Ortona. There they heard that Termoli had fallen to the 8th Army, so they decided to try to get away by sea. They did not fancy the idea of crossing the battle lines on foot, particularly as Ellis' feet were in a very poor condition. Leaving Ellis at a farm, Bowder went to Fossacesia to locate a fisherman who, he had been told, might be willing to provide a boat. Fossacesia was being prepared by the Germans for demolition. The fisherman seemed keen, saying his son wanted to leave German-held territory to prevent his boat being confiscated. But when the demolitions became more frequent and nearer his house, the fisherman changed his mind and said his first duty was to his family.

Then the two British officers met a tall young man of about 27, who said he had been a captain in the Italian army, and a stout man of about 50. They said they knew a man

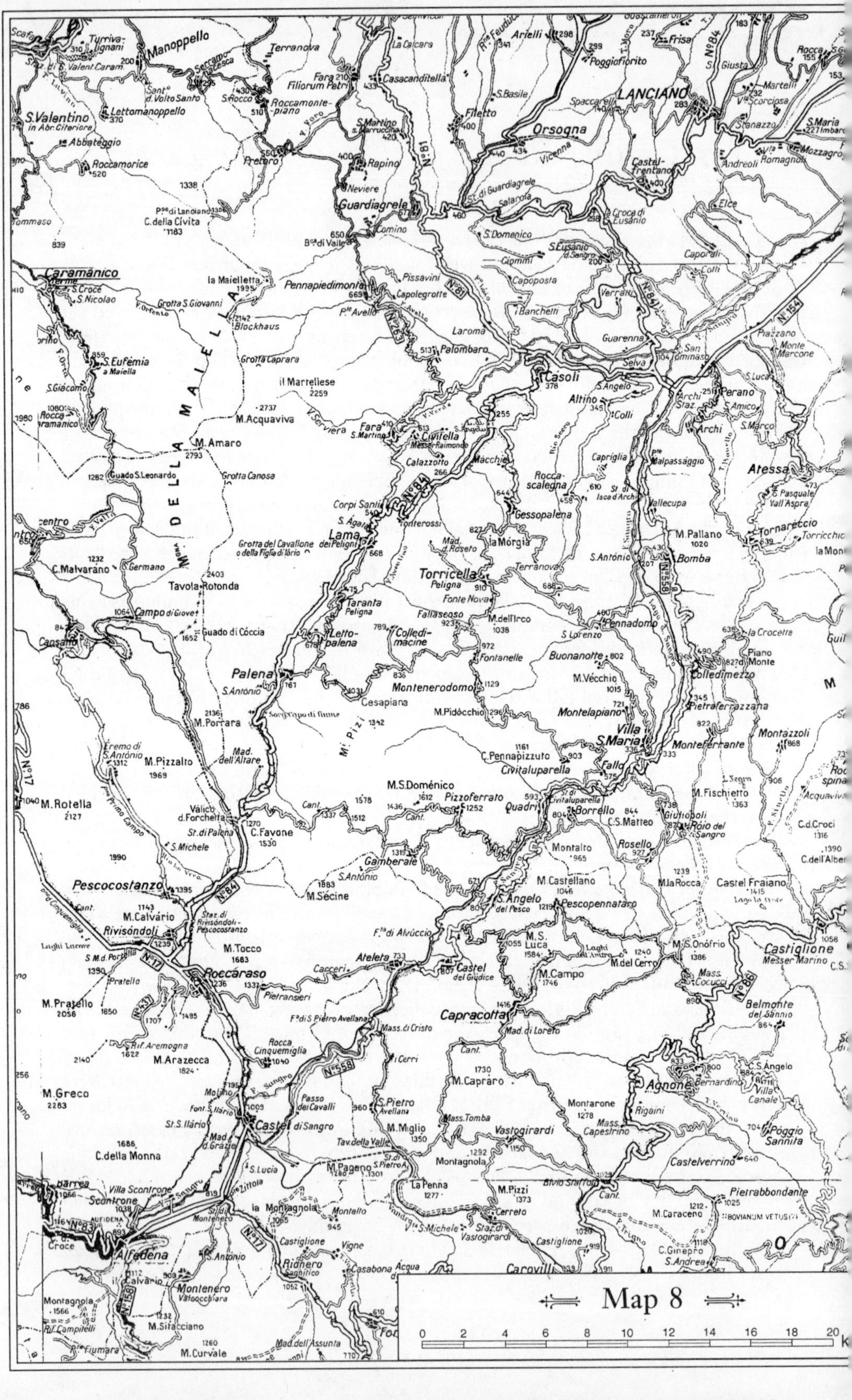

Manoppello
Turrivalignani
S.Valentino in Abr. Citeriore
Lettomanoppello
Abbateggio
Roccamorice
Serramonacesca
Terranova
Fara Filiorum Petri
Casacanditella
Roccamontepiano
S.Martino s. Marrucina
Rapino
Pretoro
Guardiagrele
Arielli
Poggiofiorito
Frisa
LANCIANO
S.Basile
Filetto
Orsogna
Castel Frentano
S.Maria Imbaro
Mozzagrogna
Romagnoli
Andreoli
Elce
S.Domenico
S.Eusanio d.Sangro
Capoposta
Caporali
Caramanico Terme
Pennapiedimonte
Capolegrotte
la Maielletta
Blockhaus
Grotta S.Giovanni
S.Eufemia a Maiella
Grotta Caprara
il Martellese
MONTAGNA DELLA MAIELLA
M.Acquaviva
M.Amaro
Fara S.Martino
Civitella Messer Raimondo
Palombaro
Laroma
Casoli
Altino
Guarenna
Selva
Perano
Archi
Atessa
Tornareccio
Torricchio
Calazzotto
Gessopalena
Rocca scalegna
Lama dei Peligni
Corpi Santi
Grotta del Cavallone o della Figlia di Iorio
la Morgia
Torricella Peligna
Bomba
M.Pallano
Campo di Giove
C.Malvarano
Tavola Rotonda
Guado di Coccia
Taranta Peligna
Lettopalena
Colledimacine
Pennadomo
Colledimezzo
Palena
Montenerodomo
Buonanotte
M.Vecchio
Montelapiano
Villa S.Maria
Pietraferrazzana
Monteferrante
Montazzoli
M.Porrara
M.Pizzalto
M.Rotella
Valico d.Forchetta
C.Favone
M.S.Domenico
Pizzoferrato
Quadri
Borrello
Civitaluparella
M.Fischietto
Roio del Sangro
Rosello
Gamberale
Pescocostanzo
M.Calvario
Rivisondoli
M.Secine
S.Angelo del Pesco
Pescopennataro
M.Castellano
Castel Fraiano
M.Tocco
Ateleta
Castel del Giudice
Castiglione Messer Marino
Roccaraso
Capracotta
Belmonte del Sannio
M.Pratello
M.Arazecca
Rocca Cinquemiglia
M.Capraro
Agnone
M.Greco
Castel di Sangro
S.Pietro Avellana
Vastogirardi
Poggio Sannita
Castelverrino
Barrea
Scontrone
Alfedena
la Montagnola
Montenero Valcocchiara
Rionero Sannitico
M.Pizzi
Cerreto
Castiglione
Carovilli
Pietrabbondante
M.Caraceno
BOVIANUM VETUS
M.Curvale
M.Sifacciano
0 2 4 6 8 10 12 14 16 18 20

Map 8

in Ortona who would take them in his boat to Termoli. These men were enthusiastic and seemed to have plenty of money and were prepared to spend it. So they set off for Ortona where they met the boat owner and his two well-built sons. Bowder wrote, 'They owned two small boats and the captain started negotiations. The outcome was that we would be taken to another man who had a larger and more seaworthy boat. The negotiations with this man seemed to be getting nowhere, until it was explained to the owner that Peter and I were important British officers and the Allied Governments would be most grateful for our safe return (Peter was a captain, I was a lieutenant!). Furthermore we would gladly pay £20 each in sterling. This part of the undertaking was made known to us *sotto voce* by the captain. The final outcome was that the boat would be available the next evening, weather permitting.'

Seven p.m. 15th October arrived and they made their way in darkness down to the beach. There were nine in the party, including the two sailor sons to actually sail the 16-foot boat, and two others whose homes were in Sicily. There was quite a commotion on the beach as the women-folk had come to say farewell to their men. The moon rose and Ellis and Bowder thought they were very exposed to anyone watching from the shore. They pushed the boat out and clambered aboard. Sail was raised about a mile out to sea. They made slow but steady progress south on the forty-mile journey to Termoli. The stout man was sea-sick, made worse by the captain talking about fat pork! Bowder's worry was that they were not certain that Termoli was in British hands. One of the sailors had heard on the Fascist radio news that it had been recaptured by the Germans. In the early dawn they heard shelling and saw tracer being fired inland. When they arrived off Termoli they dropped anchor, being undecided what to do. They could see and hear gunfire on the shore, but there was no way of telling in whose hands the port was. Then a German 'plane flew in only a hundred feet up, and dropped some incendiary bombs on Termoli and was engaged by light anti-aircraft fire. This showed the port was in Allied hands, so they sailed in and hailed a frigate anchored in the harbour. They were invited aboard for breakfast. A great moment—it was the 16th October.

Geoffrey Stavert with three others walked fast using roads whenever they proved quicker. A boy on a bicycle gave them a good map. At Altedo, villagers lined up and loaded them with food as they passed. They came to a bridge guarded by a German sentry. A boy got the villagers to walk over in a group with the four escapers hidden in their midst. They reached the Adriatic in eleven days. Their route was between Fermo and the sea, until near Montefiore di Aso they found a Major Powell with two other S.A.S. soldiers who told them there would be a boat pick-up in twelve days' time. About two hundred other ex-prisoners were in the area waiting to go. On the appointed night they made their way across the main road and railway and down to the beach, with a German sentry just up the road. For over two hours a light was flashed in a special sequence. At 2.15 a.m. they heard the muffled sound of a rubber boat which took them to a larger boat. So they made their escape.

Ian Bain, who had jumped off a lorry taking him from Macerata to Rome, went to Fermo. There he became involved in plans for a mass escape by ex-prisoners which came to nothing. Having managed to borrow some money, he and three others obtained a boat. He was joined by five Other Ranks and on 19th March 1944, the boat party reached an R.A.F. unit at Ponte della Penna.

John Hall, walking south with two companions, was recaptured on 3rd November. Having been sent to Fara nel Sabina, he escaped again by climbing through a half-bricked-up door and through three wire fences. He walked to Alofreddo and was then looked after by several Italian families. After being there for several weeks German pressure increased and Hall moved to the vicinity of Cisterna. On 30th April 1944 he and an American airman walked to the mouth of the River Sisto. Here they acquired a boat which they rowed to the island of Zannone. The next day the Italians arranged for them to go by sea to Naples.

It is always easy to look back in hindsight and say what should have been done. In retrospect there is no doubt that, for those whose ultimate aim was to rejoin the Allied forces and not go to Switzerland, the best plan was to start walking soon after the Fontanellato prisoners had split up into small parties. This had two important advantages. It was probable that, at the time the escapers reached the area of the fighting, the front would still be relatively fluid, there would be wider gaps between German positions and a better chance of German withdrawals. That was certainly true up to about the middle of November. When the outposts had been driven in and the main Gustav or winter line occupied, the Germans had no intention of withdrawing unless forced out of their very strong positions. The second advantage was that there was a good chance of getting through before the wet, cold and snowy weather set in. Of course, the main disadvantage of an early start was that one had to walk, perhaps, up to another hundred miles.

Of those who did undertake the long walk probably the first to start, and certainly the first to get through, were 'Toots' Williams, Ted Pryke and Hugh Jobson, joined on 11th September by Ian Shaw. They never changed out of battledress; their boots were nearly new at the start and worn out by the time they crossed the Sangro. The weather was good until the last week. Keeping west of the Apennines in the early stages, they then moved in a more easterly direction via Montereale and Campotosto Lake, crossing the Pescara by the hydro-electric company bridge east of Popoli on 7th October. The following day they were across the Sangro west of Casoli. On the 10th they nearly ran into a group of Germans at a petrol dump in a wood near Castiglione. They were saved by a thunderstorm. They crossed the River Trigno at dusk and spent the night near Monte Falcone. The Italians were still in their farms, so they were given a good hot lunch on 11th October. In the afternoon they crossed the River Bifurno on a small footbridge just north of Casacalenda, where they met two other British officers, one Ronnie Borradaile from Fontanellato. After sleeping for twelve hours they climbed a small hill to watch the battle. That night the shelling increased and they heard heavy traffic indicating a German withdrawal. Early on the morning of 13th October they watched the Germans blowing a bridge over the Bifurno near Guadialfiera. Having been joined by Borrodaile and his companion Blair, they walked on to Casacalenda and were the first of the Allies to enter it. They were cheered by the villagers. A Canadian scout car came to the village and took them back to Brigade headquarters. They reckoned the distance walked was about six hundred miles in thirty five days. Later they met George Lascaris and Leon Blanchaert who had been with Lt.-Col. Mainwaring on the journey south.

Colonel Mainwaring was also one of the very first starters. He knew very little Italian, but Blanchaert spoke Italian well and Lascaris was fluent in the language. Mainwaring had invited Jack Comyn to join them. He had been acting as his assistant. But Comyn decided to stay with his 8th Hussar colleagues. As he said, 'It was one of the biggest mistakes I ever made.'

Changing into civilian clothes and carrying emergency rations of a tin of bully beef, meat roll and biscuits, Mainwaring's party set off in an easterly direction, passing Parma and Bologna to the south and took a line near the coast. Their cover story was that they were Italian soldiers who had been in Yugoslavia and were walking home. The escape had had such a dramatic effect on Mainwaring that he had lost the power of speech. Mainwaring wrote, 'We walked uninterruptedly except for thirty six hours in which we stopped at Cesenatico in an attempt to find a boat.' They then followed a more inland route, and crossed the German forward area at Casacalenda where they met the K.O.Y.L.I. at about 9.00 a.m. on 13th October.

Another early starter was the Norman Rogers and A. A. Jones pairing. They walked fast, sometimes going on through the night, so they could use the main roads. After walking to near Florence and down the Tiber valley to Todi, they gave themselves three days rest a little south of Camarata, while Rogers had his shoes repaired. Thereafter their route lay by Leonessa to near the Gran Sasso to Assergi and Ofena to the Pescara River which they crossed on a footbridge, then to the west side of the Maiella, where they ran into a German training exercise. On 17th October, as there was a moon, they continued walking till dawn, tiptoeing through Pacentro at midnight to Bugnara and up into the mountains, where they were helped by shepherds. This was a common experience of Allied escapers.

As several others did, they went through Frattura to Scanno which was full of Germans. Norman Rogers was affected by stomach trouble on 19th October. North east of Opi they had to wade knee-deep through a river and then walk in full view of a main road on which all types of German transport—horsed, wheeled, trucks, motor-cycles and bicycles were moving. Jones' diary records, 'Since yesterday noon our way has led through a beech forest, with the leaves turning every imaginable gold and brown; we are in no mood to admire nature, but this Meta district is very beautiful. All our thoughts are on one thing only, pushing on and making distance. We find ourselves unable to sit over a meal for longer than a quarter of an hour.' They came within a hundred yards of a German line-laying party. Then suddenly they saw a German walking towards them. Jones wrote, 'We turned about and slowly retraced our steps. After going some hundred yards with Norman in the lead ... I could feel the Jerry just behind. I used what little Italian I knew to good effect "*Aspett un momento,*" Norman turned round, I stopped and the Bosche R.S.M. went striding by.' This incident was an example, often repeated in the experiences of other escapers, that the Germans, more often than not, could not recognise British ex-prisoners, dressed as Italians, for what they were; whereas the Italians could tell instantly. Beyond Picinisco they were given food by a man who ran four confectionery shops in England prior to 1930. On 22nd October they met a man who promised to guide them to within twelve kilometres of Venafro. They went on through Tozzili and Pozzili, taking off boots and trousers to wade the River Volturno. The area was full of Germans making preparations to withdraw by blowing up hydro-electric plant and setting booby-traps. The villagers fled to the fields taking as many of their possessions as they could. At last on 25th October Jones' diary records 'We saw German armoured cars patrolling their front and crossed their path during an interval. We were nervous that patrolling infantry might shoot us on sight and, hearing the voices of American troops, we hailed them. The response we heard was "Gee, these guys speak English." Our long journey was at an end.'

In October, after Drew Bethel and the two Grenadier Guardsmen whom he had met had got away from a German search party by jumping into a waterfall, they reached Frosolone to find the village on fire. The panic-stricken people were driving their livestock before them up the hill. The people were starving and so were the escapers. Dawn revealed long grassy slopes falling away south-east for about three miles to the plains of Campobasso. On the hill were many peasants, driven from their villages below, with their livestock. Among them were a dozen escaped prisoners-of-war. Below were the German positions. They had a grandstand view of a British attack which started in mid-morning, and watched German gunners and infantrymen in half-tracks withdrawing at mid-day. It was agreed that the escapers would try to cross the lines after dark. The

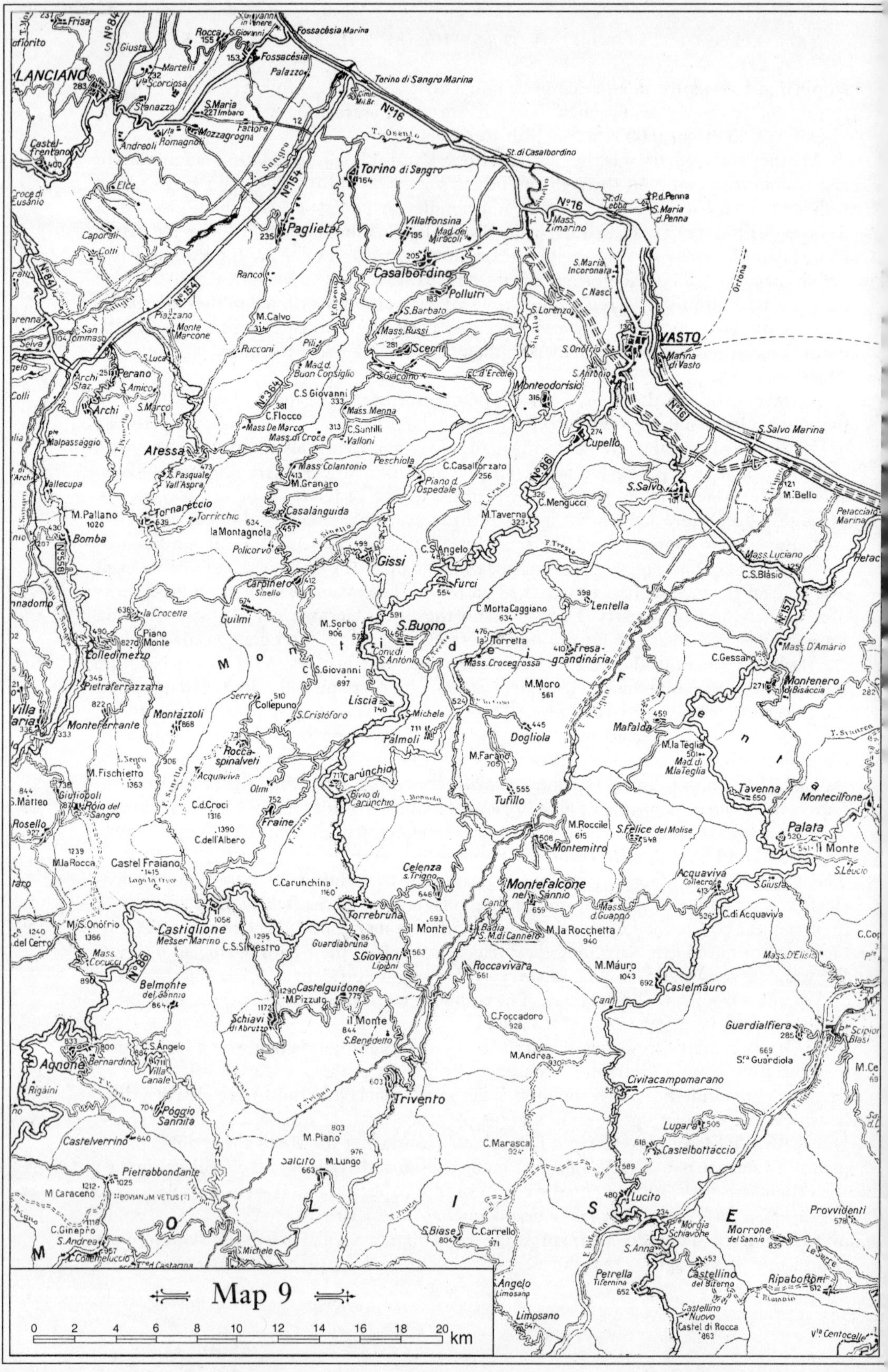
Frisa
LANCIANO
Rocca
S.Giovanni
Fossacèsia Marina
Fossacèsia
Palazzo
Martelli
Torino di Sangro Marina
Stanazzo
S.Maria
Imbaro
Fattore
Mozzagrogna
Castel-frentano
Andreoli
N°16
N°154
St.di Casalbordino
Torino di Sangro
Elce
Paglieta
Villalfonsina
Casalbordino
Pollutri
S.Maria Incoronata
Croce di Eusanio
Caporali
Cotti
Ranco
San Tommaso
Selva
Piazzano
Monte Marcone
M.Calvo
S.Barbato
Mass.Bussi
Scerni
S.Lorenzo
VASTO
Marina di Vasto
S.Onófrio
S.Antonio
Monteodorisio
Perano
Archi
Archi Staz.
S.Amico
S.Marco
Rucconi
Pili
C.S Giovanni
C.Flocco
Mass De Marco
Mass.di Croce
C.Santilli
Valloni
Mass.Menna
Atessa
S.Pasquale
Vall'Aspra
Mass.Colantonio
M.Granaro
Peschiola
Piano d. Ospedale
C.Casalforzato
Cupello
S.Salvo Marina
S.Salvo
M.Bello
Petacciato Marina
Malpassaggio
Vallecupa
M.Pallano
Bomba
Tornareccio
Torricchio
la Montagnola
Casalanguida
Policorvo
Gissi
C.S.Angelo
C.Mengucci
M.Taverna
Mass.Luciano
C.S.Blàsio
Carpineto Sinello
Furci
Guilmi
la Crocetta
Colledimezzo
Piano Monte
M.Sorbo
S.Buono
C.Motta Caggiano
la Torretta
Lentella
Fresa-grandinària
Mass.Crocegrossa
C.Gessaro
Mass. D'Amàrio
Montenero di Bisàccia
Pietraferrazzana
S.Giovanni
Liscia
Collepuno
S.Cristóforo
Villa Santa Maria
Monteferrante
Montazzoli
S.Michele
Palmoli
M.Moro
Dogliola
Mafalda
M.la Teglia
Mad. di M.la Teglia
Roccaspinalveti
Acquaviva
Olmi
M.Fischietto
Carùnchio
Bivio di Carunchio
M.Farano
Tufillo
Tavenna
Montecilfone
Giuliopoli
Roio del Sangro
S.Matteo
Rosello
C.d.Croci
C.dell'Albero
Fraine
M.Roccile
Montemitro
S.Felice del Molise
Palata
Il Monte
S.Leucio
M.la Rocca
Castel Fraiano
C.Carunchina
Celenza s.Trigno
Montefalcone nel Sannio
Acquaviva Collecroce
S.Giusta
C.di Acquaviva
Torrebruna
Il Monte
M.S.Onófrio
Castiglione Messer Marino
C.S.Silvestro
Guardiabruna
S.Giovanni Lipioni
Badia S.M.di Cannero
M.la Rocchetta
Mass.d.Guappo
Mass.Cocucci
N°86
Belmonte del Sannio
Roccavivara
M.Máuro
Castelmauro
Mass.D'Elisio
Schiavi di Abruzzo
Castelguidone
M.Pizzuto
il Monte
S.Benedetto
C.Foccadoro
Guardialfiera
S.ra Guardiola
Agnone
Bernardino
C.S.Angelo
Villa Canale
M.Andrea
Rigaini
Póggio Sannita
Trivento
Civitacampomarano
Castelverrino
M.Piano
M.Lungo
Salcito
C.Marasca
Lupara
Castelbottaccio
Pietrabbondante
M Caraceno
BOVIANUM VETUS
Lucito
O
L
I
S
E
Provvidenti
C.Ginepro
S.Andrea
C.Collemeluccio
S.Michele
S.Biase
C.Carrello
Morgia Schiavone
S.Anna
Morrone del Sannio
S.Angelo Limosano
Petrella Tifernina
Castellino del Biferno
Ripabottoni
Limosano
Castellino Nuovo
Castel di Rocca
V.la Centocelle
M o n t i d e i F r e n t a n i
0 2 4 6 8 10 12 14 16 18 20 km

Map 9

two Guardsmen wanted to go on together. Bethel tossed up with an R.A.F. Wing-Commander for which of them should go first. Bethel lost and he waited an agonising five minutes for the other to get clear. He walked slowly down the slopes, stopping frequently to listen. The night was dark. After going a considerable way he heard the clip-clop of a donkey coming up the path. He hid in the side of the lane. Then he saw the silhouettes of British steel helmets. He called out 'I'm English—escaped.' They were Canadian soldiers laying telephone lines. They calmly replied 'Just keep on down the lane and you'll come to Battalion headquarters.' He was through.

After Tony Davies and the South African Hal Becker failed to turn up at the rendezvous in the woods (Davies had been wounded and recaptured and Becker had been shot), Toby Graham and Michael Gilbert went on. They saw a camp fire and a German called out to them in English, but they ran off, avoiding the bullets fired at them. There was heavy German traffic on the Roccaraso to Pietranserai road and there were many Germans in the latter village. They tiptoed past a German bivouac area. Challenged by a sentry in Pietranserai, they managed to bluff him. It was pouring with rain and it was already dark, so they took shelter in a wash-house and debated what they should do. Gilbert wanted to stay in the village in spite of the Germans; Graham was for going on. They compromised by agreeing that, if they were unable to find shelter in ten minutes, they would push on. They found the door of the third barn they tried was unlocked, so they crept in on to the top of a heap of straw. Absolutely exhausted, they soon fell asleep. Some hours later an Italian furtively came in to feed a sow which he was concealing from the Germans. They spent the next day watching the Germans who were about a hundred strong and were billeted in every house.

Graham and Gilbert were on their way again by 4.00 a.m. the next morning. Many German foraging parties were looking for anything they could lay their hands on. Italians they met thought they were mad attempting to cross the Sangro; hundreds of German vehicles used the road running beside the river. Obviously crossing the road in daylight was too risky, so they waited till after dark. It was raining hard when they came to the Sangro and the water was rising fast. They took off boots and socks, and luckily found a shingle bank where the water was no more than thigh deep. They came to a farm. When the door opened they were pulled inside quickly. The eight people inside were naturally very scared, as Germans had twice come searching for prisoners-of-war. But the son said he would guide them past German anti-aircraft posts and over Monte Capraro in the morning. The front line was between the Trigno and Bifurno rivers.

They left at dawn the next morning mounted on donkeys, and by mid-day had successfully passed the German gun area. They circled round Agnone which was held by a battalion of the enemy. After struggling through and getting lost in thick woods, they met some charcoal burners. One said they could sleep in his barn, though it was within a hundred yards of a German anti-aircraft position. The charcoal burners were accepted and not harassed by the Germans. One guided them across the road early the next morning and pointed out the way. By a stream they met a miller, a remarkable ex-major who had escaped from Abyssinia, to Eritrea, over the Red Sea, through Arabia, Iraq, Syria, Turkey, across the Aegean, through Greece, Albania, and back to Italy. They walked through beautiful country with orchards red with fruit. The owner of a wattle hut told them of a man called Pasqua who made a business of guiding people through the lines and were instructed to go to his house at 6.00 p.m. Here were seventeen people—Italians, French, Greeks and Czechs, several of whom were drunk. They, like Toby Graham and Michael Gilbert, had agreed a price with Pasqua for the job. The people were carrying suitcases, packs, paper bags and other paraphernalia. The party crossed the Trivento ridge and at 2.00 a.m. reached a cottage where they were given a hot drink. Pasqua explained that it was dangerous to go through at night because they might be fired on by the British, so they set off again at 6.00 a.m. Gilbert and Graham, pushing on ahead of the others, went over the last ridge and walked down to Lucito. This was not occupied permanently by the British, and as there was a barber's shop in the village the two English officers went in for a shave. In walked a Canadian sergeant. It was the 1st November.

Denis Gibbs, Norman Girling, Rex Smith and Sergeant Turner, who had joined the officers, passed to the west of Avezzano 'lake.' When crossing the main road and railway near Tagliacozzo they almost ran into a party of Germans. Soon after they had to cross open ground in full view of a German officer who took no notice. They were making for a mountain hut when they were stopped by a kind Italian, who took them to his family in the village. It was a large extended family and they all had a complete disregard for the Germans. They followed the Abruzzi motto, 'A kind heart and fear nothing.' Gibbs thought it was the best family they had met on the whole journey. They were given large supplies of bread and cheese, which made the sacks very heavy as they were still carrying tinned food from the camp as emergency rations. They skirted Capistrello and were frequently advised to stay to await the Allies. They were told lurid stories of those who had gone earlier being recaptured. It later turned out that most of these stories were unfounded. On 28th October they enjoyed an evening meal with the Duke of Rocca who was a refugee from Rome.

A 4.00 a.m. start on 2nd November was the beginning of a long tiring day in which they just avoided running into a German party salvaging a wrecked aircraft near the main Atine to Pescasseroli road. That night they slept in the open with a fire going all night. The 3rd November proved to be their longest day and their biggest trial of endurance. They were aiming for La Meta mountain but never seemed to reach it. Eventually they walked right over the summit, 7,270 feet high. Now they could clearly hear the sounds of gunfire, then of digging and the voices of German working parties and the engines of compressors.

They decided to wait till dark and climbed up again into some cover. At dusk they heard the Germans collecting their tools and moving off to more central posts, from which came the smell of cooking. So that night they slipped through between these posts.

A steep slope took the escapers down to the River Volturno which at that point was small and narrow. On the other side was the Venafro to Castel di Sangro road. They had a steep climb up, now marching by compass, and whenever they stopped for a short rest, they soon got cold. Coming across a cave, they rested for an hour, but it was too cold to stay. On again by compass, over steep hills, rocks, muddy tracks and woods. As daylight came Gibbs' party found themselves on top of a precipitous hill overlooking a narrow deep valley. Then they met an Italian who told them that one end of the valley was not occupied by Germans. He took them to his house where they were offered an enormous meal, the biggest since they were captured. They had walked from 5.30 a.m. on 3rd to 7.00 a.m. on 4th November.

The next day the four escapers left at 4.45 a.m. and moved warily for three hours. They met an Italian who gave them the good news that all the Germans had gone in the night, having blown the bridges on the Isernia road. Small parties of peasants began to appear with joy on their faces. Soon after they met the Carrier Platoon of the King's Own Yorkshire Light Infantry at the blown bridge near Isernia. Gibbs described their condition as 'filthy dirty, unshaven, very long hair, clothes torn and toes coming out of their boots.' At the British headquarters they met Gerry de Winton, also from Fontanellato. Later they met Lt.-Col. 'Dean' MacDonnell, who had also been in PG49.

George Ord, after being re-captured near Pistoia, escaped over a wall of a Fascist H.Q. on 15th October while the sentry's back was turned. He continued walking south, meeting another officer. They crossed the River Sangro and met Allied forces on 13th November.

Douglas Flowerdew had jumped off a German truck when being taken to Sulmona. He found himself in steep wooded country heavily populated by Germans. By now his boots were unwearable and he was walking barefoot. He saw a man in the open door of a cabin who called out to him in German. Luckily he did not come out to investigate. Some shepherds gave him some bread and water, but would not let him stay. After an exhausting march through the night, in which he became light-headed with cold and fatigue and again had to run off from approaching Germans, he met a very kind man who took him to his home, gave him some meat and put him to bed. He stayed there for four days. Though pressed by his host to stay until the battle had moved on, he felt rested and his morale was restored, so he decided to move on. On 20th October he was guided to Civitella, where he found the whole village busy hiding food from the encroaching Germans. Flowerdew was told of some British officers, a Sergeant Major and a Chaplain, who were hiding in a shack in the hills. They turned out to be two Indian V.C.Os., a Sergeant-Major and a Corporal who had been the regimental mullah. The Italians were frightened of them and would not feed them. Flowerdew had a little money and was able to buy a sheep. They were joined by three South Africans. Quite soon he found he was running a sort of transit camp, with Gurkhas, South Africans, two British parachutists and even two British Brigadiers, with their batmen and an Italian guide, coming in, staying for a few days and then moving on. At one time he had twenty-six mouths to feed. So on 6th November he decided to move on, taking the Indians with him. After a difficult scrambling walk south, they came to some houses, where they sheltered from the heavy rain. Suddenly the mullah shouted 'Sahib! *Tedeschi.*' They ran off up the hill till they found a hiding place. After waiting an hour, they went back, to find the Germans had taken away five men.

On 12th November Flowerdew, the mullah, two Gurkhas, a Scottish R.A.M.C. private and an Italian set off to try to get through. Douglas Flowerdew was wearing sheepskins which kept him warm, but were extremely heavy when wet. About midnight they heard German voices and a fusillade of bullets from sub-machine guns lit up the air. After hiding for ten minutes they moved on. At 1.30 a.m, the moon came out from behind the clouds and by its light they could see their objective—a two-headed mountain.

Flowerdew saw a cigarette packet on the ground and picked it up—'Luckies,' but he could not be sure if that meant they were through. After scrambling down an almost sheer slope, they came to Venafro. At first there seemed no one about, but eventually they were taken to an American Military Police headquarters. The next day the Scotsman, the Italian and the remaining Gurkha, who had become separated, turned up.

Hugh Thompson got through the lines in the same area of Venafro on 20th November when he came into the positions held by the 1st American Rangers.

Binks Forster had been walking with Henry Armstrong and Bill Reid. In early November they met George Ord in the village of Opi and he joined them. But they found four together was too many, so Forster and Ord went on together. They made good progress to Villetta Barrea where they were taken in by a brave family, as there were Germans in the village. From there they could take food forward to a cave on Monte Chianno which was snow-covered. On 12th November they left their hosts in Villetta Barrea and moved up to the cave where they spent the night. The next night they moved

Map 10

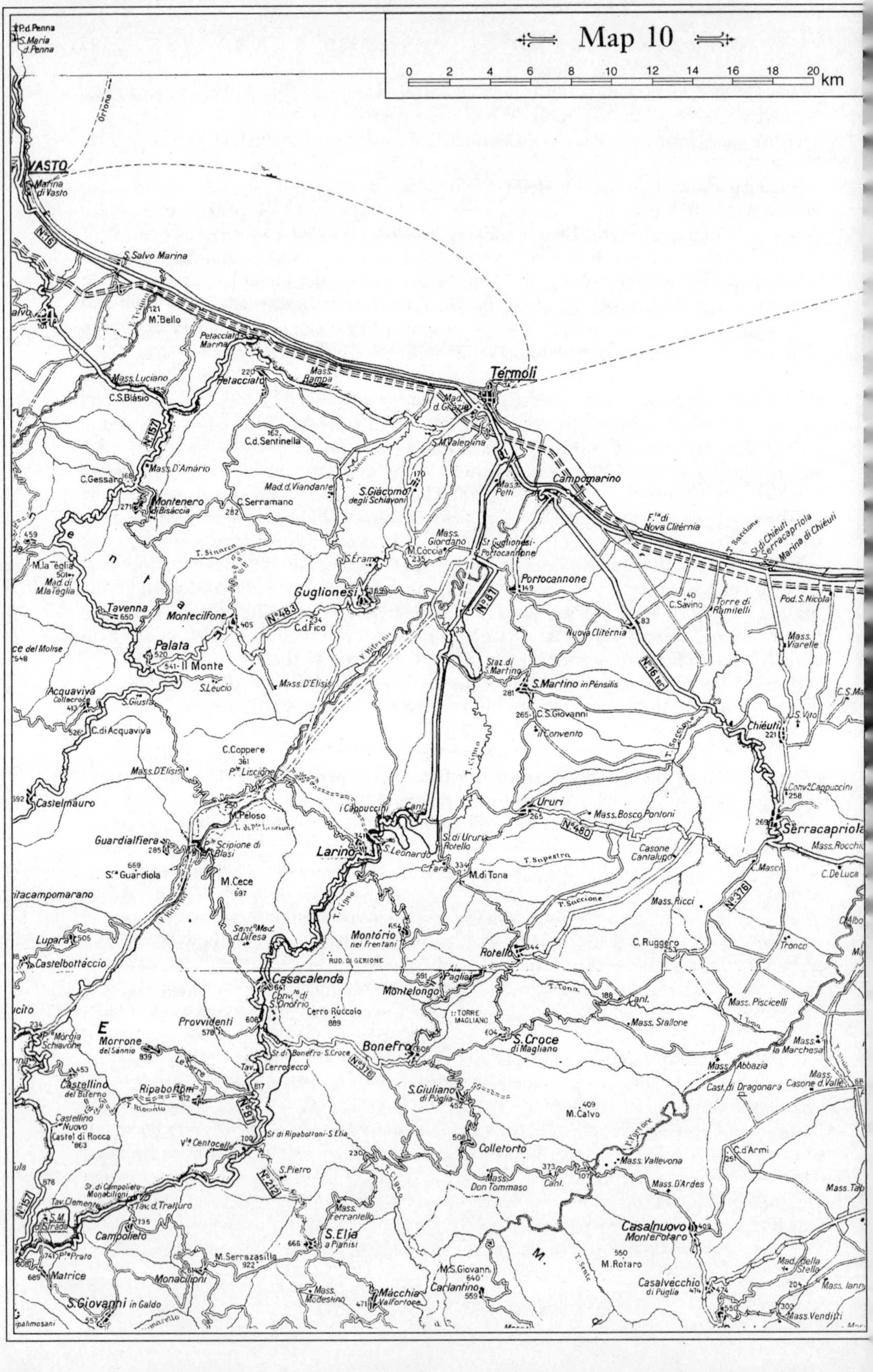
0 2 4 6 8 10 12 14 16 18 20 km
P.d.Penna
S.Maria d.Penna
Ortona
VASTO
Marina di Vasto
N°16
S.Salvo Marina
M.Bello
Petacciato Marina
Petacciato
Mass.Luciano
C.S.Blásio
Mass.Rampa
Térmoli
Mad. d.Grazie
S.M.Valentina
N°157
C.d.Sentinella
Mass.D'Amário
C.Gessaro
Montenero di Bisáccia
Mad.d.Viandante
S.Giácomo degli Schiavoni
C.Serramano
Campomarino
Mass. Petti
F.te di Nova Clitérnia
St.di Chiéuti
Serracapriola
Marina di Chiéuti
Mass. Giordano
M.Cóccia
St.Guglionesi-Portocannone
S.Éramo
T.Sinarca
Guglionesi
Portocannone
N°87
N°483
Tavenna
Montecilfone
C.d.Fico
C.Savino
Torre di Ramitelli
Pod.S.Nicola
Nuova Clitérnia
Mass. Viarelle
Palata
Il Monte
S.Leucio
Mass.D'Elisis
Staz.di S.Martino
S.Martino in Pénsilis
N°16 ter
Acquaviva Collecroce
S.Giusta
C.di Acquaviva
C.S.Giovanni
il Convento
Chiéuti
S.Vito
C.Coppere
Pte Liscione
Mass.D'Elisis
Castelmauro
i Cappuccini
Cant.
Conv.to Cappuccini
Ururi
Mass.Bosco Pontoni
N°480
Serracapriola
Mass.Rocchia
M.Peloso
Guardialfiera
Pte Scipione di Blasi
Larino
S.Leonardo
St.di Ururi-Rotello
T.Sapestra
Casone Cantalupo
C.Fara
M.di Tona
C.Masci
C.De Luca
Sta Guardiola
M.Cece
T.Saccione
Mass.Ricci
N°376
Lupara
Castelbottáccio
Santo Mad. d.Difesa
Montorio nei Frentani
C.Ruggero
Tronco
Rotello
RUD. DI GERIONE
Casacalenda
Conv.to di S.Onofrio
Montelongo
Aia Pagliai
T.Tona
Cant.
Mass.Piscicelli
Provvidenti
Cerro Rúccolo
TORRE MAGLIANO
Mass.Stallone
Pte Mórgia Schiavone
Morrone del Sánnio
St.di Bonefro-S.Croce
Bonefro
S.Croce di Magliano
Mass. la Marchesa
Mass.Abbazia
Cast.di Dragonara
Mass. Casone d.Valle
Le Serre
Tav. Cerrosecco
Castellino del Biferno
Ripabottoni
S.Giuliano di Puglia
M.Calvo
Castellino Nuovo
Castel di Rocca
Vte Centocelle
St.di Ripabottoni-S.Elia
Colletorto
F.Fortore
Mass.Vallevona
C.d'Armi
S.Pietro
N°212
Mass. Don Tommaso
Cant.
Mass.D'Ardes
Mass.Tab
Sr.di Campolieto-Monacilioni
Tav.Clemente
S.M. d.Strada
Tav.d.Tratturo
Mass. Ferrantello
Campolieto
S.Elia a Pianisi
Casalnuovo Monterotaro
M.Rotaro
M.Serrazasilla
M.S.Giovanni
Carlantino
Mad. della Stella
Pte Prato
Matrice
Monacilioni
Mass. Modestino
Mácchia Valfortore
Casalvécchio di Puglia
Mass.Iann
Mass.Venditti
S.Giovanni in Galdo

slowly forward, hiding when necessary under rocks in the German lines. There was a full moon which gave them enough light to pick their way past a minefield and down to the River Sangro. They crossed this without too much difficulty and at 10.00 a.m. on 14th November they ran into a British infantry patrol.

Peter Langrishe, walking alone since David Buchanan had been forced to drop out with bad feet at Fano, had passed to the west of Aquila. One day he walked with a mule train owned by a muleteer called Mario, finishing up at the remote high-lying village of Casamaina, where Mario provided an excellent meal and a bed for the night. On 14th November, after a wet exhausting walk, he reached Castrovalva. Here a kind old widow lady called Maria Divito took him in, dried his clothes, and fed him. She told him Castrovalva was a jumping-off point for getting through the line. Next morning he met several other ex-prisoners waiting to cross the lines, which were only about fifteen miles away.

The start of the final march was delayed several times by very bad weather. An Italian guide said the route through Alfedena was still open. But on 17th November the party, made up of twenty British, South African and American ex-prisoners and about sixty Italians carrying large suitcases, set off up hill to Frattura and on to the deserted hamlet of San Lorenzo. Here Langrishe found Gervase Nicholls and Geoffrey Phalp in company with a young Dutchman. The next morning the party aimed for Monte Greco, which meant a stiff climb through snow which was two feet deep by the time they paused for a rest at an Alpine hut. Off again, ever upwards, to the summit of the ridge. Here they could see the River Sangro and a wide open valley stretching away two thousand feet below them.

The guide went forward to do a recce, but he never returned and they heard later that he had been shot by Germans—they were on their own.

Just below them was an 88 mm. gun dug into the hillside, registering on the distant ridge. This told Peter Langrishe where the Allied positions were, but they still had to get through the hazards in between. They divided up into groups of six to eight escapers. They sent the Italians off to the left towards Castel di Sangro, hoping they would engage the attention of the German patrols, which they did. Langrishe's party moved off after dark about 8.00 p.m. to descend the hill in single file. He wrote, 'We were helped to keep straight by the "firework display" of a fierce battle round Isernia, a few miles to the south-west. We avoided the dug-in 88 mm., though it was unnerving to hear a telephone ringing in a dugout almost beneath my feet. We reached the river; it was raining fairly hard and we had no choice but to wade across in single file. It was running fast, about twenty-five yards wide and up to four feet deep, but we were all soon across. So far no wire, no f.d.l. [foremost defended localities], no mines; nothing but rain and the battle near Isernia. Almost too good to be true.'

They went across the plain very cautiously and by about 5.00 a.m. on 19th November they were at the foot of the ridge. At the top they found field telephone wires which, by the manner in which they were laid, could only have been British. Langrishe and an American fighter-pilot went on for another hour. In Langrishe's words, 'Coming up a track was an elderly Italian with two cows. I asked him "Are there any Germans in the village?" He replied "*Niente—Americani!*" We were through!' Later they were taken to the headquarters of a Ranger battalion and in due course learned that all the party got through except the Italians.

V. C. Amos also got through on the 19th November. He and six others had walked south. A German and a Fascist whom they encountered became suspicious and arrested them. Seeing they outnumbered the enemy, the prisoners overpowered them and escaped, continuing on south until they met British troops.

Before meeting Peter Langrishe, Gervase Nicholls and Geoffrey Phalp came to the small village of Santa Maria, where there were a number of other British ex-prisoners. Others from Fontanellato arrived, including John Measures, 'Mac' MacLean and E. N. Strickland with two Other Ranks from the camp. Because of rain and snow they were at Santa Maria for a week. During this time Nicholls bought a sheep for two-hundred-and-forty lire (about £4), had it cut up into joints and cooked. With the bread they had saved, they reckoned they had enough food for a week.

Marcus Kane-Burman had joined them and on 18th November he, Nicholls and Phalp set off with a blanket each and as much food as they could carry. MacLean said he would wait for John Measures who had gone to another village to have his boots repaired. They made for Frattura which they reached successfully in spite of the snow. But Measures and MacLean never arrived, and they heard Santa Maria had been occupied by the Germans soon after they had left and most of the prisoners had been re-taken. At Frattura they met an Italian guide who said he had led several parties through the lines. Early next morning the large party moved off. They moved slowly and were making a lot of noise. Two majors in the party who had a compass and a detailed map said they should push on on their own, because it would take several days at the present rate of progress. Nicholls and Phalp agreed and they made a détour away from the rest of the party. Half-an-hour later they heard sounds of shooting and shouting and reckoned the main party had walked into trouble. Making good progress, they were coming down off the highest ground in the afternoon.

They then agreed with the two majors that it was better to travel in pairs, so they let them go on ahead. Reaching lower ground the snow turned to rain and they had only one more hill to climb before reaching the Sangro.

Nicholls wrote, 'We were hurrying down a thinly-wooded hill side, when suddenly round a bend appeared three German soldiers barely fifty yards away. They called out, but we turned and almost flew back up the hill, zig-zagging. They shouted at us to halt and fired at us with their rifles and started to chase up the hill after us, but it would have taken an Olympic runner to have caught us. They were probably cooks or maintenance men. After a while we stopped and lay in a thicket to regain our breath. All was quiet, so after a decent interval we continued on our way down the hill, but making a détour.'

As darkness fell they continued moving very slowly. As their eyes had got accustomed to the darkness, it was not too difficult to avoid the sentries at the German gun positions, who stamped their feet, whistled and often were smoking.

It was a cloudy, wet night with a watery moon. In the middle of the night shells began landing in the area of the German gun positions. This enabled them to make quicker progress, as they thought the sentries would have their heads down. They came to the railway in the valley in the early hours of the morning, and crawled slowly forward down a track which led under the embankment. Suddenly there was a loud explosion and the smell of cordite. They thought it was a grenade or a stray shell. But they had set off a mine and, amazingly, were unhurt. Eventually they came to the river which was flowing fast, but where they crossed it was only about two feet deep. They came to an island and found there was more water to wade through. After that they went on south with great caution as they did not want to run into patrols. The rain continued to pour down and they were soaked to the skin. Nicholls said, 'We were too excited to feel either the wet or the cold. We realised we were probably safe, but didn't take any less care.' As dawn was breaking a few hundred yards beyond a lake they came upon a troop of 25-pounder guns. Geoffrey Phalp said, 'By God, Nick, we've made it.'

Maurice Goddard and Erik Hampson moved across a great plateau deep in snow. Emerging from woods in which German ammunition dumps were concealed, they were suddenly confronted by a party of German soldiers. They had to continue and the Germans took no notice of them. This was another example of the Germans being unable to recognise Allied soldiers in Italian civilian clothes. Near the village of Opi was a battery of German artillery. Though very nervous, one family provided food and let the escapers sleep in their hay loft. They were wakened early next morning with the news that the Germans were searching the village. So Hampson and Goddard had to make a hasty exit and hide in cover down a hillside. Later they met a shepherd in his hut busy cooking sheep meat, who gave them some and let them spend the night there. The shepherd said the Germans had evacuated all civilians from villages forward of Opi and Villetta Barrea. Next morning, when making good progress along a hillside, they were fired on by about twenty Germans, but they were able to hide in a cave.

Later, when running into some cover, they almost stepped on a figure, giving them a tremendous shock. He turned out to be a Free Frenchman who asked if he could join them. They could not refuse. Goddard wrote, 'We were brought up sharply on the edge of a gorge which dropped almost vertically several hundred feet to the river. Now in a state of exhaustion, having had no real sleep for about three days and none at all during the previous twenty-four hours, we decided to make the descent. Showers of stones and boulders went crashing beneath us ... then we became aware of the roar of the river below us ... which became deafening and must have completely veiled the sound of the miniature avalanches we were causing; We had good reason to be thankful, because to our dismay we saw a small group of figures on the far side of the river ... we presumed them to be the enemy. Rational thought should have persuaded us to go back up ... but exhaustion and desperation drove us on, accepting that recapture was almost inevitable ... At the bottom there was no cover and we found ourselves separated from a party of five German soldiers by the torrent, some thirty feet across. They were outside a hut, one chopping wood, one cleaning a rifle, and the others preparing food. We watched them for some moments, unable to believe that we had not yet been seen; then, as realisation dawned, we crouched and ran along the narrow track towards a bend, expecting every moment to hear and feel shots, but none came and we rounded the bend safely. To this day, I believe the hand of Providence guided us that day ...'

They crept into a rock sangar and were able to light a fire and prepare some food, although they were only two hundred yards from the German hut. After a short sleep they prepared to cross the river. When darkness fell, they stripped naked, tied their boots and clothing round their necks, and tested the depth of the water with long staves, and found it to be about chest high. Goddard continued 'Using the staves as a link between us, Erik went first, then myself and the Frenchman last. The icy water was like an electric shock, but it was the force of the current which was the more alarming. One slip and there would be no chance in the boiling stream of regaining a footing. When Erik was almost across the Frenchman slipped and grabbed me and, had not Erik stood firm, we might all have gone but, with his help and the staves, we made the far bank.' They dressed where they stood, Goddard and Hampson now donning battledress which they had been carrying the whole long journey. Creeping past the German hut, they climbed uphill, then hearing dogs barking they thought they saw one in front of them.

Fearing it was a guard dog, they 'froze' for some time, then realised it was a sheep! Pushing on, they came to a wide shallow river bed and then a railway station and what seemed to be a deserted village. They let a patrol pass a few yards from them, not knowing if they were Germans or British. At first light, as they were sheltering from rain at the edge of a wood, the Frenchman jumped up and shouted, *'Un soldat Anglais.'*

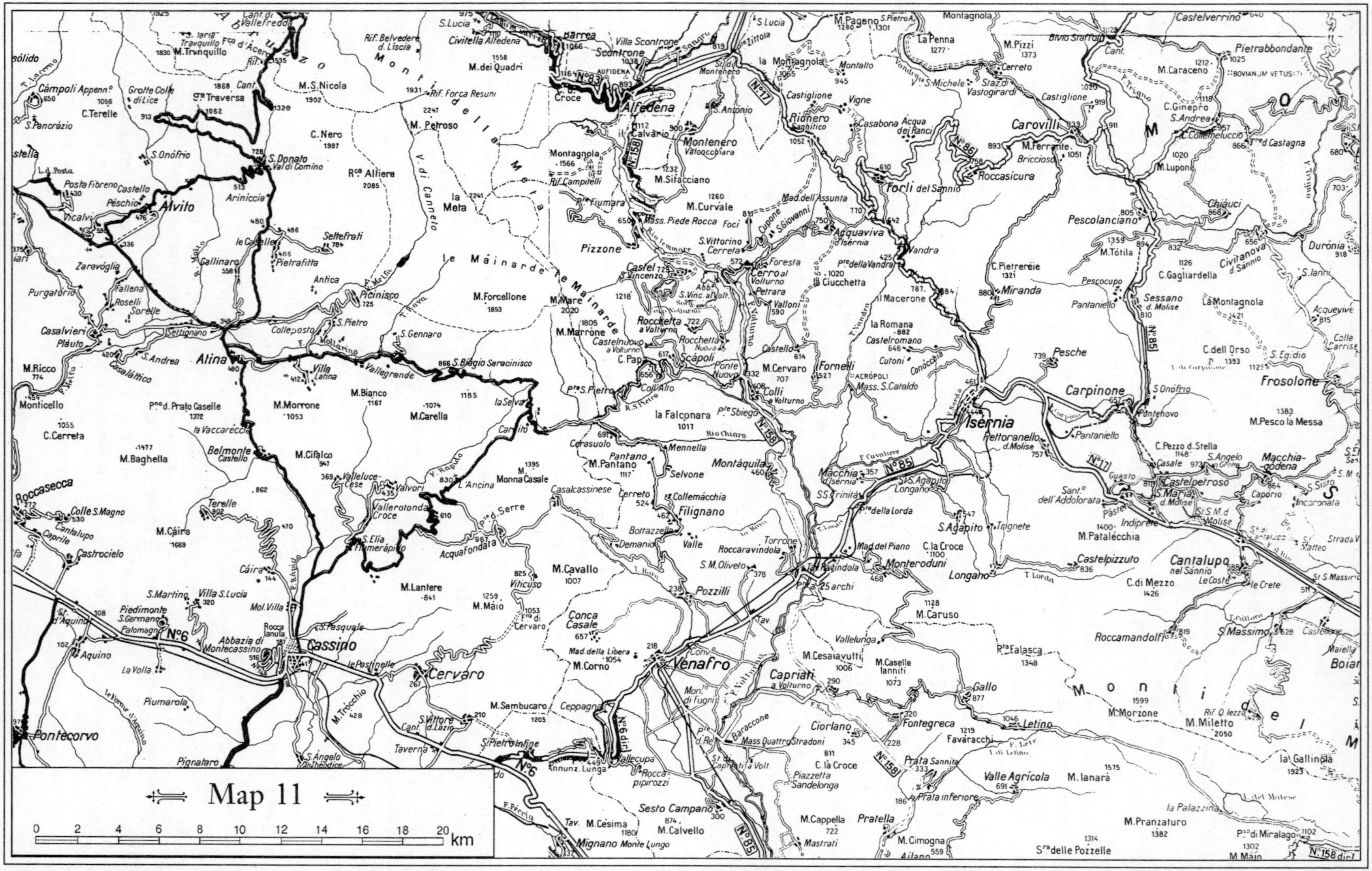

Map 11

0 2 4 6 8 10 12 14 16 18 20 km

It was undoubtedly a British soldier in battledress, with steel helmet, webbing equipment and a rifle. Goddard described their actions, 'Without more ado we careered across the field shouting and waving as we went. What we must have looked like in our unshaven and bedraggled state I can't think. But we achieved surprise and the poor chap made no attempt to move or challenge us. He was a runner with the forward company of the Northamptonshires with the British 5th Division. It was the morning of 1st December and we were home, if not dry.'

Richard Carver had been walking with Lt.-Col. 'Dean' MacDonnell. Approaching the Pescara River they met Major Gordon who had been in Chieti camp. He was trying to collect ex-prisoners to take them to the coast for a rendezvous with a M.T.B. MacDonnell decided to go with this party. As it happened, the M.T.B was intercepted and sunk, but the Naval officer in charge managed to swim ashore and, with the 'Dean' and some others, commandeered a fishing boat in which they succeeded in reaching Termoli.

Carver met a South African, Jim Gill, and they went on together, crossing the Pescara by the hydro-electric dam just as 'Toots' Williams' party had. It was now early November. They spent three nights in mountain huts. Walking the last bit at night, they met a small party of Germans when crossing a road. They looked at the escapers suspiciously but took no action. At dawn they were in a deep valley dominated by the village of Roccascalegra. They met a young man and a boy, whose pig the Germans had just stolen. They invited Carver and Gill to their farmhouse that evening. There they met a remarkable man called Donato di Gregorio who offered them a hiding-place and food. This turned out to be a sort of cave made by two huge boulders. They stayed there for three weeks. Donato wanted to get back to Naples where he lived, but he had to wait for his brother's funeral. It looked as if the Germans had withdrawn, so Gill set off on his own, and got safely through the lines. Carver and Donato set off on 3rd December, crossing the River Sangro by crawling across the sleepers of a demolished railway bridge. They reached the small town of Atessa without encountering either friend or foe, and not even a minefield. The American officer in charge of Allied Military Government was very surprised to know that his headquarters was the first Allied unit the escapers had met. Donato di Gregorio was a very brave man who risked his life protecting Carver and Gill. After many delays he succeeded in returning to his family in Naples.

Jack Moore, Wilfred White and Ian English reached Corvara, a little way north of the River Pescara, on 21st November, having been walking for six weeks. Several Italians they met warned them they would be mad to try to cross the river as the Germans were watching every crossing-place. But the next day they talked to a British and a South African soldier who had been south of the river and had just returned. They said crossing the Pescara was no problem, but living the far side was very difficult. The Germans were in every village, their patrols were very active, some ex-prisoners just in front of them had been fired on, and food was scarce. So, very reluctantly, Moore, White and English decided to wait north of the river until the 8th Army advanced, at least as far as Chieti. This was expected to be quite soon.

In the event they were in the Corvara—Colli area for three weeks. During this time they saw several demonstrations of Allied air-power, bombing German positions, near Pescara and Chieti. But the German presence was increasing and night raids on farms were becoming more common. They heard of one soldier who had to jump out of a window just as the Germans came in the door. On the night of 11th December there was shooting and rounding up of young Italians quite close to the farm they were staying at. That decided them to move on south. They crossed the Pescara without difficulty on 13th December over the hydro-electric dam which had been the route of several other parties of escapers. After two days they were on the eastern slopes of the Maiella, wandering round in circles, completely lost in thick mist which was to last for the next nine days. During this period they met Douglas de Cent who had been a prisoner in Sulmona and Bologna camps. With him was Gillian Gensini, who had been married to an Italian and lived in Florence. She had been arrested and imprisoned but had got away at the Armistice. Encounters with Germans were a daily occurrence. Moore and English were fired on but managed to get away under cover of trees. One day the five escapers were doing domestic chores, collecting wood and charcoal, and trying to cut up meat with razor blades, when they were approached by a young German soldier with his cocked rifle at the ready. He walked round looking at what they were doing. Gillian Gensini asked him in Italian what he wanted. The German, probably not understanding Italian, made no reply. He went off to summon a colleague and they both stood and stared for some time at the escapers who tried to look unconcerned while having their hearts in their mouths.

On 22nd December the mist lifted and at last they could see the country below them to the east and south-east. They watched an infantry and tank attack on Orsogna after heavy air and artillery support. They could also see where the shells from German guns were landing, indicating the British positions. They decided there and then to try to get through that night. The route chosen was down a track past two German guns, across the Rapino to Penne Piedimonte road, up over a ridge, across the road from Guardiagrele and down, bearing east of south to the Lajo stream which runs into the River Aventino near Casoli.

They set off at 6.00 p.m. as it was getting dark, and successfully crept past the German guns whose crews they could hear talking. Soon after they encountered a succession of walls enclosing small fields which were difficult to negotiate, and the party was in danger of getting split up. The night was intensely dark and they went too far to the right. Consequently they became involved in extremely steep and dangerous clay screes. English wrote, 'We started to descend into the ravine and immediately we were in difficulties. The surface was loose and when one tried to get a foothold the earth fell away ... It took Jack and me about a quarter-of-an hour to descend about ten yards. We looked back and found the others were not following. They were having a frightful time further up. Gillian had got into a position where she could move neither forward nor back ... Jack and I managed to climb back up and help the others ... another twenty minutes scrambling and sliding down brought us to the bottom. Here the mud was so soft we sank in over our ankles ... We started to climb again, but about halfway up Jack got stuck. I managed to find another way and then hauled him up. It was a matter of going a yard or two, then hauling up the person behind you, then staggering on for another yard or two. After what seemed an interminable time we reached the top and, to our immense relief, saw a field in front of us.' Apart from an encounter with a German patrol in which both sides lay and looked at each other for some time, the remainder of their journey was slow but uneventful. Using the Lajo stream as their guide, they went up and down one small ridge after another; until suddenly they were challenged 'Halt, who goes there?' When told 'Friend' the sentry said, 'Give the password.' White and English explained why they did not know the password. The soldier came up and scrutinised them carefully. He probably had not seen such walking scarecrows before. They had come into a troop position of the gunners of the 1st Airborne Division.

As Jack Kempton and Tom Craig were approaching the front lines they met a partisan named Luigi. They thought it better to travel by night, aiming for Guardiagrele and Casoli. Trooper Baker, who was keen to try to get through the lines, joined them. Craig's feet, which had been painful for some time, now turned septic. So on 30th January, 1944, when Kempton and Baker decided to make an attempt, Tom Craig decided to stay where he was. Luigi thought the safest route was by Guardiagrele down to the River Aventino and across this to Casoli, which they had heard was in British hands. The most dangerous part was the cemetery at Guardiagrele, the place where the three Garhwali officers were to be recaptured on Easter Day, where the Germans had machine gun posts on the south-east, south and south-west boundaries. They took an hour to crawl through the cemetery. Once through it they came to scrub and a wooded area which gave good cover. They descended 1,500 feet through rough, stony country. When in sight of the river, they were greatly surprised to hear the cry of a baby. They went over to a broken-down cottage where the sound came from, and found a woman nursing her baby. She said both the Germans and the British had tried to persuade her to move from the cottage in No Man's Land. But that was her home and she refused. But she did tell them of a safe route to where they could ford the river. Luigi had to leave them, but Kempton and Baker, taking great care, reached the river and crossed it, and soon afterwards came into a Brigade headquarters. Here they were suspected of being spies. This had serious repercussions. When Kempton got back to Liverpool, he was arrested and put into Walton Gaol until his identity could be established. Fortunately this did not take long.

Tom Craig was joined by Tom Wildy, who had been walking with Bill Bowder. When Jack Kempton left them to get through the lines, Craig and Wildy stayed another month, partly to give time for the former's feet to improve. At the end of February they followed the same route as taken by Kempton and Baker, and managed to get through successfully.

Ronald Mann spent three months of the winter at Frascara in the Gran Sasso region with the family of Vittorio Massara. Having met an American fighter-pilot called Roane, he decided to attempt to get through the lines. On 14th March they were guided by Paulo from a nearby village who had friends in a small place in the foothills of the Maiella. There they found a party of nine Italians, but there was no guide. Trudging through deep snow, they made for Grotto del Uomo Morto (Dead Man's Gully). On the way they encountered some Germans, but Mann and Roane managed to stay back and got away. They then tried another route. But the snow was waist deep and very slippery and they were forced back. It took them eighteen hours to reach the foot of the mountain.

After a night in a hay-loft, Mann went to Sulmona to meet a professor who, they heard, organised escape parties. He agreed to join a party leaving for the Maiella that night. This was made up of twelve Italians, three South Africans, a Scots soldier, Mann and Roane with three guides. Having had a night march through snow, they spent the next day in a good mountain hut. Two of the guides left in the morning for some reason and had not returned by 8.00 p.m. The third guide had not been over the route. An energetic little Italian called Mario joined them. He made a business of taking parties through and was annoyed there were so few ex-prisoners. He charged five thousand lire for each. He said he had led parties of two hundred.

They left the hut at 9.00 p.m. Though there was no deep snow, the climb was extremely steep. One of the South Africans collapsed, his legs having given out. He was helped by Roane and Paulo, but he could not continue, and went back. Mann described the next two hours as 'a nerve-wracking nightmare.' They reached the top at 1.00 a.m. in thick cloud. The wind was icy and everything froze. Then they were caught in a blinding blizzard. Both the South Africans collapsed completely with hypothermia. They had to be rubbed vigorously for several minutes before they came round. As they began to descend, the wind was less fierce and the mist was thinner. The South Africans revived. When the dawn came, they could see the ground ahead and Mario recognised where they were. Dropping down into a steep-sided valley, they came to a road running

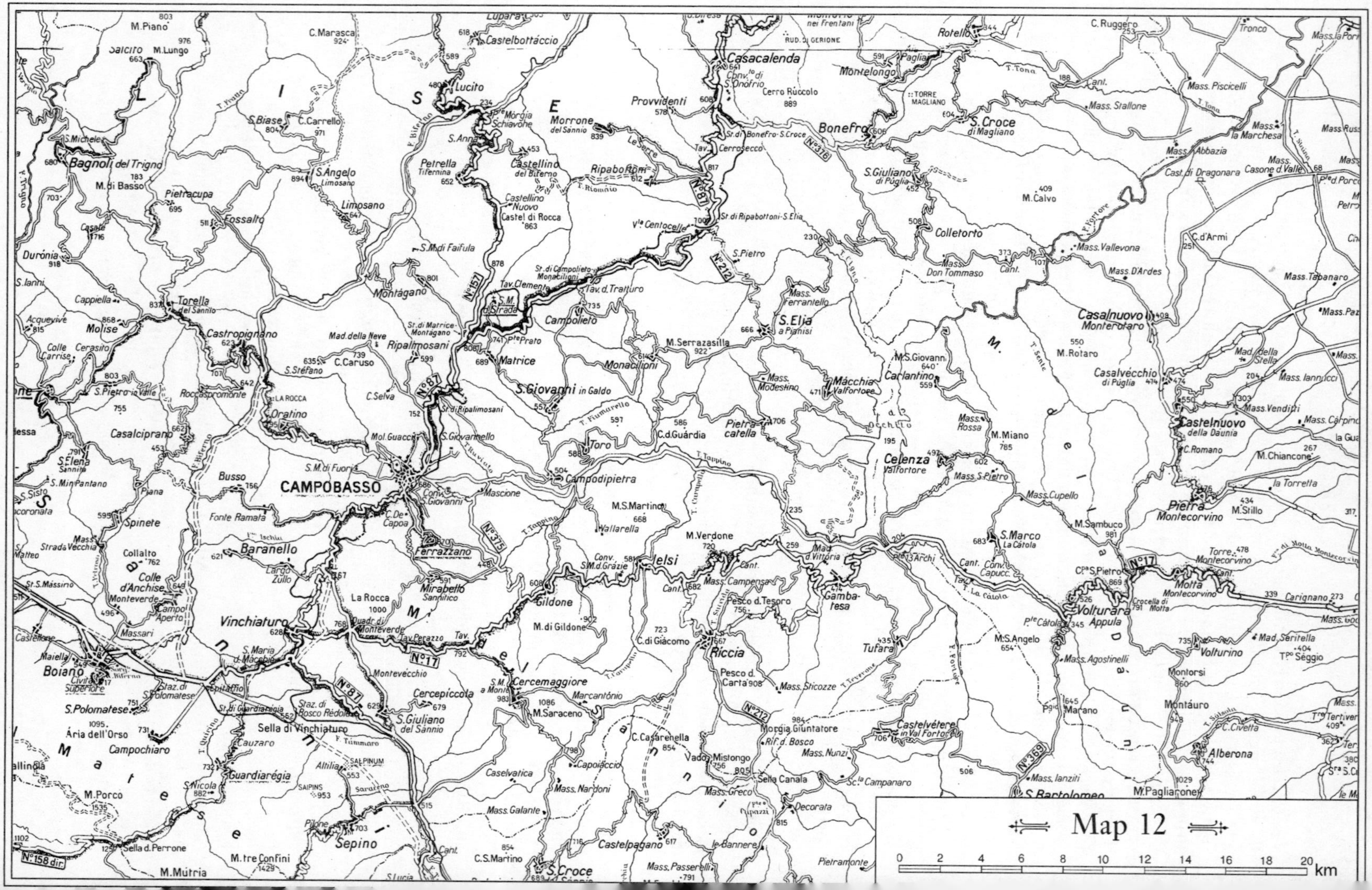
Map 12
0 2 4 6 8 10 12 14 16 18 20 km
CAMPOBASSO
Bojano
Vinchiaturo
Riccia
Jelsi
Gildone
Cercemaggiore
Ferrazzano
Mirabello Sannitico
Baranello
Busso
Oratino
Castropignano
Torella del Sannio
Ripalimosani
Matrice
S.Giovanni in Galdo
Campodipietra
Toro
Monacilioni
Campolieto
Pietracatella
S.Elia a Pianisi
Macchia Valfortore
Carlantino
Celenza Valfortore
S.Marco La Catola
Volturara Appula
Motta Montecorvino
Pietra Montecorvino
Casalnuovo Monterotaro
Casalvecchio di Puglia
Castelnuovo della Daunia
Colletorto
S.Giuliano di Puglia
S.Croce di Magliano
Rotello
Bonefro
Montelongo
Casacalenda
Provvidenti
Morrone del Sannio
Ripabottoni
Castellino del Biferno
Petrella Tifernina
Lucito
Castelbottaccio
Limosano
S.Angelo Limosano
S.Biase
Fossalto
Pietracupa
Bagnoli del Trigno
Duronia
Molise
Casalciprano
S.Elena Sannita
Spinete
Colle d'Anchise
Campochiaro
Guardiaregia
Sepino
S.Giuliano del Sannio
Cercepiccola
Gambatesa
Tufara
Castelvetere in Val Fortore
Volturino
Alberona
Castelpagano
S.Croce
N°17
N°87
N°157
N°212
N°375
N°376
N°369
N°158 dir.

through a ruined village where the bridge and part of the road were blown. They went towards Palumbaro and were stopped by an Italian soldier who took them to an Indian officer. Ronald Mann said it took several days for him to realise fully that he was free.

B. W. Nicholls stayed in the Monte Sirente area for four months. Joining up with an R.A.F. officer, they crossed the Sulmona valley on 12th March, 1944, and tried to cross Monte Morrone, but, having no guide, they were beaten back by soft snow. But a second attempt across the Maiella was successful and they reached Allied lines on 18th March.

Charles Simpson, walking with several others, reached Cagliano. Advised by an Australian Air Force officer who was helping escapers to stay in the area, they remained there till March, 1944. Then Simpson moved to Sulmona where there were many ex-prisoners in hiding. He found a guide and got together a party of escapers who successfully reached British troops at Taranta on 25th March.

Hugh Sillito walked with a companion from the Fontanellato area to Mariano. Here he fell ill and had to lie up for three weeks. At the end of September he and a French refugee went to Stia, then by train to Chiusi, and later walked to Filettino. He stayed in that area from December, 1943, to April, 1944, keeping in touch with several other ex-prisoners. Finally he led three Other Ranks through to the British lines at Vastogirardi on 16th April.

Tom Preacher, like many from PG49, went to Bardi with one companion. He then decided to go on alone and reached Frattura. He joined other escapers in an attempt to cross the lines on 13th December, but he and his former second-in-command, Ross McLaren, who had got away from Viano, were re-captured. Four days later they got through the window of their cell. They spent the rest of the winter hiding in the Lecce di Marsi area. On 30th April, 1944, they set out on a four-days' march to cross the lines. Although they came under Allied fire and two of the party were wounded by anti-personnel mines, they successfully reached Allied troops.

John Woods had been living partly with the partisans and partly in Popoli all winter. He had several hairbreadth escapes and the Germans were definitely on the lookout for him. A substantial reward was posted for the capture of '*Capitano Inglesi.*' One day in late May he and some of his partisan friends looked down from a mountain and saw the Germans blowing up the Pescara—Rome railway. They knew immediately that the Gustav line was crumbling and the Germans were withdrawing. Woods and his friends then parted, the former to head for the lines as quickly as he could, and the partisans to round up German stragglers and prevent further sabotage. After a few hours' march John Woods met a British jeep. He was taken back to Popoli to confirm the Germans had withdrawn and to act as a go-between with the partisans. Then he was driven to the nearest British unit. He wrote, 'A new problem then arose. I had no tangible evidence of my identity (his British identity discs had been seized when he was arrested in Popoli), was in poor condition physically and at first was unable to converse in English. There is some irony in the fact that for months I had been in danger from my perceived inability to appear Italian, whereas now the English were sceptical that I was one of them.'

C. D. 'Kit' Patterson, who had been in charge of the Red Cross parcels store in the camp, got away with W. Pringle. After about ten days they met an Italian who was organising people to go south by train. He turned out to be a Fascist and had several prisoners re-captured, including Pringle, but Patterson managed to avoid capture. He went up into the hills, moving around. Fortuitously he met his batman who had been in an Other Ranks camp nearby. Eventually in June, 1944, they managed to reach the positions of the Polish Division in the Ancona area.

Stuart Hood, who had been very active with the Partisans in Chianti, was ordered to go into Siena to act as liaison officer when the town fell to the Allies. At the gates was a German sentry, and, as he walked past him, Hood felt sweat breaking out at the base of his spine. After a haircut and a photograph for his identity card as an auxiliary policeman, he was given a flat off Via Montanini. For a few days he was on holiday, which he spent exploring the town. At night he lay listening in terror to the gunfire. Hood wrote, 'One morning before dawn, there was a scuffling noise of feet in the street. I looked out and saw the German rearguards falling back through the town, deliberate, unhurrying, dragging their light anti-tank guns behind them. For half-an-hour or more, the town lay in the greying light, silent and empty. Quiet figures in long grey coats began to slip along the walls ... they were in single file with rifles at the ready. The town woke and came out into the streets to greet the liberators.'

The French army took over Siena. Stuart Hood reported to the divisional Chief-of-Staff, giving him as much information as he could. Then he boarded a truck going back to base. He had the frustrating experience of being treated as a prisoner, being put in a French prisoner-of-war cage beside the Germans. Back at Naples he was screened by Security and passed the test. In the Seventies, Stuart Hood was made an honorary citizen of Campi Bisenzio, the little town near Florence where the Partisans came from, and a member of the National Association of Italian Partisans.

Bill Monteith, after living with partisans in the Bardi—Borgo val di Taro area, had had enough by late 1944, so crossed the lines and came upon the Americans in Livorno. This was another case of an ex-prisoner's identity not being accepted. So 'I went to bed supperless and "bed" was a cold marble floor. I remember thinking that was the only time in the previous year that I had been refused a meal and a bed.' Monteith did not blame the Americans as he had no real means of identification. However, by next morning they had overcome their doubts and were extremely helpful. A huge breakfast of bacon, eggs and maple syrup, some badly-needed new clothes and he was put on a flight to London.

Robert Williams, who had been in the Torsana area for some months, heard in late October, 1944, from Captain Holland, an S.O.E. officer, that an agent of I.S.9 was being sent to guide ex-prisoners through the lines. Williams decided to go, but his companion, Terry Philipsz, declined. The guide arrived a month later. He was an ex-*Alpino*, Sergeant Attilio Parma, who said he had crossed the lines eleven times. At the rendezvous were Captain H. D. Fleming, R.A.M.C., who had been in Fontanellato, and an American Air Force sergeant mechanic, William Russell. The party walked south for fourteen hours a day for three days. Williams said, 'This forced march with ill-fitting boots gave me such stiffness and blisters I hope never to have again.'

The enemy held outposts on a line of peaks above the Serchio valley, and the plan was to make for a gap between them. Hundreds of refugees and partisans, complete with women, children, mules and sheep, had already crossed in that area. At the bottom of the final hill they spent the last hours in a peasant's ramshackle hut, drinking *grappa* and meeting a red-bearded priest carrying a pistol at his waist. Apparently the house belonged to a black-marketeer who moved between occupied and liberated Italy, getting cigarettes from the Americans in exchange for eggs, and selling them north of the lines. The last climb was long and painful and only the *grappa* kept them going through snow and mist. Then they waited for daylight as Sergeant Parma thought it would be safer to approach the Allied positions in daylight. Soon after dawn they walked through woods to a house where the peasant owners gave them some coffee. Then on to a bridge over a stream guarded by Partisans, to whom Parma gave the password. So Williams and

Fleming reached Barga and the U.S. 92nd Negro Division on the 6th December, 1944. Terry Philipsz remained at Torsana until the Allied armies liberated the area.

The Fontanellato Plaque

The plaque shown on Plate 1 is on the gatepost of the old PG49. It reads:—

This plaque records the fortieth Anniversary of the imprisonment of English and Allied prisoners of war who were interned in Campo Concentramento PG 49. The people of Fontanellato who after the Armistice on the 8th September 1943, helped them and hid them at the risk of severe repercussions.
Fontanellato 11 September 1983.

The Buti Epilogue

by Anthony Laing

ON 21st December 1943 Jack Clarke and I went down to an apartment in Florence, the home of the Valvona Buti family. The mother Pam was British, born in England of Italian parents. Her Italian husband was imprisoned in England as an enemy alien. In spite of having owned a sizeable and respectable business in Manchester for many years, he was considered a danger to the country! Pam had a son of eighteen called Kim and a daughter Toy of about nine. The household included Antonia Pilser, an Austrian governess, and Erland Hindson, a South African gunner Captain. On the 4th January we were joined by Captain E. W. Mumford, 3 Gurkhas, also ex-Fontanellato.

Despite our treatment of her husband, Pam gallantly placed herself and her family at very considerable risk by sheltering Allied ex-prisoners. Between 24th September and 1st March 1944 she looked after four Americans, eight British, a South African and a British officer in the Indian Army.

After an abortive journey to Venice and Padova and return to Florence, Jack, Teddy and I finally left the Buti family on 21st February to try to reach Switzerland. Before leaving we warned Pam that it was now too dangerous for her to continue to conceal Allied prisoners. She had done enough already. But in full knowledge of the dangers, she took in two Americans and a British private soldier on 26th February.

On 1st March the Republican Secret Police raided the apartment. They left Toy in the care of Tonia and took Pam and Erland. As they were going down the stairs under guard this very brave lady turned and, to reassure her little daughter, said, 'Don't worry, Toy, I may not be back for supper tonight.'

Erland was handed over to the Germans and Pam was taken to the St. Verdiana prison for women. Kim was captured the next day and taken to Le Murate prison.

Tonia telephoned Toy's godfather in Bologna. He was a member of the *Partito d'Azione* and in touch with the partisans in his area. He advised that she should take Toy away from Florence immediately, as the Fascist Police were known to torture children in order to obtain information about their parents. He arranged for them to be received in a safe house in Merano in northern Italy and, after a while, near Como.

Meanwhile Pam was having a very uncomfortable time in prison in appalling conditions. As a British subject it was hoped she would not be put to death, but this was by no means certain. Also she had lost touch with her family and had no idea whether Kim was safe or not. Kim, in fact, was still in prison, but was now working under the Germans in a forced labour gang, mining the bridges and on fortifications of Florence.

One day the St. Verdiana prison was stormed by the partisans in order to release one of their agents, code named 'Tosca,' who told her rescuers of Pam Buti's plight and the reason for her imprisonment, saying 'Please take her too,' and they did. They kept her in a safe house.

The partisans brought Pam news of Kim. One morning when the gang were working, the German sentry barked out an order to which one of the Italian workers had failed to respond. The sentry had raised his rifle to shoot him, but Kim immediately interceded in fluent German, asking the sentry not to shoot the man who had not responded because he did not understand German. As a result of this Kim was appointed as interpreter to the group of gangs.

The partisans had discovered that one German was susceptible to bribery, and that for a certain sum he would be prepared to allow Kim to escape. Pam had absolutely no money, so she gave her wedding ring and gold watch and the partisans made up the difference. So Kim duly disappeared. He was brought to his mother, but it was some months before they were reunited with Antonia and Toy.

After the war the Allied Screening Commission, of which Lt.-Col. de Burgh was appointed Head, examined and reimbursed genuine claims from Italians who had helped Allied servicemen. A copy of Pam's claim form is attached, written by Toy at the time in an exercise book. Pam specifically stated that she did not seek recompense. Eventually she, Toy and Mario Nappini, who had supplied us with food, money and helped us in so many ways, were invited to a ceremony in Florence where Pam and Mario received rather unimpressive Alexander Certificates. A copy of Pam's is reproduced below. This was all our ungrateful Government gave them and many other deserving cases.

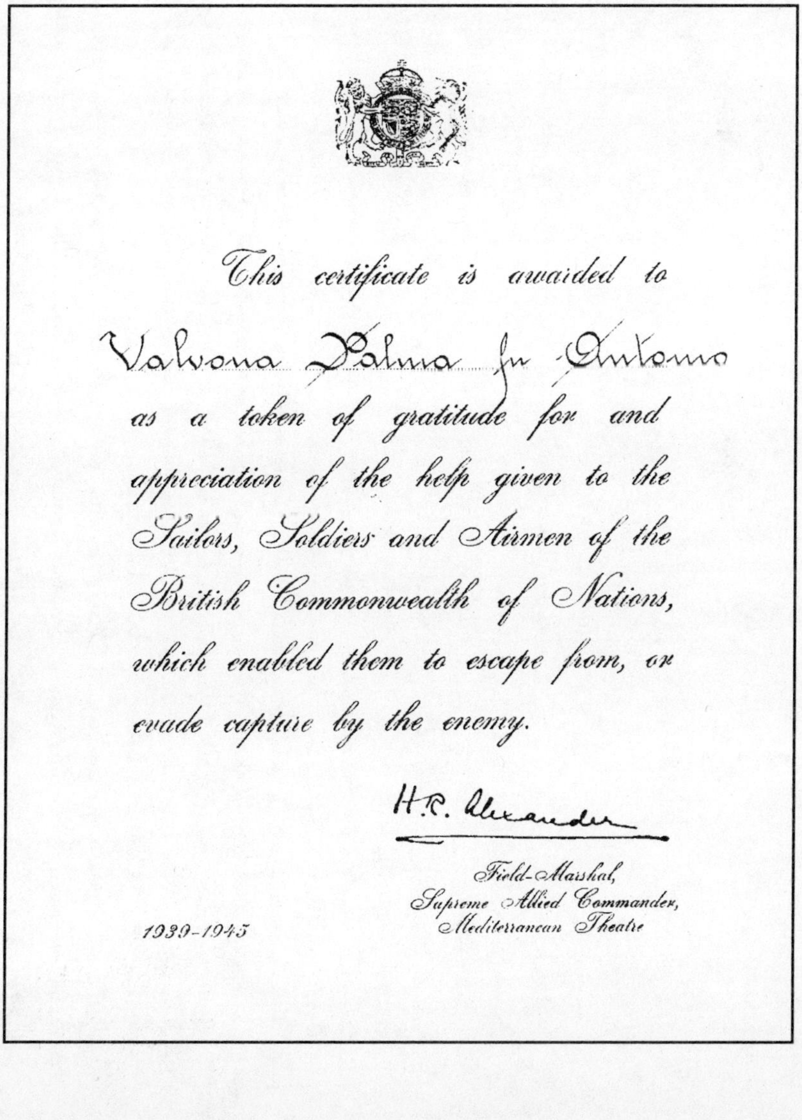

This certificate is awarded to

Valvona Palma fu Antonio

as a token of gratitude for and appreciation of the help given to the Sailors, Soldiers and Airmen of the British Commonwealth of Nations, which enabled them to escape from, or evade capture by the enemy.

H.R. Alexander

Field-Marshal,
Supreme Allied Commander,
Mediterranean Theatre

1939–1945

Allied screening commission (Italy) C.M.F.

(A)

1 Cognome del richiedente (stampatello) VALVONA Nome: Pamela Paternità: fu Anthony

Maritata in (dove applicabile) Buti. 3 Indirizzo del Richiedente (Stampatello) Comune FIRENZE Via o frazione 8 Via Ciro Menotti. Provincia Firenze. 4. Assistenza data nel Comune: Firenze-Fiesole. Via o frazione 8 Ciro Menotti - S. Brigida. Viale Alessandro Volta 10

(A)	NAZIONALITÀ	MATRICOLA	NOME	GRADO	Corpo o arma	cibo fornito DA	cibo fornito A	Alloggio fornito DA	Alloggio fornito A	Vestiario forn.	Denaro forn.	
I	American		John Askembeau	P.V.T.		24.9.43	25.9.43	24.9.43	25.9.43	//	//	I°
II	American		Daniel Leger	P.V.T.		24.9.43	25.9.43	24.9.43	25.9.43	//	//	II
III	British (English)		Harry Magnoland	P.V.T.	R. Signals.	15.10.43	22.10.43	15.10.43	22.10.43	Vest. Completo	£ 200 -	III
IV	British (South African)	1060.34	Erland Hindson	Capt.	S.A. Artillery	16.11.43	1.3.44	16.11.43	1.3.44	Vest. Completo	£ 300 -	IV
V	British (Scots)		Michael Mc Allister	P.V.T	R. Camerons Highland	16.11.43	20.11.43	16.11.43	20.11.43	Vest. Completo	£ 300 -	V
VI	British (English)	5508438	Eric Nethercoat	C.P.L		1.12.43	20.12.43	1.12.43	20.12.43	Vest. Completo	£ 200	VI
VII	British (English)		Stanley Ball	P.V.T	Goldstream Guards	1.12.43	20.12.43	1.12.43	20.12.43	Vest. Completo	£ 200	VII

(B) Siete stato il solo a provvedere il cibo durante il periodo dichiarato? (In caso contrario dichiarate in quale misura avete contribuito e i nomi di coloro) Fino al Natale 1943 ero sola; poi, Mario Nappini mi ha aiutato di nutrirli ed ha anche fornito loro del denaro.

(C) I prigionieri hanno vissuto in casa vostra (~~[illegible]~~) - Si - ma per due o tre giorni dovevano assentarsi da casa mia perchè venivano visite da me i quali non era prudente far sapere la presenza in casa mia dei prigionieri

(D) Avete ricevuto denaro o altro dai prigionieri o da altre fonti? (In caso affermativo precisate). No.

(E) Tutti i documenti e le lettere originali scritte dai prigionieri devono essere allegate a questo modulo. Precisate quali sono i documenti allegati: Lettere da taluni o dalle madri di loro.

(F) NOTE: Ero presa prigioniera il 1 Marzo 1944 con il Cap. Hindson. Il giorno dopo fu preso Eric Nethercoat. Stanley Ball ha raggiunto l'Inghilterra. Degli altri non abbiamo ricevuto altre notizie. Mio figlio fu fatto prigioniero il 2 marzo

Data 5-10-45 Firma del richiedente Pamela Buti *TESTIMONIO (cognome e nome stampatello) Antonia Pilser

Firma del testimonio: (NOME) Gianna Buti Indirizzo del testimonio Via Ciro Menotti 8. Occupazione del testimonio: Studentessa

*Il testimonio deve essere possibilmente il parroco o il sindaco.

Richiedente: Pamela Valvona Indirizzo Via Ciro Menotti 8: Comune: FIRENZE Paternità: fu Anthony

	NAZIONALITÀ	MATRICOLA	NOME	GRADO	Corpo o arma	Vitto fornito DA	Vitto fornito A	ALLOGGIO forn. DA	ALLOGGIO forn. A	Vestiario forn.	Danaro forn.	
I	British (English)	3909163	Reginald Robert	P.V.T.		1-12-43	20-12-43	1-12-43	20-12-43	Vesti Completo	£ 3.00	I
II	British (English)	129873	Anthony Laing	Lieutenant	R. E.	21-12-43	21-2-44	21-12-43	21-2-44	Vest. Incompleto	//	II
III	British (English)	66750	W.J.J. Clarke	Lieutenant	R.E.M.E	21-12-43	21-2-44	21-12-43	21-2-44	Vest. Incompleto	//	III
IV	British (Indian)	AI° 632	E.M. Mumford	Cap.	3rd Gurkha Rifle	4-1-44	21-2-44	4-1-44	21-2-44	Vest. Completo	//	IV
V	American	34397600	Kenneth Markham	C.P.L.	U.S. Rangers	26-2-44	1-3-44	//	//	Vest. Incompleto	//	V
VI	American	3126245	Arthur Lyons	P.V.T.	U.S. Rangers	26-2-44	1-3-44	//	//	Vest. Incompleto	//	VI
VII	British (English)	55-12495	Kenneth Woods	P.V.T.		26-2-44	1-3-44	//	//	Vest. Incompleto	//	VII

NOTE: Reginald Robert Kenneth Markham, Arthur Lyons, Kenneth Woods furono catturati dai fascisti in Viale Alessandro Volta 90 il 2 Marzo 1944. Laing, Mumford e Clarke hanno raggiunto la Svizzera e di là sono andati in Inghilterra

Some People of the Fontanellato Area

For this I am indebted to the writings of Professor Marco Mainardi in his book *L'orizzonte del Campo.*

DR. GUISEPPE Sambataro, who was the town's doctor, an anti-fascist and a member of the underground movement, wrote, 'It [the help given to the prisoners of Campo PG49] was the generous and enthusiastic gesture of a village which Fascist propaganda had not succeeded in winning over to the German ideal. It did not make the Italians hate the English.' The country had never wanted the 'German war,' and this feeling showed itself as a demonstration of affection and a wish to help the Allied officers.

After two days in the dried-up bed of the *Torrente Rovacchia*, the large group of prisoners began to break up into small parties. Paulo Scerni was the first to invite and house fourteen prisoners. His example was quickly followed by neighbours in a widening circle. The people of nearby Soragna, San Secondo and Fonterino were soon involved. Most Italians knew where the prisoners were. But no one betrayed them. The only exception were a few pro-German Fascists who passed on information to the Germans. This exacted exemplary punishment on those who were assisting the prisoners.

Ermes Arduini recounted, 'I went down with my mother to the Rovacchia. The prisoners had escaped without a thing, and we took them some things, some of which we had found in the Orphanage.'

Feeding the large number of escapers soon became a problem. The bakers Incerti and Maccagnoni baked seven hundred loaves for distribution in the area. The dairy farmer Riccardo Abrati, at Dr. Sambataro's request, gave the prisoners two hundred kilos of milk.

Bruno Gotti looked after an Englishman and an American. They hid in the fields by day and ate in the house in the evenings. Sometimes they tried to help with farm work, but were obviously unused to manual work. Gotti also helped an English prisoner with brown hair, and two older officers who were later recaptured in a German search.

At Torchio, a hamlet between Fontevivo and Castelguelfo, there was a midwife who housed an Englishman for some time. This man could speak no more than a few words of Italian. One day the Germans arrived and placed a machine gun covering the house. The midwife said, 'Be careful, the Germans are here,' and then, feeling ill, retired to bed. When there was a knock at the door, the Englishman opened it and said, '*Avanti accomodateri* (make yourselves at home).' The Germans searched everywhere and found nothing. The English prisoner then went up into the hills.

The Germans raided all the houses near the Rovacchia, and there were many arrests. On 15th September the Germans returned to Fontanellato, searched the convent, the garden of Gandini where some prisoners had lived in the garden shed, and houses near the castle.

Renata Avanzini was asked by two prisoners if she could dye their uniforms. After some difficulty she found some dye and dyed the uniforms black. The prisoners said, 'Now we are real Fascists.'

Reno Casalini, who had housed several prisoners, told how his father arranged with a naval officer for a party to travel to La Spezia in the hope of finding a boat. They were driven to Parma by Snr. Arduini whence they went by train to La Spezia. But no boat could be found, so they returned to Casalini's house. On 23rd November the Germans arrested Casalini's father Cornelio, and took him to the *Cittadella* in Parma. In spite of severe interrogation and beatings, he never said a word. The Germans were then disposed to release him, but the Italian court refused and he was transferred to Castelfranco Emilia. He was later put on a list to be shot as a reprisal. Fortunately this was not carried out. His wife was also arrested and imprisoned. They did not regain their freedom till October 1944.

After the first euphoria and hope of the arrival of the Allied armies, the Germans exerted an ever-tightening grip on the area. It was only natural that morale suffered, and the people were less inclined to help the prisoners. Many of the latter left the area either making for Switzerland or south into the mountains.

As well as the spontaneous help given to prisoners by many individuals in the Fontanellato area, the Parmesan Resistance, part of the All Italia Committee of National Liberation, became increasingly active. The aims of the N.L.C. were to gather arms and to protect those who had got out of prison camps from the danger of recapture by the Germans. In the first instance the need to find secure hiding places led to the creation of *case di lalitanza* (escapers' houses). This brought open support for the Resistance.

The valleys of the rivers Stirone, Ceno and Taro held many inhabitants who had spent some years in Great Britain. Therefore many ex-prisoners gravitated to these valleys.

Men of the Parmesan N.L.C. made early contact with Snr. Skof (Wanda Newby's father) and Dr. Sambataro, both strong anti-fascists. Both were arrested in October 1943. Skof managed to be freed, while the doctor feigned appendicitis and was taken to hospital, from whence he escaped to the mountains to join partisan groups.

The Salsa group of the Parmesan N.L.C. organised and assisted several prisoners to move from the plain to the Bardi area. German motorised units were moving round the Pellegrino—Salsa district, but the Italian guides ensured a safe passage for the prisoners. One of the first to shelter English soldiers was Francesco Berni, the prefectural commissar. Several officers spoke highly of his efforts. In due course the partisans became very active in the area and actually established a 'free zone' in June and July 1944. They always kept in close touch with the many Allied ex-prisoners. The Assistance Committee organised the issue of ration cards and helped the escapers to buy goods in the shops. In Fornovo Taro, Lazzaro Bazzoni from Mariano di Pellegrino (later to be shot with his wife in Milan in March 1945) established contact with the N.L.C., and organised supplies of food and clothing, and even went on an errand to Fontanellato to collect some officers' belongings. This help continued until the end of March 1944. Five officers from PG49, among several others, were R. N. Brooke, John Burman, H. D. Holworthy, John Taylor and Jack Younger. In March Bazzoni received information that the Fascist police were going to raid the Mariano district, and the Englishmen had to leave, some to the south and at least two to Switzerland, being guided by Bazzoni on to a train under the noses of the Germans.

There was one shocking case which reflected extremely badly on an English prisoner. One officer, moving round the countryside near Fontanellato, took it upon himself to make enquiries about German movements, and was well informed on the whereabouts of Allied prisoners and the Italians who were sheltering them. In due course he was arrested. Quite contrary to orders, this officer kept a diary in which were the names and addresses of Italians who were helping British prisoners. He had stayed with the Baruffini family for about three weeks and again later on. Then he was some time in Parma. In this diary were the names of Andrea Baruffini, Alice Belmore di Cannetolo, Volumnia Ugolotti, Alberto Guerino, Dr. Ravazzoni from Parma, Maria Oppici of Pieve di Cusignano, Paride Tonella and Lino Maiardi.

As a result of the discovery of the diary, Baruffini, Volumnia Ugolotti a nurse attached to Dr. Ravazzoni's surgery and the doctor himself were arrested. A search of Ugolotti's house revealed several diaries kept by the British officer. In his interrogation Dr. Ravazzoni confessed to having helped the officer and having taken him to his nurse's house. The following night Dr. Ravazzoni took his own life, leaving a letter denouncing many people who had helped prisoners and 'rebel elements.'

Andrea Baruffini's house was surrounded by Fascist militiamen, and he was taken to Francesco prison in Parma. While he was there, the prison was bombed and he could have escaped. But he refused, being frightened the Fascists would take his children. His daughter was already in prison. From Parma he was taken to Fossoli, and later to Bolzano, reaching Mauthausen concentration camp on 5 July. He died there on 11 April 1945.

Smugglers' Way

A Story of our escape over the Monte Rosa

by Lieut.-ColonelH.G. De Burgh, D.S.O., O.B.E., M.C.

WHEN all the Fontanellato prisoners had dispersed from the Bund, Colonel Dick Wheeler and Captain Reggie Phillips, my two staff officers, and I began our own bid for freedom. Our plan at that time was to try to get to Genoa and thence by boat, possibly a neutral vessel, to Corsica or some other place in Allied hands. But when one is escaping, plans do not work out quite as expected. We were taken to Fidenza by Dr. Guiseppe Sambataro, then to Milan by Gaudini Remo, and subsequently were conveyed up to the valley of Aosta by Captain Camino. From here many other deep and narrow valleys ran up to the Swiss Alps. We did not want to go to Switzerland, where we thought we should be interned for the rest of the war. But by now Germans and Fascists were searching for escaped prisoners and all movement in north Italy was being watched, so we were gradually forced up one of these valleys towards the mountains. We began to fear that a party of three was too conspicuous, so Dick Wheeler went off on his own. He eventually succeeded in negotiating one of the passes alone and arrived in Switzerland.

Reggie and I rested for a while to ease my foot, in which I had an old wound; also, having been in hospital for six months, I was not particularly fit. We then began our long walk to a village at the end of the valley, which we had been told was a winter sports resort of Italians in peace-time. We thought we should be able to hide in this lonely valley and eventually join a guerrilla band. It was a glorious day and the country was quite beautiful and untouched by any suggestion of war. There were thick woods everywhere, and the road wound up the hillside, on which grew a profusion of mosses, ferns and little coloured flowers. At intervals clear cold water cascaded down the rocks and across or under the road. It was all so peaceful and so beautiful that one had to remind oneself that one was an escaped prisoner-of-war and that either death or another prison was waiting round any corner. One thing very important in escaping is to be inconspicuous.

Our clothes were all right, but it was not always possible to wash and shave. I carried a razor, soap and brush in my waistcoat pockets, and in odd streams in the mountains we made our toilet so as to look as local as possible. We developed very sore feet, owing to the town shoes we wore. The shoes themselves were becoming conspicuous in a part of the world where everyone wears mountain boots. So we kept to the fields and along the river-bank, where we could take off the offending shoes and dip our aching feet into the icy snow water.

Here by the river we ate what food we had to the incessant accompaniment of the cow-bells. These I hated; I wanted the silence after the noises and worries of war, prison camps, and escapes. However, one got used to them, as to everything else, in time.

The mountains were closing in on both sides to a point where the sun shone brightly on the snows. I said to Reggie 'Thank God! The valley ends. We stop in that village.' [This was probably Frachey, in the Val d'Ayas.]

'Thank God, too, from me,' said Reggie. 'If I don't stop, my feet will; they are just burning. How is your leg?' 'Bloody, but unbowed,' I said, as we walked on. A village lay ahead of us. It was quite lovely. Red roofs, timbered houses, and up the mountain-sides gay chalets dotted here and there in emerald-green open spaces in the pine woods.

Farther up were a few more chalets showing dark against the snow. As we entered the main street we saw by a bridge Alpini troops in their grey uniforms with yellow facings, their small felt hats with feathers stuck in them. They were examining all civilians. 'Reggie,' I whispered out of the corner of my mouth, 'This looks like the end.'

'Hell!' said Reggie. 'Go on as if we owned the damned place,' and we did, hardly glancing at them. And got away with it.

Frightened by this episode, we walked on past several small hotels, until well out the other side of the place. There was one building ahead with a large notice, 'Hotel Breithorn'; another, a sort of chalet, stood across the road. 'I stop here,' I said, 'whatever happens.' Reggie said nothing.

I went up the steps of the hotel and found the office. A woman jumped up nervously, and before she could speak I asked if she knew French. She did. I said, 'I want two rooms.' She said I could have one, with two beds, in the chalet. I agreed, and we were taken across by an old fierce-looking maid. We ordered a bottle of red wine, drank it, and fell into bed, having ordered some dinner to be sent over later.

I could not sleep. I don't think I ever slept much on the whole trip. I was too tired physically and mentally. Not only was escaping a strain, but there had been the responsibility over a period of weeks for the preparation of plans to prevent several hundred British officers from being taken to Germany; the final mass escape and organisation of food, clothes, and concealment till all could get away in various parties.

All this had now produced a sort of numb mentality, so that I lay half unconscious and woke unrested. Reggie slept and slept. Next morning at about seven-thirty coffee and rolls were brought to us. We got up and went out. It was beautiful. A forest of pines and other trees grew up both sides of the narrow valley; down the middle wound a fast-running river about twenty yards across in places, but narrowing and widening at times. In some places it was fairly smooth and shallow, but with deep pools; at others a rushing torrent over rocks.

By climbing a little way up the eastern side we could see away to the Matterhorn, or Monte Cervino as it is called locally, and nearer at the end of the valley the Breithorn. They were shining white with snow; except for the top of the Matterhorn, which looked like a great jagged black tooth. One more village lay beyond the pine woods, tucked into the sharp angle where the valley ended. A track led up to one of the passes into Switzerland.

That evening the proprietor of the hotel and his wife came to see us. They told us that they had thought we were French, but now realised we were English. They were very frightened and said we must go away as the Fascists were up looking for escaped prisoners. I said we would not go unless they produced guides to take us over the mountains. They said we could not pass over now as it was too late in the year. The weather would be bad and the snow deep and soft. I said in that case we must stay and that anyway I didn't really want to go over at all. They left us, saying they would find guides.

We stayed in our room, but when local people began to visit us we found that everyone knew that two English officers were there in the village. The ladies brought us woollies, thinking we were going over the Alps. The woollies belonged to their fifteen-year-old daughters and so were not very adequate. Reggie was presented with a small piece of fur, either cat- or goat-skin. I never discussed where he wore it.

Apart from these 'comforts,' we were dressed in light summer suits, silk shirts, socks and shoes, and had no other garments of any kind.

We waited in vain to meet guides which the hotel-keeper had promised, and eventually we met a 'beautiful' young Italian officer who spoke English. He had the best 'pansy' winter sports kit on, and his fair curls were arranged tastefully under and around a white cloth cap. We christened him 'Blondy' at once. He told us that he was escaping too; we asked 'what from,' but this appeared tactless and we got no answer.

During the course of conversation he said he was in touch with two brothers who might take us over if we wanted to go. We told him we were not thinking of going to Switzerland. We didn't trust him anyway. Later that evening an Italian lady came and told us that a party of Australians were in a deserted house farther up the valley. We went to see them, and later managed to get an Italian Alpini soldier to guide them to the main pass, where he said they, being ordinary soldiers in uniform, would not be stopped. These Australians told us that more were on the way up, so we decided to see them over before doing any more about our own future. The last party to arrive told us that they had heard on the wireless that prisoners were to go to Switzerland, from where they would be repatriated.

This decided us, and I sent Reggie to contact 'Blondy'; for we were told that as civilians or officers we should not get through the guards in the place where the soldiers went. 'Blondy' came, accompanied by two Italians. He said they were willing to take us, but it was a long and dangerous journey, and they looked with contempt at us and asked where our kit was. We told them. They laughed. After much weary argument and trouble we got some ancient mountain boots.

Then we were ready to go. After many false starts, owing to bad weather, we started at two o'clock one morning. Just before we began the climb, 'Blondy' informed us that the other two were smugglers and must be paid. We had a little money and agreed, but the nature of our guides' calling did not give us much confidence in our safety and I was quite expecting to be 'done in' at any convenient place. Through the dark pine woods, aided by sticks, we panted up a narrow path at times almost perpendicular. Three thousand feet we went that night. We arrived at a farm in an exhausted state. A drink of hot stinking milk revived us and we slept in the cowshed with the cows. It was warm.

The following night we started off again, sore and stiff now; it was painful. Another farm, and here the farmer had been in Australia for many years. We stayed for two days, wandering about the mountain waiting for the clouds to lift, and trying by gentle exercise to get aching muscles fit for the journey again. Each night we hoped to start, but it was not until the third that the Italians got out their ice-axes, ropes, and crampons to go. It was cold and clear; up we went above the forest-line over bare rocky ground in misty moonlight.

At about three in the morning we halted by a small lake which shone like a burnished shield of black metal. We had a mouthful of brandy and struggled on again. Now we were under the frowning brow of a great massif, on top of which were frontier posts. We had to move silently and were unable to use our steel-shod sticks to help us on the steep sloping hillside. The path had disappeared and we began to cross the many moraines in which every stone and rock was flat and edge up. The painful struggle over these was accompanied by slips between them, when feet and ankles were wrenched and bruised agonisingly.

We were getting into snow; there was ice on the rocks and the wind was bitter. The way here was one great mass of stone and rock tumbled as if by an explosion, and we climbed or scrambled on the slippery ice, tearing hands and knees. Most of the nails were gone from my ancient boots and they leaked. Dawn was breaking. We halted again to eat. I had nothing. 'Blondy' gave us some bread, and Reggie had a tin of sardines. We never managed to get the smugglers to produce food for us, and they always seemed surprised when we took theirs; however, they never refused to give some.

It was too cold to sit long, exhausted though we were, and we could find no shelter from the Arctic wind. As we went on the tumbled rocks disappeared more and more into snow, until we were knee-deep in it. I was desperately thirsty and sucked icicles, which 'burnt' my mouth so that I was unable to eat. On the top of a high peak we halted again, and in spite of utter weariness we were astonished at the sight around us. Below, a few hundred feet, was a sea of billowing, pure-white cloud. Out of it great jagged black islands of rock, like giants' teeth, stood up towards the sky. On the east the whole was tinged with a lovely pink darkening to red near the rising sun.

We gazed in silence for some time, refusing to listen to the Italians when they wanted to push on. It was a sight few people had ever seen. We were out of the world. I felt we were part of the heavens, and a curious detached feeling came over me that little men crawled about below but were like ants, not part of my life. Then the Italians began to jabber, and I said to Reggie, 'I'll never pay any attention to my mountain-climbing friends again. I don't believe they've even dreamed of this, much less seen it in their little expeditions. Do you realise that we've seen the dawn from the top of Monte Rosa in summer suits?' 'No one will believe it,' said Reggie. 'I probably shan't believe it myself, if we ever do get down to the world again.'

We turned to resume our trudging through the snow, and I soon forgot the glory I had seen in my concentration on putting my feet into the steps of the man in front. This made the going easier, as he had stamped the snow down, and my feet did not sink softly at each step.

By now the backs of my legs and thighs were almost giving out. They were a compound of pain, a chill aching pain, and my foot and twice-broken ankle were on fire. Even the guides were weary and silent now, and 'Blondy' was failing badly. Later he fell with a loud cry; I didn't even look round. He made a great fuss. As we went on I said to Reggie, 'Is he badly cut?' 'Good Lord, no; he's spoilt his beautiful trousers, that's all.'

I had forgotten how wonderfully he was got up in his winter sports outfit.

The snow was getting deeper, so we all walked or plodded in the footsteps of the leader. The going was difficult and much of it dangerous. Often we were on an almost perpendicular wall of snow, leaning on our sticks, which we thrust in above us, and stamping a foothold for each foot in turn. To lose balance, or a false step, might precipitate us all down a slide of a thousand feet or more, with a final dive into space and a crash on rocks below.

On we struggled, up, always up, and the white glare on the snow just under my nose made my eyes ache. Sometimes I said 'Stop!' and for a few breaths we halted; once or twice Reggie said it. But mostly we plodded on praying; at least I did. I prayed all the time, 'God give my knees strength to go ten yards more,' and each time I looked up the top was farther off. I don't think I was conscious all the time. I remember looking at Reggie's drawn yellow face and thinking he wasn't.

At last we rounded a turn at the top of a small glacier and two hundred yards away was a hut. It was one of those used by Alpine clubs for expeditions. It had been broken into. The entrance was heaped with snow, and we had to dig our way into the living-room. There were piles of wet and sodden blankets. The small kitchen, however, was shut and dry. There was some wood, and soon a fire was going in the stove. The Italians got a bucket of snow, melted it, and put sugar in. We all had a hot drink. I got my boots off, and, rolling myself in the blankets, tried to rest.

I only lay aching; whichever way I turned was pain. And then I began to shiver. I shall never forget that shivering; the agony of it was worse than being wounded. Reggie slept till he got cold. Then we both shouldered the Italians away and sat right over the stove. Through the window the sun was bright and everything clear, so clear that we could look down upon the valley we had left. Reggie said—'If I had a glider I would go down and never climb again.' I felt I'd like to sit down and slide away on that smooth white surface rather than move again. But we had to move one way or other now.

After an hour we set off again, this time up a long glacier with some horribly sinister-looking black cracks in it, towards the pass twelve thousand six hundred feet high over which we must go to Switzerland. It does not sound much to climb from ten thousand five hundred to twelve thousand six hundred feet over snow and ice, sometimes going up, sometimes going down; it was to be a dreadful journey.

Our first attempt was a failure. As we reached the top of the glacier the sky darkened, snow began to fall, and the wind, that ice-cold wind, to drive through us. We were roped now. The Italians put on blue goggles, scarves and gloves. We had no goggles or coverings for heads or hands. Our thin clothes were no protection. The storm became a blizzard; my hands went black. I was so cold that I didn't feel cold. Soon we could hardly see twenty yards and at last, on a slope so steep and frozen that we had great difficulty in remaining on it at all, we realised that we were lost.

Like all Italians, the three began to shout and argue. Then we stood or rather leaned against the ice, hardly daring to move. At last I ordered them to go back. I was angry, but I dared not lose my temper in case I slipped down the precipice. I hardly dared turn round. At last we were back on the glacier, but now we could see nothing, for the driving snow blinded us At first we followed our footsteps, made coming up. They gave out, and only the little holes our sticks had made, which had not filled with snow yet, enabled us to find our way back to the cabin. I often afterwards wondered at which period we were nearest death, but I never got it worked out.

The agony of our thawing out is a thing neither of us will ever forget. I think our brains must have remained frozen or else fear would have prevented us from ever doing the last part of our journey three days later.

The Italians now said it was useless to go on, the weather would last for days. We said we would not go back. The guides said it was madness, that the last date for crossing was the 15th of September in ordinary times, and now it was the 25th. We sat silent and let them shout.

Then at last they said they would go back for food, and that when they returned, if the weather was not suitable, we must go back. I agreed, and off they all went, leaving us a small loaf, some cheese, and some sugar. 'Blondy' was like a girl going to a ball; he brought out the most wonderful kit from his rucksack, arranged his curls under his white cap, and that was the last we saw of him as his scarlet wind-jacket disappeared down the snow.

We were now left alone. We stoked the fire, and, wood being scarce, held a conclave on the order in which we should burn parts of the hut to keep warm. The lavatory door went first. Two days we stayed listening to the howling wind and watching the snow, and wondering if our rocking cabin would blow away. We had no light other than the stove, and we hadn't, or wouldn't have, enough wood to keep it burning all the time. I don't think we talked much. I was too tired to sit up and too cold to lie down; and what agony that shivering was! The ice-cold chill of the wet blankets was terrible, so we sat at the stove till we could sit no longer, then lay down while the warmth lasted to try to sleep. We didn't talk, but sometimes we discussed how easy it would be for the smugglers to leave us or finish us off.

The third day dawned brighter; the wind had dropped and the snow seemed to be stopping. We had nothing left to eat and very little sugar for the hot water. We both thought, but neither mentioned it, of what would happen if the guides did not come back.

At about mid-day the sun was bright and there was no wind or snow. I suddenly had a craving for a pipe. Neither of us had anything to smoke. Matches were few and we began to fear to let the fire out in spite of shortage of wood. We shaved and washed and walked about in the sun, getting warm for the first time for ages. We got quite angry if we thought one or other was neglecting the fire, or neglecting to watch down the mountain for the Italians. But especially we got angry if we thought the other was holding the door open too long when passing through, thus letting any warm air out.

At about four o'clock the Italians came back—without 'Blondy.' They laughed contemptuously and said he was in bed. They brought us no food as they said we must go back, that it was now impossible to go farther. Sadly Reggie and I agreed to abandon the trip. So on the 27th of September we started back to Italy again. It was all clear and beautiful and I felt we should be going the other way. I said so to Reggie. He agreed, and we stopped. Reggie told the Italians we refused to go down. After much argument we got them back to the hut for one more night. It was too late to start now, as the trip was dangerous, and we must have daylight and enough for them to get back. They dare not risk being taken by either Italian or Swiss guards.

We settled down again for the night, it having been decided that unless there should be a clear sky and stars it would be impossible to go on. I did not sleep. All night I watched the window. If I ever prayed in my life I prayed for a star that night. So did Reggie, though I didn't know it then.

It must have been about 4 a.m. that something shone on the glass. I couldn't believe it, then I saw it was not on the glass and it was 'A STAR.' I leaped at the recumbent Italians and kicked them up. Until daylight we watched that star. I never took my eyes off it. And at daylight, under a clear shining blue sky, we started up the glacier once more.

We went up the same way as we had on the first occasion, crossing the sinister crevasses by the same snow bridges. The greenish ice-walls shone brighter in the sunlight. The leader felt his way continually with his ice-axe, stamping on the 'bridges' to test the bearing power of the snow, and 'packing' it down with each foot when he found it held. Occasionally one leg would go through and we hung back ready to take the strain on the rope if he went down. At last we were past the place where we got lost in the blizzard; on the other side the snow was soft and deep and we were in it to our knees, a very tiring progress being made.

I tried to walk in the footprints of the man in front, but it is not easy to adjust one's paces like that. I kept thinking of Kipling and everything gone but the will to hold on. I had not thought of the meaning of those things before, or if I had, there had been no understanding of it.

We were climbing all the time, so steep a slope that one was almost leaning against it and fearing all the time that one might start an avalanche. We had heard the rumble of one or two far below us. We came to a knife-edge stretching away and up in front of us, rising five hundred feet or more. On the right nothing, black rocks a thousand feet below; on the left a slope of shining white snow almost perpendicular. I stared fascinated at the edge so narrow that it looked impossible. But on we went, and I know my tired brain could not register enough fear or I should never have been able to go another step. On this hair-raising climb one false step by one of us would probably have meant dragging the whole party down to death. Castor and Pollux, two great twin heights, were behind us and the Lyskamm lay ahead and above. As we mounted over eleven thousand feet I began to feel slightly sick, and now I had to call frequent halts;

not only was my leg hardly alive, but my heart was giving some trouble. One of the smugglers kept turning to ask me if I was all right. He was anxious; for if anything went wrong with one of the party it meant an almost superhuman task by the others to get the sick one along, whether forward or back.

Somehow I kept going, but the short halts were now every few yards. At long last, dazed, I reached the summit of that climb. I sat down; almost in a stupor I heard someone saying *'Svizerra.'* He might have said China for all I cared. The Italians produced a bottle; it had a little liquid in it. I gazed at it listlessly, but Reggie grabbed it from them and handed it to me. I took a mouthful. It burnt horribly all my mouth and throat and all the way down, but the pain of that pulled me together. The alcoholic effect was nil. Reggie drank and gave the bottle back to the guides.

There was hardly any snow on this side for some distance and we were going down. The relief to my legs was indescribable, but it didn't last long; the pain transferred itself to tired knees, and after a time I began to long for a climb again, when there was no jerking and jarring of downward progress.

We were on a well-defined path leading towards the valleys, and, beginning to take an interest, I saw the Gornergrat and the entrance to the valley down which lay Zermatt—Switzerland! The realisation came now, suddenly—we were in Switzerland.

As we descended we came to more snow. We had come out from a sheltered cup, and suddenly I looked hard at what lay between us and that pleasant valley. We were on a great glacier. Now the rope, which we had discarded above, was put on again, and crampons and ice-axes were once more ready for use by the guides. We, of course, had our walking sticks only.

The glacier was known as the 'Grenz,' and, as we afterwards heard, as the 'Man-eater.' Once again we trod the lovely white virgin snow, threading our way round the black yawning crevasses or crossing the snow bridges over great chasms of green ice and dark depths. I looked fearfully down into some, wondering how far down one could fall if the treacherous white wig of snow with hanging icicles, like ringlets, which overhung the green walls, should give way under us.

Soon we appeared to be so close to the black rocky river valley beyond which lay Gornergrat that I felt the end of the journey had come. In fact it was nearly our own end which we were meeting.

We halted and looked across. The Italians pointed to a path on the hill beyond the dry valley—the path to Zermatt. They showed us that we must go up to the right to the foot of a black mass of rock, the right bank of the glacier, and down this we were to climb into the valley. They were anxious to go back. They had to use the daylight, and also they were afraid of being captured by the Swiss patrols. We said a grateful farewell and paid them what we had. They had come much farther into Switzerland than we had bargained for, and so we unroped and off they went.

Reggie and I stood a moment watching them negotiate a particularly dreadful ice-wall which we had crossed by cutting steps for hands and feet. Then we turned and started on the last lap, walking blithely across the snow. Then I went through—I flung out my arms and by the grace of God they held, but my legs and body were dangling in nothing. Reggie came behind me; I told him to go away or we'd both go, but he heaved me out—I don't know how.

I got to my feet, and without looking at the hole turned and went on. Suddenly in a clear patch of smooth unwrinkled snow I went down again. This time I had a dream as the snow dropped from under me. As I fell I threw myself back clutching, but the snow came with me and down I went. My thoughts were numb and detached, but I remember wondering whether icicles grew upside down and if I should be impaled.

Then I crashed; I knew no more for seconds, it must have been. The snow had broken my fall, but I had not got away scot-free. My left arm was injured. I was more anxious than frightened now. It was gloomy but not dark, and a trickle of water ran below me and under the ice. Far above was daylight and sun and silence. The walls about me graded from black to dark green as the ice rose towards the light.

I thanked God it was early morning and the light would last. Probably longer than my life. It was cold with a dead cold and my body seemed to steam. The steam froze and formed a thin coating of ice all over me. I got up and moved along the narrow passage of the crevasse; as I moved I stumbled over a long block of ice. I looked down. In a thin casing of frozen glass lay a man. I could see his shadowy form and his face; his eyes were shut; he was grinning. It did not impress me much; I wondered who he was and passed on. There were two more, One I saw very clearly, young and fair-haired, in what appeared to be an Italian uniform.

He was looking at me; his eyes were open and he smiled. I liked him. I felt he was glad to see me. I sat down on his—his what?—his robe of ice and, nursing my broken arm, began to talk to him. But suddenly I found that I, too, was gradually becoming robed in ice. I got up, and, working arms and legs, broke it off. As it cracked away my body steamed and I felt icy-cold, which I had not done when in the ice. I thought 'These three are warm enough,' and then I pulled myself together and said 'Live, you must live; fight, damn you—fight' and I fought. I fought against drowsiness. I fought against the silence and the gloom of the ice-walls. I fought against the desire to join my friends in their ice happiness, their freedom from worries and misery.

I fought—why? But I did; and doing so kept myself warm. No—not warm—alive. Then I sat down at the feet of my friend the Italian and talked to him. He had some medals. One leg was broken; it was twisted under him so that, unless you looked closely, he appeared to have only one leg. He had a great bruise over one eye, and his hands were black. I looked at mine; they were black too. I wondered why. And then I found the coating of ice on me again. Now I panicked; I stood up and shouted. Then I stopped in horror; the shouting came back dead at me. Dead from those horrible translucent walls of solid ice. I thought 'Now I must die—all responsibility is over—all I have to do is sit down with my friends here and be happy.'

'No, no,' I shouted. 'I won't give in; I will fight as I have fought all my life. I—will—fight!'

The cold dead mist, made by the sun on ice and snow, began to sink down upon me. The light above was fading. I could not see my friend in his ice any more. I was ceasing to feel the cold. Almost I had died when—crack!—down came a load of snow and ice. I was quite angry, I was being disturbed! I tried to turn to my friend and found I could not move. I was frozen to his pall—to his tomb. I had sat so long I was frozen there and I didn't care.

Someone was making a noise. I felt angry. I moved, and my ice clothing cracked away. I thought that one of the other bodies had got up. No—it was someone else. He said—'Move, move, or you will die!'

I laughed, and my ice cracked—it was quite thin still. That was all I remembered for a long time.

I became fully conscious again on the snow with the burning of brandy in my mouth and throat. Reggie and the Italians were standing by me. I sat up. I stood up rather bewildered. Reggie said, 'Feeling better? I shouted and got the guides back. Thank God they have come; we can't get on alone.' We were roped up again and on we went.

When they had left us they had said we'd be down in half an hour. It took them four hours to find a way down. I have been afraid in my life, but never so afraid as I was during that journey down the 'Grenz.' Now we came to where the glacier broke as it curved into the valley. We zigzagged round and over a horrible network of crevasses, jumping many great cracks, not knowing if the snow would hold as we landed, sometimes on ridges of ice so narrow that only perfect balance prevented one from pitching over into the next fissure. Many times we thought we should never get over the great gaping chasms, and sometimes it was only by cutting steps in the walls of ice for hands and feet that one by one we slid dizzily along from one side to the other, never daring to look down.

At last we were actually at the bottom. But still I could not free myself of fear and went slowly, after the Italians had again left us, prodding with my stick. I saw Reggie striding on and pulled myself together and joined him.

We were soon picked up by a Swiss patrol. I didn't know whether they were Germans, and I didn't care. They gave us all their rations and sent for a thermos of hot tea to meet us later. We got to Zermatt on the 29th of September and took a room with a bath. That bath got overworked that night, and we rested. I didn't sleep properly for many days. I was too exhausted. In my half-waking hours I wondered whether it was all real or only a dreadful nightmare.

From Zermatt we went to Visp, or Viege, where we were put in a Hospice just outside the town. We interested ourselves in the soldiers of our own army and Dominions who drifted over other passes and were collected at Visp, to be fed, rested, and to some extent clothed. It was October; all had been very lightly clad and were now, for the most part, in rags. Many of the men came over with almost bare feet, bleeding and frost-bitten. Some had not come at all; the gaping crevasses had claimed them; surprisingly few in view of the complete lack of food, clothing and mountain equipment.

Before leaving Visp I called to thank the Swiss officers for their kindness to us all. One of them said—'Why not? If it had not been for the Battle of Britain in 1940 there would be no Switzerland.'

From Blackwood's Magazine *No. 1561, November 1945, Vol.258.*

On leaving a Train outside a Station

by Anthony Laing.

THE GERMAN guards herded us out of the trucks and across the rails of Frosinone Goods Yard and we stumbled towards the train. It cannot have been easy for Hugh Fane Hervey, for he had down one of his trouser legs an axe which had luckily been left unattended by a stove in the Transit Camp. A small group of us surrounded him as we approached the train which was composed, except for the front and rear vans, of long box wagons totally enclosed such as are seen in First World War photographs bearing the inscription *'8 Chevaux 40 Hommes.'* The two small wagons at either end of the train had windows and little raised roofs with glazed observation panels all round. These were obviously the guards' vans and reduced the possibility of escaping through the roof.

We clambered aboard the last van, next to the rear guard's van, to discover from the plentiful floor-covering that the last inhabitants had definitely not been *hommes.* As Frosinone was a railhead, we thought that the cattle had probably been pillaged by the Germans in northern Italy and brought south to feed their troops. In the centre of each side there was a pair of heavy sliding steel doors which were padlocked on the outside. On either side of the doors at high level there were long open ventilating slots about nine or ten inches high secured with vertical steel bars and an infill of barbed wire, otherwise we were totally enclosed by solid hardwood planking two inches thick. In the centre a cut-down oil drum had been thoughtfully placed for us to relieve ourselves.

We made our way to the left hand forward corner of the wagon, away from the guard's van, while the Germans continued to press more and more in until I am sure that we were many more than forty *hommes.* Hugh hid the axe within our floor-covering, which was just as well because, shortly after, the wagon was searched without anything being found, even though the guards had a couple of Alsatian dogs. The doors were slammed shut and padlocked. The ventilating slots did not admit much light and we tried to sort ourselves out in semi-darkness.

We had already drawn lots. Hugh was naturally to be the first to jump followed by his R.A.F. friend Garrad Cole, with Jack Clarke third, me fourth, Don MacAuley fifth, and so on. When the train got under way Hugh started to cut a hole in the front end of the wagon about two feet in from the corner and about a foot above the floor and we took it in turns to help him. When the train stopped we stopped and there were many stops, some of long duration. At each stop we filled the cutting with dung from the floor. Sometimes the guards patrolled with their dogs up and down the train. During several halts the doors were slid open and cursory checks were made but these were defeated by our camouflage, the overcrowding and the dim light in the corner. The last two factors plus the swaying and jerking of the wagon combined to make the work quite difficult. However, one thing in which all P.O.W.s will normally co-operate fully and enthusiastically is an attempt to escape and even greater overcrowding and discomfort was readily tolerated elsewhere in order to make room for the work, and as evening came someone kindly produced a torch to enable work to continue.

With the open vents, the noise under way was only just tolerable and the streams of cold December air chilled us to the bone. After a day of stop-go, both by the train and the axemen, we entered the suburbs of a large city and stopped in a large marshalling yard. As at every stop some were hoisted by others so that, gripping the bars, they could look out of the vents until the guards made us retire. We agreed that we were in Rome. Only sixty miles in a day! Clearly our train was of very low priority but this was to our advantage. In a fast train we might now be over halfway to the Austrian border.

We passed the night in the marshalling yard in dreadful squalor and very cold but at least warmer than when we were under way. Finding one's way to the oil drum in near darkness without disturbing or hurting somebody was nearly impossible, though tolerated with a groan and a sort of sleepy understanding, though real sleep was also impossible especially in our excited state as we contemplated escape

Throughout the night we were jostled by shunting as other wagons were added and our comparatively short train became very long. Finally there was a very heavy air raid not far away which, believing ourselves to be safe within the open city, we cheered at the top of our voices, which disturbed the guards and dogs who in turn silenced us. We all felt very much better after this encouragement from the R.A.F. and our futile though natural gesture. With any luck the bombing might have destroyed the railway line ahead which would delay our departure for Germany. Under such circumstances one tends to clutch at straws!

Throughout the following morning there was more shunting, the oil drum was emptied by two of us under guard and we were given some food and water. We were unable to do anything until we got under way, which we did in the afternoon, and then we were reluctant to start cutting in case our efforts became visible externally, so we did not start again until after dusk. Thankfully it was dark early.

Meanwhile we discussed various plans of action and it was naturally agreed that we would all walk back from the train. Walking away from the enemy was not only sensible but it would also enable us to assist anyone who might have been injured in the fall, and link up in pairs, I with Jack Clarke. We discussed plans for every possible eventuality, tried to monitor our progress through the ventilation slots, tried to recall how two parachutists in our camp had taught us how to fall and when not thus occupied or chopping, tried to rest.

The train was rolling along fairly consistently in late evening when Hugh finally broke through and, after we had trimmed the hole, he squeezed through followed by Garrad Cole and Jack Clarke. My turn!

The hole was little more than a foot wide and eighteen or twenty inches high. It was not wide enough to get my shoulders through horizontally so that, having put my head and an arm through, I had to rotate my body through ninety degrees to get my body partly out. I was then able to rest a hand on the buffer below to support my body as I squeezed further out until I could get my other hand out and place it on the wagon wall in front. I was surprised that, although it was a dark night, I could see very well because of the many sparks generated by the clashing of the buffer pistons and the grinding of the wheels on the rails.

Although the train seemed to be travelling at a fairly constant speed the distance between the wagons was constantly changing as they continually jostled into each other. This was very unhelpful as I got first one foot out onto the buffer and then, with both hands working their way up the wagon in front I managed to raise my body hand over hand and thus extract my second leg.

Leaning on the front wagon I then had to shuffle my first foot on the buffer casing, avoiding the very active buffer piston, to make room for my second foot, which action was impeded by a loose, flapping boot sole. Still leaning on the front wagon and without hand-holds, I took a very deep breath, pushed myself free from the front wagon into the upright position and, balancing for a moment on the buffer, jumped …!

Contributors of Accounts

In addition to the ex-prisoners of PG49 whose stories appear in their books listed in the Bibliography, the following have contributed accounts of their adventures:

Peter F. Barshall, R.A.
G. R. M. (Bill) Bowder, R.A.
Noel H. Burdett, R.A.
Richard O. H. Carver, R.E.
Dermot R. C. Chichester (Lord Donegall), 7th Hussars
Gerald Churchill, 12 Lancers
Douglas Clarke, R.A.S.C.
W. J. (Jack) Clarke, R.E.M.E.
Tom S. Craig, R.T.R.
Mrs. Jean Davis *re* her husband W. J. (Pat) Davis, R.A.S.C.
R. (Reg) Dickinson, R.A.F.
J. (Jock) I. Donagher, R.A.
T. D. (Binks) Forster, R.A.
Michael F. Gilbert, R.H.A.
Eric S. Hopkins, Green Howards.
Derek S. Iles, R.A.F.
A. A. Jones, R.A.
J. (Jack) A. Kempton, R.T.R.
Anthony R. Laing, R.E.
Mrs. A. Measures *re* her husband John B. Measures, A.A.C.
W. (Bill) N. Monteith, R.A.F.
E. (Ted) H. Mumford, 3 G.R.
C. D. (Kit) Patterson, R.N.F.
Tom I. Pitman, 11th Hussars
R. (Bob) Smyth, R.A.
Peter Stericker, D.C.L.I.
Hugh H. Thompson, R.A.
Tom D. Vickers, C.G.
H. T. (Taffy) Wilcox, R.A.
G. T. (Toots) G. Williams, D.C.L.I.
Robert N. D. Williams, 4 G.R.

The photographs have been contributed by:

P. J. D. Langrishe (Plate 1, top; Plate 2, bottom), Ian English (Plate 1, bottom), Hugo De Burgh (Plate 2, top), Toby Graham (Plate 3, top) and Anthony Laing (Plate 3, bottom; Plate 4).

Recaptured

In addition to those mentioned in Chapter 11, the following officers from Fontanellato are also known to have been re-captured:

S. N. Floyer-Acland; R. E. Adlard; A. S. M. Alcock; G. A. F. Archdale; H. D. Armstrong; A. H. Austin; G. K. Barber; F. E. Bardell; C. G. Barker; C. C. Bass; R. I. Bell; J. A. Berry; R. G. V. Black; P. V. Board; W. Bowker; A. M. Boyd; E. G. Brett; B. H. Brookes; V. A. Buist; E. O. Burne; M. A. Callaghan; N. Carr; R. F. L. Chance; J. A. Clarke; M. M. Clifford; J. N. Colbeck; F. G. Cook; M. P. D. Cruickshank; A. P. Davies; F. J. Dolphin; J. F. Dugdale; C. P. Dumenil; J. Duthie; J. M. Eadie; C. E. H. Edwards; H. P. Edwards; D. B. Erskine; A. N. Evans; D. C. G. Seymour Evans; L. N. Everett; J. W. Fairbrass; F. N. St.J. Fairhurst; R. S. Ferguson; J. A. Fleming; K. A. Fraser; D. Futrell; M. A. Gibb; J. H. Gibson; A. S. Gilbey; A. C. Glover; E. A. Graham; B. H. Grant; T. D. Grocock; N. T. Gulliver; P. N. Gunn; H. R. Haig; R. Hargreaves; J. W. Hartley; F. R. Lewis-Heath; N. J. Hellings; A. Hill; R. H. Hill; P. A. T. Holme; H. Holmes; K. de C. Holroyd; J. A. Horner; H. Houghton; T. A. Hoyle; D. H. E. Jeston; A. Jewson; R. S. V. Johnstone; C. H. Jones; F. P. Jordan; P. H. Joscelyne; P. G. King, L. B. Krailing; M. W. Lacey; W. E. Lamaison; A. G. Lees; W. H. H. Lewis; W. G. Lowther; S. E. Lyndon; D. R. Macaulay; J. B. Measures; K. D. Miller; B. Mills; J. E. Mills; T. W. Mills; C. M. Milner; B. D. Moody; J. Moore; G. F. Oldham; C. V.´Olding; A. D. Orme; G. B. Pearce; J. T. Philp; E. Player; E. G. M. Popple; J. H. Poynton; W. Pringle; R. B. Reid; W. A. Reid; H. T. R. Renwick; M. J. Field-Richards; A. Roberts; M. G. Roberts; V. J. Roques; R. J. Sage; G. A. Saunders; C. A. G. Simkins; J. W. Simpson; B. J. Smith; N. L. H. Smith; P. E. C. Smith; C. J. N. Stanford; A. D. Steven; L. Stewart; E. N. Strickland; J. Tennant; P. S. Thursfield; T. Tufnell; J E. Tull; D. P. Turnage; A. C. Tute; P. J. Vine; G. E. T. Watson; A. F. L. Wells; H. Wharfedale; H. E. Wheeler; M. H. E. Williams; J. D. Winchester; P. L. Winchester; W. E. Wright; J. H. Wyatt; R. S. Young.

E. & O.E.

Honours and Awards

The following received Honours and Awards for actions taken during the period from the exit from PG49 to their rejoining the Allied forces.

Lieut. V. C. Amos	193718	Mention in Despatches
Capt. J. H. Baddeley	130342	Mention in Despatches
Lieut. I. G. Bain	149348	M.B.E.
Lieut. J. A. Ballantyne	229558	M.B.E.
Pte. C. F. Botha	21753	Mention in Despatches
Gnr. A. C. Butler	105606	Mention in Despatches
Lieut. W. J. F. Clarke	66750	Mention in Despatches
Capt. D. Derozhinsky	EC 422	M.B.E.
Fl./Lieut. J. D. Hall	41176	Mention in Despatches
Major H. J. Fane Hervey, M.C.	140579	Bar to the M.C.
Capt. D. G. A. Flowerdew	44838	M.B.E.
Lieut. P. G. Glendenning	293853	M.B.E.
Capt. S. C. Hood	194501	M.B.E.
Capt. W. O. James	127676	M.B.E.
Lieut. E. A. Kiaer	130209	Mention in Despatches
Lieut. A. R. Laing	129873	M.C.
Lieut. P. J. D. Langrishe	121709	Mention in Despatches
Lieut. F. W. H. Lockett	165411	M.B.E.
Major F. S. H. Lowsley-Williams	35427	Mention in Despatches
Lieut. R. G. H. MacLean	90788	M.B.E.
Lieut. R. E. Mann	160661	Mention in Despatches
Lieut. B. W. Nicholls	187606	Mention in Despatches
Lieut. G. R. K. Ord	124188	Mention in Despatches
Capt. J. Philip	EC 1797	Mention in Despatches
Lieut. R. P. Phillips	45237	Mention in Despatches
Capt. T. Preacher	88762	Mention in Despatches
Lieut. H. D. Sillito	165918	Mention in Despatches
Lieut. C. H. E. Simpson	134908	Mention in Despatches
Capt. G. F. Spooner	79690	Mention in Despatches
Lieut.-Col. R. Wheeler	34344	O.B.E.
Lieut. J. W. Younger	114122	M.B.E.

E. & O.E.

P.G.49 Fontanellato

Nominal Rolls, September 1943

Royal Navy

Officers

Name & Rank	*Arm*
Beale, C., *Lt.*	R.N.V.R.
Hart, R. D. C., *Lt.*	R.N.V.R.
Hunt, P., *Lt. Cdr.*	R.N.
Luce, —	
McDonald, S. G., *Gnr. (T)*	R.N.
Norwood, L. W., *Lt.*	R.M.
Salmons, B. H., *Lt.*	R.M.
White, R. D. C., *Lt.*	R.N.V.R.
Wright, M. G. A., *Capt.*	R.M.

Ratings

Name & Rank	*No.*
Bishop, W. J., *A.B.*	D/JX 1295376
Cabalane, J., *Stoker*	D/KX 82031
Challis, R. H., *A./Ldg. Tel.*	P/JX 129019
Dryer, S. G., *A.B.*	D/JX 140364
Griffiths, *Ldg. Stoker*	D/KX 82819
Hunt, J., *A./Ldg. S.*	C/JX 141738
McLean, A. McI., *A.B.*	D/SSX 22068
Martindale, H., *A.B.*	D/SSX 21180

British Army

Officers

Name & Rank	*Pers. No.*	*Regt. or Corps.*
Adams, F., *Lt.*	71620	R.T.R.
Adlard, R. E., *Lt.*	90381	R.A.C.
Alcock, A. S. M., *Capt.*	87892	R.E.M.E.
Alexander, J. L., *2/Lt.*	198407	R.E.
Amos, V. C., *Lt.*	193718	B. & H.
Anderson, G. A., *Capt.*	153972	R.A.M.C.
Archdale, G. A. F, *Maj.*	40350	R.A.
Ardern, C., *Lt.-Col.*	15616	R.A.
Armstrong, H. D., *Lt.*	113954	R.A.
Ashby, M. J. F., *Lt.*	105936	N'd. F.
Astley-Cooper, D. L., *Lt.*	128778	R.A.C.
Austin, A. H., *Capt.*	69196	R.T.R.
Baddeley, J. F., *Capt.*	130342	Hamp.
Bain, I. G. B., *Lt.*	149348	Worc.
Ball, H. B., *Lt.*	87353	R.T.R.
Ballantyne, J. A., *Lt.*	229558	R.A.C.
Barber, A. A., *Capt.*	64475	Gn. How.
Barber, G. K., *Capt.*	75824	R.A.C.
Bardell, F. E., *Capt.*	73293	R.A.
Barker, C. G., *Lt.*	143532	For'ters
Barnard, C. J., *Lt.*	182286	Hamp.
Barshall, P. F., *Capt.*	90726	R.A.
Bass, C. C., *Lt.*	93630	R. Bde.
Baynham, J. R., *Lt.*	105993	Recce. C.
Beales, R. H. A., *Capt.*	116804	R.T.R.
Beazley, G. H., *Lt.*	132589	R.T.R.
Bell, C. G. B., *Lt.*	190305	H.L.I.
Bell, R. I., *Lt.*	232219	R.E.
Bennett, C. W., *Capt.*	183308	R.A.
Benson, R., *Capt.*	34896	Ches.
Benzie, W., *Lt.*	197992	R.T.R.
Berry, J. A., *Lt.*	143765	R.A.
Billany, D., *Lt.*	194884	E. York.
Bird, N. M., *Capt.*	129142	17/21 L.
Birkbeck J. W. G., *Lt*	87723	R.A.
Black, R. G. V., *Lt.*	62483	4 H.
Blair, D. A., *Capt.*	73177	Seaf.
Blake, A. S., *Lt.*	190751	R.A.
Blanchaert, L. G., *Lt.*	169526	Gen. List
Bligh, H. K. H., *Lt.*	92415	R. E
Blunt, N., *Lt.*	92988	Gn. How.
Board, P. V., *Capt.*	97195	Hamp.
Bolton A. R. D., *Capt.*	77181	Hamp.
Booth, J. R., *Capt.*	96485	Gn. How.
Borradaile, R. G., *Capt.*	63631	Cam. H.
Bowder, G. R. M., *Lt.*	132866	R.A.
Bowker, W., *Lt.*	176849	Lan. F.
Boyd, A. M., *Capt.*	125475	R.A.M.C.
Boyle, P. J., *Lt.*	124470	S.G.
Brett, D. A., *Lt.*	229045	R.A.
Brett, E. G., *Capt.*	156476	D.C.L.I.
Briggs, K. J., *Lt.*	105517	B. & H.
Brooke, R. N., *Lt.*	121340	S.G.
Brookes, B. H., *Lt.*	189797	R.A.C.
Brown, N., *2/Lt.*	201341	R.T.R.
Buchanan, D. V. G., *Capt.*	121276	R.A.
Buchanan, H. A. D., *Lt.*	124535	G.G.
Buist, V. A., *Lt.*	160006	R.A.C.
Bullett, G., *2/Lt.*	148727	R.T.R.
Bunning, J. S H., *Lt.*	190217	Hamp.

Name & Rank	*Pers. No.*	*Regt. or Corps.*
Burdett, N. H., *Capt.*	187371	R.A.
Burman, J. W., *2/Lt.*	166167	R.T.R.
Burne, E. O., *Lt.-Col.*	30666	R.A.C.
Burton, V. D., *Lt.*	214826	R.A.C.
Caffyn, W. D., *Capt.*	117868	E. Surrey
Callaghan, M. A., *Lt.*	105557	A.A.C.
Cameron, A. G., *Capt.*	137928	Cam. H.
Candler, J. H., *2/Lt.*	165737	D.C.L.I.
Canning, J. G., *Capt.*	129105	R.A.
Caraher, E. F. M., *Capt.*	159540	R.A.M.C.
Carr, N., *Lt.*	121257	R.T.R.
Carver, H. C., *Lt.*	108541	8 H.
Carver, R. O. H., *Maj.*	62678	R.E.
Castle, C., *Capt.*	18788	R.A.O.C.
Chance, R. F. L., *Maj.*	49821	K.R.R.C.
Chichester, D. R. C., *Capt.*	69083	R.A.C.
Churchill, G. I., *Lt.*	170576	12 L.
Clarke, D., *Capt.*	112205	R.A.S.C.
Clarke, J. A., *2/Lt.*	151669	R.A.C.
Clarke, W. J. F., *Lt.*	66750	R.E.M.E.
Clifford, M. M., *Capt.*	52113	R.T.R.
Clover, R. G., *Capt.*	91879	R.A.
Colbeck, J. V., *Capt.*	101039	R.T.R.
Collins, G. J. H. D., *Maj.*	70758	Queens.
Collis, W. L., *Lt.*	160651	R.A.
Comyn, J. A., *Lt.*	66066	R.A.C.
Cook, F. G., *Lt.*	151477	R.A.
Craddock, G., *2/Lt.*	167957	P. C.
Craig, T. S., *Capt.*	85709	R.T.R.
Crofton, K. H., *Lt.*	88193	R.A.
Crosthwaite-Eyre, J., *Capt.*	134990	R.E.
Cruddas, H. H., *Capt.*	74506	R.A.
Cruickshank, M. P. D., *Capt.*	57419	10 H.
Cutler, E. S., *Lt.*	158264	R.A.
Davies, A. P., *Lt.*	166080	R.A.
Davies, E., *Lt.*	182507	D.C.L.I.
Davis, W. J., *Capt.*	147872	R.A.S.C.
Day, G. M., *Lt.*	94508	Welch
Dean, J. G., *Lt.*	96486	R.A.
de Bendern, J., *Lt.*	131220	R.A.C.
De Burgh, H. G., *Lt.-Col.*	1229	R.A.
De Clermont, P. H. V., *Capt.*	50859	8 H.
Dennis, H. I. A., *Capt.*	95000	Gn. How.
De Winton, G. F. W., *Maj.*	91217	R. Sigs.
Dickens, G. C. H., *2/Lt.*	160014	R.A.C.
Dolphin, F. J., *Lt.*	164434	For'ters.
Donagher, J. I., *2/Lt.*	174810	R.A.
Dorrian, H. J., *Lt.*	198253	D.L.I.
Dowie, D. A., *Lt.*	244060	N'd. F.
Drayson, G. B., *Capt.*	50201	R.A.
Driffill, J., *Capt.*	137751	R.A.
Dugdale, J. F., *Capt.*	115915	R.A.S.C.
Duke, D. O. C., *Capt.*	91775	R.A.
Dumenil, C. P., *Lt.*	224636	Leic.
Duthie, J., *Maj.*	26752	R.A.
Eadie, J. M., *Lt.*	85776	R.A.
Edge, C. G. J., *Maj.*	44078	R.A.
Edwards, C. E. H., *2/Lt.*	95077	R.E.
Edwards, H. P., *Maj.*	113927	K.R.R.C.
Ellis, P., *Capt.*	159499	R.A.
English, I. R., *Capt.*	79387	D.L.I.
Erskine, D. B., *Capt.*	74712	R.T.R.
Evans, A. N., *Lt.*	125357	Gn. How.
Everett E. N., *Lt.-Col.*	20760	K.O.R.R.
Fairbrass, J. W., *Capt.*	20245	R.A.
Fairhurst, F. N. St.J., *Capt.*	66065	7H.
Fane Hervey, H. F., *Maj.*	140579	R. T. R

Name & Rank	*Pers. No.*	*Regt. or Corps.*
Ferguson, R. S., *Capt.*	74604	N'd. F.
Few, J. S., *Lt.*	162156	R.A.
Field-Richards, M. J., *Lt.*	87878	R.E.M.E.
Fleming, H. D., *Capt.*	136274	R.A.M.C.
Fleming, J. A., *Lt.*	151480	R.A.
Flowerdew, G. D. H., *Capt.*	44838	R.A.
Floyer-Acland, S. N., *Capt.*	71150	D.C.L.I.
Forgan, T. H. K., *Lt.*	140058	Ches.
Forster, K. H., *Capt.*	74732	Gn. How.
Forster, T. D., *Capt.*	132853	R.A.
Frank, G. S. W., *Capt.*	181330	Y. & L.
Frazer, K. A., *Capt.*	118766	R.A.O.C.
Futrell, V., *Lt.*	207445	R.A.S.C.
Gardner, J. C., *Lt.*	144486	R.T.R.
Gardner, P. J., *Capt.*	132595	R.T.R.
Gates, N. P., *Lt.*	89953	R. Sigs.
Gatford, H. J. H., *Capt.*	95073	R.E.
Gazeley, E. S. J., *Lt.*	105353	R.A.
Gelly, J. P., *Lt.*	145555	R.A.
Gers, R. W., *Capt.*	124523	R.T.R.
Gibbs, D. L. A., *Lt.-Col.*	34771	Queens.
Gibbs, M. A., *Capt.*	67487	C.G.
Gibson, J. H., *Capt.*	78710	R.A.M.C.
Gibson, R. P. T., *Capt.*	91219	R. Sigs.
Gilbert, M. F., *Capt.*	102700	R. A
Gilbey, A. S., *Lt.*	85281	4 H.
Gilliver, W. T., *Lt.*	160821	For'ters.
Girling, G. N., *Maj.*	63187	Gn. How.
Glendenning, P. G., *Lt.*	193853	Y. & L.
Glover, A. C., *Capt.*	143214	R.T.R.
Goddard, J. H., *2/Lt.*	138688	Buffs.
Goddard, K. M., *2/Lt.*	184287	R.A.
Goldingham, C. A., *Lt.*	132752	R.A.
Gosling, R. G., *Lt.*	220596	R.A.
Graham, D. S., *Capt.*	106681	R.A.
Graham, E. A., *Capt.*	195382	G. List.
Graham, J. W., *Lt.*	44598	R.T.R.
Graham-Cambell, D., *Lt.*	176469	A. & S. H.
Grant, B. H., *Lt.*	95074	R.E.
Green, A. J., *Capt.*	93641	R.A.
Green, J. C., *Lt.*	136031	R. Sigs.
Greenwell, W. N., *Lt.*	90772	R.T.R.
Greenwood, J., *Capt.*	90773	R.A.
Grocock, T. D., *Lt.*	128782	R.T.R.
Gunn, P. N., *Lt.*	245351	R. Bde
Gunter, P. K., *Lt.*	155853	R.A.
Haig, H. R, *Maj.*	58198	Cam. H.
Hall, A. F., *Capt.*	155614	R.A.
Hall, J. H., *Capt.*	100107	I. C.
Hammick, R. W., *2/Lt.*	235312	R.A.
Hammond, A. D., *2/Lt.*	186797	R.A.
Hampson, E. T., *Lt.*	74494	R.A.
Harbord, K. P. G., *Lt.*	77602	Buffs.
Harding, A. J., *2/Lt.*	210319	R.A.
Hargreaves, R., *Capt.*	113843	R.E.
Harris-Matthews, T., *Lt.*	158953	R. Sigs.
Hartley, J. W., *Lt.*	94252	R.E.
Harvey, C. J. R., *Capt.*	50136	R.T.R.
Heck, H. D., *Capt.*	148230	R.A.
Hedley, C., *Lt.*	169570	8 H.
Hellings, N. J., *Lt.*	244323	D.C.L.I.
Hemmings, S. J., *Lt.*	151706	R.A.
Hill, A., *Lt.*	87773	Gn. How.
Hill, R. H., *Rev.*	101746	R.A.Ch.D.
Hobbs, L. A., *Capt.*	19796	R.A.
Hockney, A. T., *Lt.*	174170	War.
Holme. P. A. T., *Capt.*	117122	Hamp.

Name & Rank	*Pers. No.*	*Regt. or Corps.*
Holmes, H., *Capt.*	69103	N'd. F.
Holroyd, K. de C., *Capt.*	89369	R. Bde.
Holworthy, H. D., *Lt.*	35450	R.T.R.
Hood, S. C., *Lt.*	194601	H.L.I.
Hoole-Lowsley-Williams, F. S., *Capt.*	35427	16/5 L.
Hope, H. A., *Maj.*	65415	K.R.R.C.
Hopkins, E. S., *Lt.*	113474	Gn. How.
Horner, J. A., *2/Lt.*	179798	D.C.L.I.
Hornsby, D. F, *Lt.*	106684	K.R.R.C.
Houghton, H., *Capt.*	141472	R.A.M.C.
How, F. R. W., *Maj.*	6830	8 H.
Hoy, J. E., *Lt.*	226189	E. York.
Hoyle, T. A., *Capt.*	37135	R.A.
Hubbard, A. D., *Lt.*	204926	R. Bde.
Jacovides, C., *Lt.*	171508	P.C. (Cyp.)
James, W. O., *Capt.*	127676	R.A.M.C.
Jamieson, A. W., *Capt.*	134462	R.A.
Jenoure, J H., *Lt.*	214532	11 H. R.A.C.
Jeston, D. H. E., *Lt.*	113749	Buffs
Jewson, A., *Lt.*	193398	Bord.
Jobson, T. H., *Capt.*	95618	D.C.L.I.
Johnston, C. G., *Lt.*	75698	R. Bde.
Johnstone, R. S. V., *Capt.*	71226	R.T.R.
Jones, A. A., *Capt.*	148305	R.A.
Jones, C. H., *Lt.*	237878	War.
Jordan, F. P., *Lt.*	220630	Recce C.
Joscelyne, P. H., *Capt.*	164126	R.T.R.
Kam, A. A., *Lt.*	70446	R.T.R.
Kearns, M. N., *Lt.*	117066	Gen. List.
Kempton, J. A., *Lt.*	7292	R.T.R.
Kerr, A. M., *Lt.*	102095	R.A.
Kiaer, E.A., *Lt.*	130209	R.F.
Kilbane, E. M., *Lt.*	140783	R. T R
Kinch, C. E., *Lt.*	186071	W. Yorks.
Kindersley, P. L., *Capt.*	99194	C.G.
King, P. G., *Lt.*	220601	R.A.
Kinsman, A. H. I., *Lt.*	200079	G.G.
Kitson, C. H., *Capt.*	148613	Y. & L.
Knight-Bruce, R. N. C., *Lt.*	198592	R.A.C.
Krailing, L. B., *Lt.*	237927	Essex
Lacey, M. W., *Lt.*	105903	R.A.
Laing, A. R., *Lt.*	129873	R.E.
Lamaison, W. E., *Lt.*	145985	R.A.
Langrishe, P. J. D., *Lt.*	121709	R.A.
Lanyon, O. P., *Capt.*	94298	R.A.
Lascaris, A. G., *Lt.*	202650	I.C.
Lawrence, R. F., *Capt.*	117520	R.A.
Lax, F. A, *Lt.*	124762	Gn. How.
Ledgard, G. A., *Capt.*	89100	R.A.
Lees, A. G., *Lt.*	217464	R.U.Rif.
Le Mesurier, J. S., *Capt.*	52966	R.T.R.
Leslie, C. D. C. K., *Capt.*	48353	H.L.I.
Lewis, E. D. T., *Capt.*	118303	R.A.M.C.
Lewis, W. H. H., *2/Lt.*	179465	RA.
Lewis-Heath, F. R., *Lt.*	162524	Hamp.
Lockett, F. W. H., *2/Lt.*	165411	R.A.
Lockwood, G. F., *2/Lt.*	162180	R.A.
Lowther, W. G., *Capt.*	53672	8 H.
Lyndon, S. E., *Lt.*	190527	R.E.
Lyon-Williams, C., *Lt.*	135067	R.T.R.
Lytle, J. H., *Capt.*	117271	Hamp.
Macaulay, D. R., *Capt.*	120188	R.A.M.C.
McCubbin, A., *Lt.*	237740	Recce. C.
MacDonald, H., *Rev.*	133401	R.A.Ch.D.
MacDonnell, F. E. A., *Lt.-Col.*	19640	Gn. How.
McKinlay, J., *Lt.*	180330	Cam. H.
Maclean, R. G. H., *Capt.*	90788	R.A.
Magee, H. A. G., *Lt.*	140885	R.A.
Mainwaring, H. S. K., *Lt.-Col.*	30735	R.A.
Mann, R. E., *Lt.*	160661	R.A.
Marshall, P. A., *Lt.*	187914	R.A.
Marshall, R. G., *Lt.*	198294	N'd. F.
Mather. D. C. McD., *Capt.*	124488	W.G.
Mathieson, G., *2/Lt.*	146183	R.A.
Mead, P. H., *Lt.*	155641	Buffs.
Measures, J. B., *Capt.*	153097	A.A.C.
Merritt, S. C., *Maj.*	111442	Gen. List.
Millar, K. D., *Lt.*	94181	R.T.R.
Millington-Buck, J. B., *Lt.*	148902	Gn. How.
Mills, B., *Lt.*	149790	R.A.
Mills, J. E., *Lt.*	176706	R.T.R.
Mills, P. C. M., *Lt.*	100376	R.E.
Mills, T. W., *2/Lt.*	176500	N'd. F.
Milner, C. M., *Capt.*	65270	R.A.
Mitchell, A. P., *Capt.*	72198	D.W.R.
Moody, B. D., *Lt.*	240677	R. Suss.
Moore, J., *Capt.*	138238	Leic.
Moore, J. W., *Lt.*	244335	R.A.
Morgan, J. L., *Capt.*	149826	S.W.B.
Morns-Keating, P. S., *Capt.*	56634	R. Bde.
Morrison, E. G., *Maj.*	106261	R.A.
Moyle, A. D., *Capt.*	108225	R.A.S.C.
Nelson, W. V. H., *Capt.*	62563	8 H.
Newby, G. E., *Lt.*	153984	Bk. Watch
Nicholls, B. W., *2/Lt.*	187606	R.A.
Nicholls, G. H., *Lt.*	132008	R.A.
Nixon, P., *Lt.*	220621	Gn. How.
Noble, R., *Maj.* *(War Correspondent)*		
Norman, D. S., *Lt.-Col.*	14022	E. Yorks.
Nott, D. H., *Maj.*	39477	Worc.
O'Brien, F. E., *Lt.*	219843	Leic.
Ockleston, C. T., *Capt.*	87395	R.A.
Ogilvie-Grant, M., *Capt.*	123875	S. G.
Oldham, G. F., *Capt.*	151450	R. Sigs.
Olding, C. V,, *Capt.*	152881	R.A.
Oliver, J. L. S., *Lt.*	77840	D.L.I.
Ord, G. R. K., *Lt.*	1214 8	S.W.B.
Orme, A. D., *2/Lt.*	155821	R.A.
Orr-Ewing, R. A., *Capt.*	53685	S. G.
Palmer, A. R. M., *Lt.*	134493	R.T.R.
Partridge, R. C., *Lt.*	153980	Welch
Paterson, J., *Capt.*	130225	R.T.R.
Patterson, C. D., *Capt.*	96257	N'd. F.
Pearce, G. B., *Capt.*	126403	D.C.L.I.
Phalp, G. A., *Capt.*	88264	R.A.
Phillips, A. L., *Lt.*	111444	R. Sigs.
Phillips, G. J., *Lt.*	140556	Som. L. I.
Phillips, R. P., *Lt.*	45237	R.A.C.
Philp, J. T., *Lt.*	117229	R.A.
Pipe, R. R., *Lt.*	203816	Hamp.
Pitman, T. I., *Lt.*	56972	11 H.
Player, E., *2/Lt.*	177321	R.T.R.
Playford, J. P., *Lt.*	93657	A.A.C.
Pool, D. A., *Lt.*	137341	Hamp.
Pople, E. G. M., *Lt.*	207513	K.R.R.C.
Porter, F. E., *Capt.*	117769	R.A.
Potts, G. B., *Capt.*	100390	R.A.
Poynton, J. H., *Lt.*	62111	R.A.
Pratt, W. E. J., *Lt.*	241193	R.A.
Preacher, T., *Capt.*	88762	D.L.I.
Pringle, W., *Capt.*	91563	R.A.

Name & Rank	*Pers. No.*	*Regt. or Corps.*
Pryke, W. D., *Capt.*	99745	D.C.L.I.
Pyman, H. D., *Maj.*	53751	For'ters.
Raeburn, E. A., *Lt.*	134216	R.A.
Ramsay, R. D. G., *Maj.*	85706	R.T.R.
Ramsay, S., *Maj.*	63322	Bk. Watch
Ramsden, C. O. I., *Capt.*	68107	R.A.
Ramshaw, W., *Lt.*	91118	Gn. How.
Reid, R. B., *Lt.*	176707	R.T.R.
Reid, W. A., *Lt.*	164177	R.A.
Renwick, H. T. L., *Lt.*	137754	R.A.
Ricketts, B. A., *2/Lt.*	173911	R.A.O.C.
Ricketts, H. O. D., *Capt.*	70589	Leic.
Roberts, A., *2/Lt.*	187904	R.A.
Roberts, W. G., *Lt.*	190623	R.A.C.
Rogers, N. C., *Capt.*	106811	R.A.M.C.
Roncoroni, A. D. S., *Capt.*	100946	R.A.
Rooke, D. R., *Lt.*	237660	E. Surr.
Roques, V. J., *Lt.*	142291	R.E.
Ross, M. P., *Capt.*	137366	Welch
Russell, A. P., *Capt.*	112119	R.A.M.C.
Sage, R. J., *Lt.*	189823	R.T.R.
Saunders, G. A., *Lt.*	89972	R.A.
Scott, F. G. R. W., *Lt.*	237399	R.A.C.
Seely, V. B. J., *Maj.*	22302	9 L.
Seymour-Evans, D. C. G., *Maj.*	58071	7 H.
Shakespear, J. H., *Capt.*	53122	R.A.
Shaw, D. F., *Lt.*	85969	R.A.C.
Shaw, I. S. M., *Capt.*	138255	Gn. How.
Sillito, H. D., *Lt.*	165918	A. & S.H.
Simkins, C. A. G., *Capt.*	88592	R. Bde.
Simms, F. C., *Capt.*	40719	War.
Simpson, C. H. E., *Lt.*	134908	R.A.
Simpson, J. W., *Lt.*	124219	D.C.L.I.
Smith, B. J., *Capt.*	188650	R.A.M.C.
Smith, B. R., *Maj.*	64524	R.A.
Smith, J. D., *Lt.*	204342	R.A.
Smith, N. L. H., *Lt.*	129493	N'd. F.
Smith, P. E. C., *Lt.*	130530	R.E.
Smyth, R., *Lt.*	90811	R.A.
Spence, H., *Lt.*	138271	Gn. How.
Spooner, G. F., *Capt.*	79690	R.A.C.
Stanford, C. J. N., *2/Lt.*	220672	17/21 L.
Stavert, G. S., *Lt.*	207341	R.A.
Stephens, T. M., *Lt.*	95606	S.W.B.
Stericker, P., *Lt.*	153955	D.C.L.I.
Sterry, F. D., *Lt.*	126805	R.A.
Steven, A. D., *Capt.*	89383	R.T.R.
Stewart, L., *Lt.*	170102	R.A.
Strange, J. P. A., *Capt.*	140567	R.T.R.

Name & Rank	*Pers. No.*	*Regt. or Corps.*
Street, A. W. M., *Capt.*	74302	R.A.S.C.
Strickland, E. N., *Lt.*	153378	D.L.I.
Stuchberry, T. O., *Lt.*	140064	Ches.
Sutcliffe, K. N., *2/Lt.*	201038	R.A.
Swain, P. B., *Lt.*	124863	K.R.R.C.
Taylor, J. F., *Lt.*	140566	R.T.R.
Tennant, J., *Maj.*	90822	R.A.
Thickett, J. A., *2/Lt.*	174827	R.A.
Thomson, H. H., *Lt.*	151377	R.A.
Thursfield, P. S., *Lt.*	124091	R.A.
Tolley, R. S., *Capt.*	159307	R.A.
Tomkins, E. E., *Capt.*	176506	I.C.
Tregoaing, R. G., *Lt.*	121687	R.A.
Tuffnell, T., *Lt.*	113725	R.T.R.
Tull, J. E., *Lt.*	177737	Hamp.
Turnage, D. P., *Lt.*	105309	D.C.L.I.
Tute, A. C., *Capt.*	47684	R.T.R.
May have assumed identity of: Westcott, F. W. A., P/O.	*109026*	*R.A.F.*
Tyndale-Biscoe, N. E., *Lt.-Col.*	11409	R.A.
Vian, G. D. S., *Lt.*	87481	R.A.
Vickers, T. D., *Lt.*	149127	C.G.
Vine, P. J., *Lt.*	234314	R.A.C.
Wakelin, H. M., *2/Lt.*	134773	R.A.
Watson, A., *Lt.*	113279	R.T.R.
Watson, G. E. T., *Lt.*	186068	W. York.
Watson, J., *2/Lt.*	145684	N'd. *Fus.*
Watson, P. D., *Capt.*	77643	D.C.L.I.
Wells, A. F. L., *2/Lt.*	95049	N'd. F.
Wharfedale, H., *Lt.*	117718	R.A.
Wheeler, A. E., *Lt.*	226193	Gn. How.
Wheeler, R. H. L., *Lt.-Col.*	34344	R.A.
White, W. S., *Lt.*	235700	D.L.I.
Whitehead, F. H., *Capt.*	200490	R.A.
Wilcox, H. T., *Capt.*	129229	R.A.
Wildy, T. H., *Lt.*	243048	Linc.
Williams, D. P., *2/Lt.*	177307	R.T.R.
Williams, G. T. G., *Capt.*	95617	D.C.L.I.
Williams, M. H. E., *2/Lt.*	177519	K.O.R.R.
Willis, A. E., *2/Lt.*	149331	S.W.B.
Wilson, D. F., *Lt.*	190654	R.A.C.
Winchester, J. D., *Lt.*	174364	Hamp.
Winchester, P. L., *Lt.*	124048	R.A.
Woods, C. J., *2/Lt.*	156774	D.L.I.
Wright, W. E., *Lt.*	165424	R.A.
Wyatt, C. E. N., *Lt.*	126348	10 H.
Wyatt, J. H., *Capt.*	205212	R.A.
Young, R. S., *2/Lt.*	194602	H.L.I.
Younger, J. W., *Lt.*	114122	C.G.

Other Ranks

Name & Rank	*Army No.*	*Regt or Corps.*
Busby, J. W. H., Dvr.	T/142594	R.A.S.C.
Ellis, J., *Pte.*	4467863	D.L.I.
Harrison, J., *Spr.*	409184	R.A.C.
Maddox, E., *Tpr.*	321416	R.A.C.
Robinson, A., *Fus.*	4275340	N'd. F.
Rogers, J. A., *Sgt.*	552878	R.A.C.
Taggart, J., *Bdr.*	6978419	R.A.

Royal Air Force

Officers

Name & Rank	*Pers. No.*
Beauclair, D. A., *F/Lt.*	40493
Beckett, S., *F/O.*	
Bridger, J. W. F., *F/Lt.*	
Black, F. A., *F/O.*	46219
Bragg, P., *W/Cdr.*	
Bratchell, D. F., *F/O.*	111534
Dickinson, H. R., *P/O.*	120070
Goode, G. E., *S/Ldr.*	81675
Gee, G. M., *F/Lt.*	89327
Hall, J. D., *F/O.*	41176
Hill, R. C., *F/O.*	63804
Iles, D. E., *F/O.*	66560
Monteith, W. N., *F/O.*	
Packington, R. F., *F/O.*	49730
Pirie, A. N., *S/Ldr.*	39643
Player, E., *F/O.*	
Rainford, R. W. B., *F/Lt.*	82213
Rippondale, F. L., *P/O.*	62005
Turner, H. J., *F/O.*	115614

Airmen

Name & Rank	*No.*
Halliwell, G. F., *Sgt.*	1050080

Canadian Army

Officers

Name & Rank	*Regt. or Corps*
Graham, A. F., *Capt.*	R.C.A.M.C.

New Zealand Army

Officers

Name & Rank	*Regt. or Corps*
Mason, D., *Capt.*	N.Z.E.F.
Napier, H. C., *Capt.*	N.Z.E.F.

South African Army

Officers

Name & Rank	*Pers. No.*	*Regt. or Corps*
Kane Burman, M., *Capt.*		S.A.A.M.C.
Whyte, D. R. D., *Lt.*	123974	

Other Ranks

Name & Rank	*No.*
Botha, C. J., *Pte.*	21753
Butler, A. C., *Gnr.*	105606
Chennells, G. J., *Pte.*	5386
Cumming, E. D. K., *Pte.*	12253
Eloff, T. S., *Pte.*	198030
Field, F. W., *Pte.*	11269
Godfrey, M. E. T., *Sig.*	110450
Grant, R. H., *Sig.*	251952
Hattingh, C. J., *Pte.*	SAP/197003
Jacobs, B., *Pte.*	87808
Jenkeson, A. G., *Pte.*	45431
Johnson, C. K., *Pte.*	142777
Lee, W. A., *Pte.*	185617
Lind, D. G., *Pte.*	75070
Louw, W. C., *L/Cpl.*	12284
Lowe, H. A., *Gnr.*	13888
Muller, J. J., *Pte.*	SAP/198347
Myburgh, W. J., *Sig.*	145827
Odendaal, G. H., *Pte.*	SAP/197033
Potgeiter, J. T., *Spr.*	141387
Prins, F. E., *Gnr.*	144061
Randles, P. J. L., *Pte.*	5268
Redmond, T. J., *Pte.*	88295
Rigby, W. L., *Pte.*	107791
Seppings, E. C., *L/Cpl.*	88940
Silbert, P., *Sig.*	82634
Silversten, A. J., *Pte.*	1704
Smith, C., *Spr.*	189570
Smith, H., *Pte.*	SPA/196377
Smith, J. K., *Pte.*	242363
Smith, W. K., *Pte.*	242475
Sparg, K. F., *Gnr.*	114748
Trollope, H. J. K., *Pte.*	12170
Van Grenning, J. N., *Sig.*	289528
Van Rensburgh, J. J., *Pte.*	79589
Viljoen, H. J., *Pte.*	79100
Viljoen, J. L., *Pte.*	241749

Indian Army

Officers

Name & Rank	Army No.	Unit
Abbott, D., *Maj.*	AI 874	18 R. Garh. Rif.
Browne, N. Q., *Capt.*	907 AI	4 G.R.
Bruen, E. J. D., *Lt.*	LA 1254	6 Rajput R.
Davies, S. H., *Capt.*	EC 799	2 Punjab R.
Derozhinsky, D., *Capt.*	EC 422	5 Mahratta
Duncan, W. W., *Capt.*	EC 830	10 Baluch R.
Durrant, N.S., *Maj.*	AI 837	18 R. Garh. Rif.
Du Vivier, C. L. E., *Capt.*	658 AI	11 P.A.V.O. Cav.
Finch, R. J., *Capt.*	687 AI	12 F.F.R.
Fltzpatrick, T. S., *Capt.*	RO 783	R.I.A.S.C.
Fraser, l. M., *Capt.*	AI 1056	13 F.F.Rif.
Glover, W., *Capt.*	E 123824	I.A.O.C.
Goldingham, M. J. D., *Lt.*	EC 3512	18 Cav.
Houghton, H. W., *Maj.*	255 IA	7 G.R.
Leach, E. R., *2/Lt.*	EC 775	I.A.C.
Meares, J., *Capt.*	662 AI	I.A.C. (18 Cav.)
Mumford, E. N., *Capt.*	AI 632	3 G.R.
Philip, J., *Capt.*	EC 1797	7 Rajput R.
Philipsz, T. G., *Capt.*	RO 3454	5 Mahratta
Smith, R. J., *Capt.*	EC 1240	4 G.R.
Stephenson, A. T., *Capt.*	760 AI	18 R. Garh. Rif.
Walker, J. M. P., *2/Lt.*	EC 1283	I.A.C.
Werner, R. L. H., *Capt.*	EC 189	4 G.R.
Whitaker, G. A., *2/Lt.*	EC 1343	10 Baluch R.
Williams, R. N. D., *Capt.*	1093 IA.	4 G.R.
Willis, A. G. R., *2/Lt.*	EC 1357	11 Sikh R.

Other Ranks

Name & Rank	Army No.	Unit
Rolland, E. V., *S. Cndr.*	7872040	I.A.O.C.

United States

Name & Rank

Allen, L., *War Correspondent.*

E. & O.E.

Bibliography

Abbott, Lt.-Col. Denny: *Winter Holiday in Italy*. The Garhwali, 1952.
Absalom, Roger: *A Strange Alliance*. Leo S. Olschhi, 1991.
Barber, A. A.: *Interim in Italy*. Privately published, 1945.
Comyn, J. A.: *Episodes*. Private circulation, 1994.
Davies, Tony: *When the Moon Rises*. Leo Cooper, 1973.
English, Ian: *Assisted Passage*. Privately published, 1994.
Flowerdew, Douglas: *Finding the Way*. Bee-Line Graphics, 1988.
Foot, M. R. D and Langley, J. M.: *M.I.9*. Bodley Head, 1979.
Gibbs, Denis: *Apennine Journey*. Gale and Polden, 1951.
Goddard, K. M.: *Inside Out*. 'Gunner,' The Journal of Royal Artillery, 1978.
Graham, D. S.: *Escapes and Evasions of an Obstinate Bastard*. Private circulation, *n.d.*
Hood, Stuart: *Pebbles from my Skull*. Readers Union, 1964.
Kindersley, Philip: *For You the War is Over*. Midas Books, 1983.
Lamb, Richard: *War in Italy 1943-45. A Brutal Story*. John Murray, 1995.
Langrishe, P. J. D.: *The Long Walk Out*. Private circulation, 1994.
Mann, Ronald: *Moving the Mountain*. Aldersgate Production, 1995.
Minardi, Marco: *L'Orizzonte del Campo*. Casa Editrice Mattioli, 1995
Newby, Eric: *Love and War in the Apennines*. Hodder and Stoughton, 1971.
Newby, Wanda: *Peace and War*. Collins, 1991.
Nicholls, Gervase: *The Long Walk to Freedom*. Private circulation, 1994.
Watson, Peter: *Mountain Highway*. Private circulation, *n.d.*
Woods, John: *Capitano Inglese*. Private circulation, 1995.
Woods, Rex: *One Man's Desert, The Story of Capt. Pip Gardner V.C., M.C.* William Kimber, 1986.

Index

See also Appendices 6 and 8

Designed and Set
in 10 point Ehrhardt leaded 1 point
by
Langlands Edition
Loughborough, Leicestershire

Front Cover Painting
by
W. G. Cameron-Johnson and Ronald Mann

Printed and Bound in England
by
The Cromwell Press
Broughton Gifford
Melksham, Wiltshire

IAN ENGLISH was born in County Durham and educated at Oundle School, where he was Head Boy in his last term. He was commissioned into the Territorial Army in 1938, joining the 8th Battalion the Durham Light Infantry. He served with them in the B.E.F. Campaign in 1940, in the Gazala battles where he was awarded the Military Cross, at El Alamein where he gained a Bar to the M.C. and at the Battle of Mareth where he was taken prisoner.

After leaving Italy, Ian English returned to the U.K. and rejoined 8 DLI in time for the D-Day Landings and the fighting in Normandy where he won a second Bar to the M.C., one of only 24 to gain this distinction in World War II. At the end of the war he was Second in Command of his battalion.

On demobilisation he went up to Cambridge University where he gained a Degree in Agriculture. He then joined Fisons Limited as an Agricultural Adviser and was with them for 30 years. Now retired, he and his Danish wife live in Wensleydale. His hobbies are bird watching, gardening and military history.

His own escape story, *Assisted Passage—Walking to Freedom, Italy 1943*, was published in 1994.